A Summer On The Riviera

A Summer On The Riviera

Rachel Barnett

First published in Great Britain in 2023 by

Bonnier Books UK Limited
4th Floor, Victoria House, Bloomsbury Square, London, WC1B 4DA
Owned by Bonnier Books
Sveavägen 56, Stockholm, Sweden

Copyright © Rachel Barnett, 2023

All rights reserved.
No part of this publication may be reproduced, stored or transmitted in any form or by any means, electronic, mechanical, photocopying or otherwise, without the prior written permission of the publisher.

The right of Rachel Barnett to be identified as Author of this work has been asserted by her in accordance with the Copyright, Designs and Patents Act 1988

This is a work of fiction. Names, places, events and incidents are either the products of the author's imagination or used fictitiously. Any resemblance to actual persons, living or dead, is purely coincidental.

A CIP catalogue record for this book is available from the British Library.

ISBN: 9781471415296

This book is typeset using Atomik ePublisher

Embla Books is an imprint of Bonnier Books UK
www.bonnierbooks.co.uk

*For the best friends anyone could hope to have –
my Fossilers Four*

Chapter One

Bella glanced around the cabin – it was smaller than she'd imagined, cramped, and she wondered why she hadn't realised she would be sharing with another member of the crew. At least there was a porthole in the room, a tiny oval of blue light. Dumping her rucksack on the lower bunk she sank down beside it and took a deep breath. This was really happening. A new job, a new challenge. Maybe even a new life.

Life begins at the end of your comfort zone – one of her brother's favourite phrases chose that moment to pop into her head. If Jay had said it once, he'd said it a thousand times, and she wondered how much of her decision to change direction had been to do with him and his encouragement.

Several years' worth of covering every aspect of hotel work – working silver service dinners and fine dining occasions at The Magnolia, then for the last couple of seasons, managing the entire waitstaff and catering department – hadn't exactly felt like living outside anybody's comfort zone. Not to Bella, anyway. Unless you counted an early brush with disaster when she was almost fired for speaking to a guest as she served their potatoes.

While she had spent years folding napkins and arranging petits fours, dealing with last-minute staff illness and guest tantrums, her brother – they weren't biologically related, but had been adopted together – had nearly finished medical school. Although his route into the medical profession hadn't been easy, and finances were tight, he had brains to spare and was loving life at London's King's College. Their parents were puffed up with pride at his achievements, and she could understand why. Jay's star was set very firmly in its ascendancy – more than that, he was working towards something he'd always dreamed of achieving.

Meanwhile, Bella had become very proficient at keeping her mouth shut while serving potatoes. To her credit, she could manage even the tiny baby new ones, covered in melted butter and sprinkled with the most delicate strands of chopped chives, despicably keen to roll away from her spoon and fork combo. Catching them up into groups of five was harder than it appeared – it took skill, as did placing the treacherous little marbles on each plate in exactly the same spot without dripping melted butter onto anyone's Jimmy Choos.

But was knowing a terrine fork from a cake fork, and having an intricate knowledge of the difference between the shapes of red, white and dessert wine glasses really something to write home about? The thought that being able to head off a staffing disaster due to an outbreak of flu, accommodating last-minute menu changes from demanding diners, and sitting behind a desk ordering cavolo nero and new tablecloths might be the sum total of her worth had become unsettling. Continuing at The Magnolia while the years spooled away into the future couldn't truly be the way she wanted to spend her life.

It was ironic, really, that while her parents had done everything they could to help Jay fly the nest, Bella had been left with little choice but to stick around, ignoring a deeply embedded yearning to travel. To see the world, not just the view from The Magnolia's sun terrace. Burying it deep, because there was no way she would ever manage to earn that kind of money on her hotel salary. And fully understanding there was no way she could ask her parents to help support her, when every spare penny was already winging its way to help with Jay's living costs. Which was why landing this job had been such a dream opportunity.

Was it possible today was the start of more than a new job? Could she unpack more than her belongings, and begin to believe she had discovered a way to earn her way around the world? Or, at least, the parts of the world that butted up against the sea?

A plink from her mobile had Bella checking her messages.

This one was from Jay, suggesting she was going to "kill" this new job, and he wasn't the slightest bit jealous of her. He took great pains to explain how little he cared that she was sailing around the Med for the summer getting – as he put it – "an epic tan", while he would be spending every waking hour in scrubs, bathed in artificial strip lighting.

She began to type a reply.

'You can't leave your stuff there – that's my bunk.'

The unexpected voice made Bella start, her finger slipping across the screen as she looked up to see a lean blonde woman, hands on hips and standing firmly in the doorway, a proprietorial expression on her face.

'Yours is the upper one.' The woman advanced into the cramped space, pulling open some tiny doors to reveal a couple of miniature cupboards. 'Your stuff can go in here.'

Sliding her bag onto the floor, Bella held out a hand and did her best to ignore the line of frost advancing in her direction.

'Hi, it's nice to meet you. I'm Bella.'

'I know who you are.' The handshake was terse. 'Jean-Philippe said you'd arrived. I'm Mel. Second stewardess. You know we have less than twenty-four hours until the guests arrive, right? There's still plenty to do and you're the one in charge.'

The one in charge . . .

'The captain's waiting for you – he's got the manifest for the charter guests.'

'OK. Thank you so much.'

The frost retreated from the cabin as Mel left. Bella sank back onto the lower bunk, considering for the first time since she'd left home the full extent of the role she'd taken on when she accepted this job.

Chief stewardess. Although the charter yachting industry didn't seem to have caught up with the rest of the world where equity in job titles was concerned, Bella was more focused on what the job itself would entail. Like a cross between being a hostess, silver service waitperson and ultimate facilitator for whatever the yacht's charter guests – or owner – required. Hospitality at its very finest. This yacht was referred to as having seven-star service, with every whim catered for, and Bella was now in charge of everything that happened inside it, while witnessing first-hand the beautiful scenery of the Mediterranean Sea. It had all seemed very doable, in theory. Most of the work she'd been doing for years on dry land – how different could it be to achieve it on a yacht? If this worked out, and the tips were as good as everybody told her they were, she would then be able to fund some winter travel, maybe find work on other boats, in other parts of the globe. The start of a new life.

It also sounded like it could be fun.

She supposed the wobble of nerves was only natural – this was the furthest away from home she'd ever been, and she knew nobody aboard *Blue Sky*. The interview with the captain had taken place over the internet and she had no idea what to expect from any of the guests – or the rest of the crew for that matter. After her brief and rather chilly chat with Mel, it looked likely Bella was going to have her work cut out with at least one staff member.

She just needed to take a breath, remember the calm poise she'd cultivated to keep musket balls of potato on a shallow spoon, and smile. With a serene, balanced approach, the rest of it would surely fall into place. That was going to be her theory, anyway.

After shoving her luggage onto the upper bunk, Bella slipped her mobile into a pocket and untied her hair, running fingers through its length in place of a brush – which was still buried deep somewhere inside her bag. Hooking some of the dark strands behind her ears, she took a quick peek at her reflection in the tiny mirror on the wall. Satisfied she hadn't smeared what little mascara she was wearing all over her cheeks and didn't look a total disaster, she headed out to locate the captain.

The entire crew had assembled in *Blue Sky*'s formal salon. Bella perched on the edge of one of three chesterfield leather sofas dwarfed by the dimensions of the room. After the confines of the crew area, the difference in the guest space was stark. The contrast between upstairs versus downstairs was evident in every polished chrome light fitting and highly glossed oak-panelled wall, in the enormous Persian rug adorning the teak hardwood floor, and the recessed ceiling with Michelangelo-esque paintings of gods and goddesses handing one another fruit. This room screamed opulence, without the slightest pretence at an apology.

To be fair, it wasn't all that different to working in a five-star hotel. Everything front of house was designed to impress the guest, while the chipped flooring and peeling paint backstage were at the bottom of everybody's list.

Clutched on Bella's lap was the earpiece and two-way radio which from here on in would be worn by every crew member, ensuring communication was consistent – and immediate. "I'll do it in a minute" or "I didn't realise I needed to . . ." didn't cut it on a superyacht any more than they did in a top-flight hotel. The only appropriate response to a request for a crew member to jump was to ask, "How high?"

The captain – Jean-Philippe Kirque – was in full swing. He had already introduced all crew members, new and old. Bella tried to take in all the names on this first pass and was gratified to note she wasn't the only newbie. This was also the third stewardess's first day aboard.

'As you know, our first charter guests arrive tomorrow, and we have much to prepare. Food delivery arrives in . . .' the captain checked his watch '. . . less than an hour, so at least one stewardess must be on hand to assist Tobias with provisioning the kitchen.'

As the briefing continued with specific tasks to be undertaken by the deck crew, Bella took the opportunity to take stock of the people with whom she would be spending – in extremely close proximity – the next three months.

If she had to hazard a guess, she'd put the captain in his early fifties. Short in stature, chunky and intense, deeply ingrained crow's feet spreading out from the corners of his eyes. He carried a rich tan that went some way towards balancing out the salt and pepper of his no-nonsense closely cropped hair and beard. She already knew he'd captained yachts for over twenty years; he'd told her as much in her interview. Before that he had served time in the navy. A lifetime spent at sea. Hopefully that meant *Blue Sky* was in the best hands.

Other members of the deck crew stood against the walls, including an engineer and bosun; there would be far more staff on board than guests.

Everyone, including the pair of well-built Greek deckhands – Yannis and Dimitri – had excellent English, the captain announced, his own accent richly continental.

Directly in Bella's eyeline, at the opposite end of the chesterfield, Mel was sitting bolt upright. Listening intently to the captain, she had positioned herself in such a way as to make absolutely sure she couldn't so much as glance in Bella's direction. Or was Bella imagining the frostiness was reserved solely for her? Maybe Mel was a naturally reserved person. Perhaps Bella should wait a while before she jumped to conclusions and not allow the insecurities she felt about the newness of everything to overshadow her perceptions. Nestled between her and Mel was the final stewardess, Jessica. Also overshadowed by the stress of the day, if the flashes of a nervous smile were anything to go by.

Jean-Philippe handed around sheaves of A4 paper, stapled at the top-left corner and covered in photos.

'Our first charter group are due on board at midday tomorrow. I think you will recognise the principal guest?'

The shuffle of papers made it over to Bella. She took a copy and passed the rest on, scanning the photos on the top sheet and nodding as she read the accompanying details. A smile crept onto her lips. She'd seen this face a hundred times – probably more – in one of her all-time favourite TV programmes. She'd avidly watched every episode of the female detective duo series, starting when she was about eleven.

'Felicia Kennedy,' the captain continued. 'The British actor who starred in many Hollywood films, and is currently playing the lead role in the television drama *Murder in Mayfair*. Please notice she doesn't drink red wine and needs all fresh flowers to be removed from her stateroom at least two hours before she retires for the night.'

He continued with his brief, but all the information was typed on the pages. She could memorise the details later. Right now, Bella couldn't stop herself from checking who else would be on board. Below Felicia's PR shot was a photograph of her husband, Nikolai. Not often seen in the press, and notorious for being private, he was a strikingly handsome older man. With a chiselled jawline and no trace of grey in a head of Scandi-blond hair, he had a faraway look in his eye, as if something of much greater import than the taking of his photograph had occurred just out of shot.

Turning the page, Bella's face lit up even further. Patti Prior, the actor who played sidekick to Felicia's character in *Murder in Mayfair*, would also be on the cruise. Patti portrayed with aplomb the role of a displaced Yank, thousands of miles from home and endlessly baffled by the British. Plus, she was the constant butt of Felicia's character's sarcasm. Undeservedly so, Bella thought, as it was habitually Patti's character who was the one to solve the weekly murder, even if she didn't get the credit for it. Patti's trademark red lipstick and even brighter auburn hair shone from the page almost as vividly as her smile.

Beneath that was a photo of someone Bella didn't recognise. Patti's daughter, Hannah. Same red hair as her mother, but no smile. A self-conscious pose. Not a pout for the camera, but definitely a calculated expression.

Bella flicked to the next page and her breath caught in her throat. She scanned the words quickly before settling her gaze back onto the photo and allowing it to rest there. Leo Kennedy-Edge. Felicia's nephew. Bella did her best to swallow, but her throat wouldn't comply with the request. Because staring at her from the page was one of the most attractive men she'd ever seen. Melting almond eyes set below eyebrows quirked in a half-question, a mop of hair as dark as her own, cut short at the sides and layered over the crown of his head. A jawline softened slightly by a beard, which appeared to require minimal maintenance, but probably took endless tweaking to make it look *that* good.

Doing her best to drag her gaze away, she turned to the final page, to see a photo of a middle-aged man with thinning mousy-brown hair and a thickening jawline. Felicia's lawyer, joining the yacht part-way through the trip, and staying for the remainder.

Bella flicked back to the front page. What a way to start her yachting career – with the first set of guests including two actresses she'd adored for years. Not to mention the glorious Leo Kennedy-Edge. This was going to be a proper adventure. She risked a glance along the chesterfield at the other stewardesses, and then across at the rest of the crew. Nobody seemed as excited as she felt, and she did her best to tamp her grin down to a manageable level, to control her levels of anticipation.

Because it was time to focus – time to remember the rules. Her rules. The rules that had enabled Bella to be successful in the roles she'd held until this point. And up near the summit of the list – even higher in the pecking order than not dropping potatoes onto designer footwear – was remembering that the guests, whether they were in a hotel, or on a boat, were an utterly different animal to people like her. That, even if they seemed nice, they weren't ever going to be her friends. The important thing was to make them happy, keep their glasses brimming, and hope for a healthy tip at the end of their trip.

Mel slid a glance around the salon. J-P was working his way through the list of guests for the first charter of the season. A beard suited him. Her molars clamped together, top set tighter and tighter against the bottom set until she felt the muscles in her jaw ache. God damn him. It grated at her to have to admit it, but he looked good.

Perhaps she should have applied for a job on a different boat, made a fresh start somewhere else. Somewhere without the history and baggage she'd built up over five years on *Blue Sky*. It would be easy enough to get second stewardess roles on any of the yachts doing the circuit; she knew the job like the back of her hand. And what had happened the previous summer – it hadn't been her fault. None of it was her fault.

Her work record was impeccable, or at least that was the way it would appear. J-P had guaranteed her that much – had gone as far as to say he'd support her applications for chief stewardess roles on other superyachts if that was what she wanted. But something deep inside Mel told her that wasn't good enough. That to metaphorically jump ship – or to be pushed overboard by J-P – weren't options she was prepared to explore. It was all too easy, too simple for him.

Yes, things would be awkward for a while, but she could cope with awkward. Forcing her jaws apart far enough to be able to wiggle at her cheek muscles with her fingers, she risked a sideways glance at Bella Mason. Brand-new chief stew. No previous yachting experience, but with an impeccable shoreside record in five-star hotels, latterly on the Cornish coast. Had J-P done it on purpose? Employed someone like Bella over Mel's head in an attempt to give her the final push she needed to leave?

Looking away before Bella noticed her stare, Mel arched defiant eyebrows and settled her gaze on their oh so illustrious captain. Held his eye when he glanced her way, allowing herself the tiniest hit of satisfaction as he momentarily stumbled over his words, and continuing to focus her attention on him while he composed himself and ran through his familiar spiel about standards, service, charter guests expecting the highest possible level of attention, nothing's too much trouble, blah blah blah. Mel crossed her arms and hoped J-P would notice the huff of her irritated sigh. She knew this bit off by heart.

Two things were crystal clear in Mel's mind. Firstly, this season was going to be anything but smooth sailing for the newbie, Bella Mason. She was all bubbly right now, with her barely suppressed puppy-dog excitement over the first set of charter guests – she was practically panting with enthusiasm. But it wouldn't be long before the reality of life on board a superyacht began to bite; it always did. And if Bella didn't crumble of her own accord, Mel might have to think up a few tricks to aid the disintegration.

Secondly, if Jean-Philippe Kirque thought he was going to sail through this season as if nothing had happened, then she was going to have to use this *Blue Sky* summer to remind their captain that she hadn't forgotten. Any of it.

Chapter Two

Bella edged the final box onto the stainless steel countertop in the galley.

'That's the last one,' she said.

Tobias, *Blue Sky*'s resident cordon bleu chef, jerked up at the sound of her voice, slamming the back of his head against the lip of the cupboard he had been stocking.

'Shite on a stick,' he said, reaching to cup the back of his head with a hand. 'Where did you spring from?'

'Oh God, I'm sorry – are you OK?'

'If you can discount the fact that we're light on the order for snapper and monkfish, one of the ovens is dicking around and the local maintenance guy hasn't been able to fix it, and I think I've sustained a mild concussion, then yes. Apart from that, I'm completely chipper.' He gave his scalp a final abrasive rub, sending messy blond hair into even greater disarray. 'Worse things happen at sea, believe me. How's it shaping up so far, being a virgin?'

'Sorry, what?'

Tobias held her gaze for a moment too long, his expression difficult to read. Then he waggled his eyebrows. 'First time on a superyacht, right?'

'Oh. I see. Yes.'

'So, how is it going?'

'Good. I think.'

'What's in the box?'

'Not sure.' Bella tugged at the folded top, unfurled the plastic bag inside and had to chuckle at the contents. 'Baby new potatoes.'

'Cold room, please. The vegetables are on the left – put them on the bottom shelf.'

Tobias put a tick against one of the long lists he had laid out beside the sinks, and she headed for the cold storage room, behind the galley.

'Fancy a coffee?' His voice wafted along the short corridor.

'I'd love one,' she called back, re-emerging to find him filling the kettle.

'How are the guest cabins? Ready for charter season round one?' Tobias mimed ringing a bell. 'Ding ding.'

'Getting there.' She'd left Mel and Jessica cleaning and preparing the en-suite bathrooms and planned to do a final vacuum and dust check later, before setting the towels and the welcome hampers on each bed. The finishing touches could wait until the following morning.

Buckets full of the most gorgeous flowers – lilies and roses in a sliding scale of hues from ruby red through all the pinks and ending with clean, sharp whites, stems of eucalyptus and sedum to ground all the colour – were ready to be arranged in vases and spread throughout the guest areas of the yacht. Bottles of Krug champagne were chilling – apparently the principal's husband's favourite – and Bella had checked through the crockery and linens, glassware and silverware, and was satisfied everything was as it should be.

Tobias handed her a mug, the aroma of fresh coffee a welcome distraction from work.

'I've checked the preference lists for lunch tomorrow. I'm going to give them antipasti. Cured meats, olives, cheeses, artichoke hearts. That sort of thing. I've got some fantastic sun-blushed tomatoes and I'll make crostini. Sound good?'

'Sounds wonderful,' she said.

'Can you pair some wine to go with that?'

'No problem.'

'Jean-Philippe is planning on taking us out of harbour and dropping anchor somewhere quieter and more picturesque in time for the food, so do you want to serve lunch on the sun deck?'

Tobias sipped from his own mug, his expression edged with amusement as he waited for her reply.

'Are you asking me, or steering me?' Bella met his mock surprise with a straight face.

'You're the virgin here,' he said, 'Not me. Feel free to pop your cherry however you see fit. You can serve it however and wherever you like, although when the weather is as calm as it's going to be for the next couple of days, it's good to get the guests on deck as much as possible. That's why they're here, after all. The ocean and the scenery, darling.'

'And the cuisine, I presume.'

'Always.' He grinned.

'Sun deck it is,' she said. 'Thanks for the suggestion.'

'Pleasure.'

'Can anyone stand around and drink coffee, or is that reserved for management?' Mel's tone was confrontational before she'd even made it fully into the galley. Shoving a bucketful of cleaning products on the floor, she reached for a mug and spooned coffee granules haphazardly. 'All the bathrooms are done, and I left Jemima, is it? Third stew—'

'Her name's Jessica.'

'Whatever. I left her polishing bed legs. Did you say you were going to do the flowers?' Mel's tone hadn't softened, and she stabbed at the switch on the kettle.

'I'm more than happy to do them. Unless you'd rather we did them together?' Bella's suggestion that they might work as a team was clearly pathetic, if the lift in Mel's eyebrows was anything to go by.

'No. You're fine.'

'OK. In that case, can I ask – where are the vases kept?'

Felicia Kennedy couldn't shift her headache. It had settled above her eyebrows the previous evening, right after dinner, and despite taking copious painkillers she couldn't seem to make a dent in it. While Nikolai suggested he take the others to the Casino de Monte-Carlo, and Patti announced she'd always wanted to go to Jimmy'z nightclub, Felicia decided to retire to their hotel suite. As beautiful as ever, Monaco's Hotel de Paris – with its curved construction and mermaids bursting from its exterior plasterwork – had promised an unparalleled night's sleep. Unfortunately, it hadn't delivered, but that was less to do with the goose-down pillows and Egyptian cotton, and more to do with the fact that she hadn't been able to shift the damn headache.

Now on the marina and heading for their yacht – *Blue Sky* – Nikolai took her hand, and she did her best to ignore the dull thud coming from somewhere behind her eyes. The smile dancing on his lips was worth her personal discomfort.

'It's like a superyacht parking lot.' Patti's voice, nasal and brash, pierced straight to the root of Felicia's headache. Her frown was unconscious, and only added to the tension already squeezing at her forehead. Thank God for her enormous dark glasses, behind which she could safely do what she liked with her expression.

'It is exactly that,' Nikolai said.

It often struck Felicia that even though it was his second language, Nikolai's command of English far surpassed many for whom it was their native tongue. Especially Americans, like Patti. It didn't seem to matter how long ago he'd swapped his native Denmark for the UK, or how many years Nikolai spent surrounded by those who spoke English as a first language – and regularly took a hatchet to the grammar book – the precision of his speech remained undiminished. And its effect on her was as strong as ever. There was something timelessly attractive about a man with good grammar. She tightened her grip on his fingers and tugged him in the direction indicated by the shore agent.

Felicia had decided to take the walk down to *Blue Sky*, rather than piling everyone into the grubby transfer bus with their luggage. She wanted to see the expression unfurl on Nikolai's face when he caught his first glimpse of the yacht, and she wasn't disappointed.

'Ladies and gentlemen, there she is,' the shore agent said with more than a touch of dramatic emphasis, gesturing to a sleek white craft moored tight to the jetty. 'Motor yacht *Blue Sky*.'

As he reeled off the yacht's statistics as if it were a supermodel, the rest of the group wandered closer. The yacht was exquisite. Even in a marina bursting with what would no doubt add up to billions of pounds' worth of boats, *Blue Sky* still managed to catch the eye. Every inch of her gleamed. Reflections and glints from the rippling bottle-blue water shimmered and played off the sleek surface, the perfect white curve of the hull. Everything was swan-white and gleaming, apart from the chrome of the handrails, shining even more brightly in the sunlight – if that were possible – and the yacht's name, emblazoned across the back in an elegant turquoise font.

Nikolai ground to a halt, pinning Felicia to the spot beside him, his hand clasped tightly around hers.

'Oh, my darling. She is stunning,' he said.

His expression was as stellar as the boat. This was why Felicia had booked the charter in the first place. She didn't spend anything like enough time with her husband; hadn't done for far too long. Her filming schedule had been brutal for years. They said you had to ride the crest of the wave until it came to shore, had to take advantage of every acting and publicity opportunity that came your way, that it was only a matter of time before the wave flattened and the viewing public lost interest. For Felicia though, the wave of celebrity hadn't ever really flattened. Instead, it had been more of a tsunami, crushing everything in its path and continuing, unabated.

In some ways, her hectic work schedule over the last few decades had been a blessing. It kept her focused and driven, had made it possible for her to try to forget some of what had come before. It had also been responsible for making her a very wealthy woman. But the price of success had been intrinsically high. Her time never quite felt her own. Moments with Nikolai were negotiated around filming schedules, and although they'd managed to snatch enough time to travel a good proportion of the globe and experience some of the best of what the world had to offer, it had never felt like enough.

She'd always planned to stop acting at some point, to

withdraw from a life lived in the public eye and spend time as Nikolai wanted, but she'd never quite managed to quit the lure of the camera.

She soaked up the uncharacteristically boyish smile that had engulfed Nikolai's features, and memories of the first time she'd seen him crowded at the front of her mind. He'd been on a boat then, too. Grinning like a teenager even though everyone had told her he never smiled.

Taking a step or two towards *Blue Sky* and with Nikolai keeping pace with her, she squeezed his hand more firmly and smiled, too.

'Happy birthday, Nicki,' she said.

Bella checked the buttons on her white shirt for probably the tenth time since the captain had given the order for all crew to dress in their whites and assemble on deck to meet and greet the charter guests. She made sure the pin on her name badge was level and fastened, then flicked a wrist to check the time. The second hand on her watch ticked through the last few seconds before midday. High noon. Time for her to start proving she'd been the right pick for this job. Time to fix a smile to her face and play her role to the best of her ability – the perfect hostess – regardless of any curveballs fired in her direction.

Twisting at the waistband of her black pencil skirt, making sure the shirt was tucked in evenly all the way around, she could see the guests on the quay, wandering towards the boat. Alexandro, the shore agent, coaxed them closer, and she could hear snatches of his conversation.

'At just over eighty metres from bow to stern, *Blue Sky* offers the ultimate in comfort and . . .'

'I wish he'd get on with it.' Tobias fiddled with the popper fastenings on his chef's whites. 'God, I hate this bit.' He slunk his hands into the pockets of his checked trousers. 'Can't wait to have this done and get on with the cooking – it's what I'm here for. Not all this hanging around like a stuffed monkey.'

Bella had to admit, standing in a row like this, waiting to greet the guests, did have the artificial nature of one of those lines at a wedding, where everyone had to greet and fawn over the bride and groom – and their relations whom you'd never previously met and would never set eyes on again afterwards. Either that or a line-up of suspects in a police holding cell, waiting to be interviewed.

Eventually, the clonking of footsteps sounded on the gangplank and the excited chatter from the guests faded as they climbed the curving stairs. First to crest the steps was Felicia Kennedy, bestowing on the captain the sunshine-bright screen smile Bella recognised so well.

'Welcome aboard *Blue Sky*. I'm your captain – Jean-Philippe Kirque. We are honoured to have you aboard. Anything we can do – let us know. Please . . .' Jean-Philippe clasped her hand, his Mediterranean accent on full throttle, then gestured her along the line-up. It appeared Bella wasn't the only one who felt like she had to put on a show.

By the time Felicia had greeted Tobias and reached her, Bella knew exactly what she was going to say. She managed a "hello" but didn't get any further. Felicia took her hand in both of hers and leaned closer.

'Is his name really Captain Kirque?'

Bella couldn't stop herself from huffing a laugh. 'Yes. It is.'

'How do you stop yourself making *Star Trek* jokes? I'm not sure I'm going to be able to help myself.'

'It's tricky,' Bella agreed.

'I almost asked him if he was going to "make it so" – but that's the other one, isn't it? Picard. Patrick Stewart. Fantastic actor – hard to believe he's in his eighties now, and still working like a twenty-something.'

Felicia still had a hold of her hand, the warmth from her smooth fingers becoming sticky in the climbing heat of the midday sun.

'Oh that we should all be blessed with his longevity,' Felicia added.

'Absolutely. It's wonderful to have you on board – we're all so excited. I'm your chief stewardess, so anything you need, please don't hesitate to ask me.'

'He wears purple slippers, you know,' Felicia said, releasing Bella's hand.

'I'm sorry, who does?'

'Patrick Stewart.'

Felicia moved along the line to greet the rest of the crew and Bella ran through her pre-prepared welcome as the rest of the guests filed past. At the end of the line came Leo Kennedy-Edge. Felicia's nephew was even more striking in person than his photograph had suggested. Striking enough to make Bella's mouth instantly dry and her palms turn slick. She hoped he didn't notice the surreptitious rub of her hand against the fabric of her skirt, in an attempt to dry the skin before she shook his hand.

She fumbled her way through her welcome, covering her suddenly intermittent brain-to-voice-box connection by plying the guests with a glass of chilled Krug and suggesting she take them on a tour of the yacht.

Timing her route to allow the deckhands an opportunity to lift luggage on board and distribute it to the correct cabins, Bella wound her way through the elegant salon and formal dining room – complete with its one-of-a-kind bespoke chandelier, each teardrop of crystal shining with a slightly different hue of blue as it fell like a waterfall from the brilliant white of the ceiling – and showed them the on-board gym and spa facilities.

'If you wish, we can bring in a specialist trainer for a tailor-made workout,' she said.

'Darling, we're here for a holiday.' Felicia drained the rest of her champagne from the flute glass. 'I mean, I expect Leo might want to give the equipment a go, keep those pecs of his perky, but the extent of my working out this week will be to tilt my deckchair to catch the best of the sun.'

'Hannah will want to work out, for sure.' Patti Prior looked at her daughter, her expression loaded. 'Won't you?'

'Sure. I guess.'

If Bella were to hazard a guess, she wouldn't imagine Hannah spent much time in the gym. She was willowy and delicate, seemed quiet and self-absorbed. Though as her gaze flicked in Leo's direction, spots of colour bloomed momentarily on otherwise pale cheeks.

'Maybe you can persuade Leo to help you,' Patti said. 'Devise a workout routine together, you know?'

Hannah's eyebrows furrowed, a flash of annoyance crossing her delicate features.

'I'd be happy to.' Leo wandered over to the equipment, checking out the treadmill and the cycling machine. He stopped by the multi-gym. 'This Ironman will be great for my knee.'

'We can also arrange for a professional masseur to come on board, if you should want some pampering.' Bella did her best to drag her gaze away from Leo, fixing her gaze on Felicia, instead.

'Now you're talking.' Felicia waggled her empty glass. 'But before all that, I think it's time for a top-up.'

Bella left the guests on the sun deck and carried the empty champagne bottles down to the galley, heading past Tobias to the cold room.

'It's going to be one of those charters, is it?' he said, his gaze remaining focused on the platters onto which he was arranging a variety of salamis into intricate fans and curling prosciutto meats into flower shapes.

He glanced up as she reappeared with an armful of unopened bottles and a bag of ice, tipping out the half-melted icy water at the bottom of the wine cooling bucket and refilling it.

'A boozy cruise?' Tobias clarified his question with a wave of a hand towards the champagne.

'Put it this way, none of them have been shy with the Krug,' Bella said, pulling out a fresh linen cloth to wrap around the next bottle.

She had stayed with them on the sun deck, ready to pour

top-ups the moment anyone's glass threatened to run dry. From her vantage point under the shade of the canopy, she'd watched the group as they leaned against the gleaming chrome railings, stretching to take in as much of the view as possible, while the captain's voice fed directly into her ear as he instructed the deck crew to cast off.

The specific boating language was something she was going to have to play catch-up with; there was no doubt about that. Although she wasn't expected to know where the anchor pockets were, or when the boat bumpers needed to be inflated ready for docking, Bella sensed it would be just as well to have a grasp of as much of what went on as possible. Apart from anything else, if one of the guests asked her a question, she didn't want to look like an idiot.

She'd watched the expressions of excitement, the heightened level of chatter from the guests as Jean-Philippe fired up *Blue Sky*'s engines and they negotiated their way out into open water. She felt it too, had been unable to smother her own excitement. They were on a *superyacht*. It hardly felt real – she was half-expecting a crew member to pull her to one side, with an apology and an explanation that it had all been a giant mistake, that unfortunately they'd got the wrong Bella Mason and she shouldn't be on board at all.

With Monaco shrinking into the background and open water surrounding them for the first time, she'd topped up everyone's glass at least twice. There weren't any teetotallers in this group. But if she had to make a prediction about who would head the leader board for alcohol consumption over the next week, surprisingly she found herself leaning towards Hannah. Although the young woman appeared mild-mannered, bordering on quiet, she'd already packed away at least three flutes of champagne, and had been halfway through her fourth when Bella headed for the galley with the empties.

Having loaded the fresh bottles into the ice, Bella tested the weight of the ensemble. Heavy, but manageable.

'How long until lunch is ready?'

Tobias twirled a final piece of prosciutto and squeezed it into the display, throwing her a glance. 'How long until we're at the captain's designated spot?'

'*All crew, all crew. Five minutes until we reach anchor point.*' Jean-Philippe's voice, tinny and distant in her ear, answered both their questions.

'Looks like it'll be ready in five minutes' time,' Tobias said. 'Do you need a hand with that?'

She tugged at the handles on either side of the large ice bucket and shook her head. 'I'll be back in five.'

Chapter Three

With the anchor dropped and the engines stilled, the gentle lapping of the waves against the hull and a slight warm breeze in her face, Felicia stared out to sea. The rest of the group were admiring the coastline. Sleek, colonial-style properties nestled against the green of Cape Martin. But Felicia wasn't here to gawp at other people's affluence. She tipped her face to the breeze and allowed her eyelids to sink.

Sensing Nikolai before she felt his touch, she leaned into him as the cool smoothness of his fingers found their natural resting place where the curve of her neck melted into the rest of her spine. He didn't speak, instead she heard the depth and contentment of his sigh.

'Happy?' she asked.

'Never happier,' he replied.

Opening her eyes, Felicia studied the undulations of the water, following its curves further and further away from the boat, until her whole vista was nothing but blue. But it wasn't only blue. It was inky in places, and in others a multitude of greens, constantly shifting – an endless variety of hues, alive and vibrant and ever-changing. Something that had forever been the largest constituent part of the planet, and would continue to be, long after everyone on *Blue Sky* was nothing but dust. She wondered what it would be like to stock up the boat with as many supplies as they could cram into it and sail away. Not simply for a week as they had planned, hugging the coastline and playing on the fringes of the Mediterranean; no, how would it feel to plot a course out into the wilds of the ocean and keep going?

It wasn't something she had ever thought about, before.

But lately all sorts of strange notions had been visiting Felicia. Crowding into her brain. Thoughts about opportunities she hadn't taken, things she'd never dreamed she might want to try. Some of them crazy, others far more mundane and ordinary. All of them with a much greater resonance than ever before in her life.

Chartering *Blue Sky* had seemed the ideal starting point to right the imbalance. It was booked primarily for Nicki – the perfect way to celebrate his sixtieth birthday – but as she stood on the sun deck and stared out into the blue, Felicia wondered if it hadn't been in part for her, too.

'If you would like to take a seat, ladies and gentlemen. Lunch is served.'

Felicia hadn't noticed the lunch preparations, had been unaware of the dark-haired stewardess, with her effortless smile and her unbounded springy youth, bringing plates of food to the table.

Nicki ran his fingers across to her shoulder before his hand dropped.

'Shall we?' he said.

Nodding, Felicia waited for Nicki to turn away, then held her empty champagne flute over the railings, hovering it there before she dropped it into the water. Watched it as it bobbed for a moment, then tipped and filled and disappeared beneath the surface.

Then she pushed away from the handrail, and headed for the table.

Mel pulled yet another dress from Patti Prior's suitcase. This one was long, covered in silky swirls of greens and pinks and cut to hide the worst of the ravages suffered by a middle-aged body. How many clothes could one woman need for a week on a yacht? Having hardly made a dent in the contents of the Louis Vuitton bag, Mel glanced into the wardrobe, checking the number of remaining padded hangers as she straightened the fabric of the capped sleeves onto the hanger in her hand.

Most of the female charter guests tended to bring a bag full of string bikinis and a bigger bag of diet pills, only outweighed by their bitchy attitudes. It went with the territory. But Patti Prior didn't conform to the stereotype, and Mel had to admit she admired her for that. It couldn't have been easy, negotiating her way through the cut-throat world of acting when the chances of her ever fitting into the expected size-zero outfits were clearly zilch.

The difference between the two actresses was stark. Felicia Kennedy was tiny – barely five-foot four on her tiptoes, and with a delicate bone structure that had allowed her to remain wafer-thin, even though she must be in her fifties. Meanwhile, Patti Prior stood at a good five-seven, without heels, and she filled the eye with more than her personality.

Mel hadn't ever watched the long-running series they both starred in. They played a detective duo, apparently, thrown together by some chance encounter and, when their investigations proved successful, were kept together by the brass upstairs even though they couldn't stand one another. She'd heard that Felicia's character spent all her time snarking at Patti's, but that the latter was usually the one to find the key to the killer's identity.

It would be interesting to see how that played out in real life. How far life would imitate art. Mel lifted another dress, eyebrows arching at its vibrant colour palette. It wasn't going to be hard to spot Patti Prior in a crowd.

Perhaps that was the secret to Patti's success. Making sure everyone knew who she was, and where she was. Refusing to apologise for herself, pushing forward and making sure to stare everyone in the eye. Because, regardless of their on-screen personas, Mel had heard all about Patti. About her very vocal condemnation of the way women were expected to appear. The boxes they were expected to inhabit. Her refusal to change herself for the industry and the resulting missed career opportunities.

Eventually, after reaching the base of the luggage, arranging toiletries in the bathroom and footwear in the wardrobe, Mel zipped up then slid the cases away into the space beneath the bed. She'd long since become accustomed to the difference in the living arrangements on board a yacht. This bed was king-sized, furnished with sheets of the finest cottons, which would be changed – probably by her – every day of the charter. Meanwhile she was bunking with Bella, in a room far smaller than Patti Prior's bathroom.

Had J-P arranged that on purpose, too? To be made to share a room with the woman who had taken the job that should rightfully be Mel's . . . It felt deliberate. She knew how calculating J-P could be. She'd seen it often enough.

After smoothing out the bedspread and turning a circle to check everything was perfect, she left the room, closing the door softly behind her. She could hear laughter coming from the sun deck. Lunch was still underway, with Bella overseeing the proceedings. Unable to suppress a wave of annoyance, Mel felt her jaw clench again, her molars squeezing together until they hurt. Fuck it. Maybe she shouldn't wait for the intense nature of life on board to bite at Bella. Perhaps she should be proactive. But how?

No doubt she'd think of something, given a little time. After all – Patti Prior wasn't the only one who'd learned how to fight for what she wanted.

With lunch cleared away, the guests plied with coffee and settled into recliners on the lower deck, and *Blue Sky* underway for their first overnight mooring, Bella allowed herself to relax. The rest of the crew squeezed themselves around their dining table in the utilitarian staff space, to eat their meal. Tobias catered for everyone on board, and clearly recognised that the needs of the deckhands varied significantly from those of the guests, as a large tray of browned sausages stood alongside a bowl of mashed potato and a pile of green beans.

'Someone needs to take some up to the captain,' Tobias said, sliding onto the end of the bench seat and helping himself to a dollop of the mash. Glancing in Bella's direction, he added, 'He'll eat at the helm.'

'Well, I can't.' To be fair, Mel was wedged between the two Greek sailors. But the tone of her voice had Bella wondering if she'd have said the same wherever she'd been seated.

'I'll take it,' said Jessica, lodging her cutlery onto the edge of her plate.

'No. I'll do it.' To be honest, Bella wasn't all that hungry – certainly not for something as substantial as sausages and mash. The heavy, cloying caramelised smell from the crisp sausage skins and the oozing buttery mash, along with the way the deckhands were enthusiastically enjoying every mouthful was doing strange things to her stomach. Getting upstairs where she could take in some fresh air suddenly felt like an extremely good idea. Tobias plated up and then handed the food to her, and she grabbed some cutlery before escaping the close confines of the space.

With the plate delivered to Captain Kirque, Bella headed outside, to the front of the boat where she could take in the panorama undisturbed. With the coast to their left – their portside, she needed to try to remember the lingo – and the expanse of blue to her starboard, Bella took some deep breaths of the fresh, salty air. Allowed the breeze to run across her face and ripple through the fabric of her shirt. Tried to concentrate on the movement of the yacht on the water, the smooth undulations, the slap of the waves against the point of the hull as it cut its path. Fixed her gaze on an indistinguishable point somewhere in the middle distance.

It took a while for Bella to realise she still felt sick. It was as if her stomach was dropping, and she had no control over its descent.

Concentrating on her breathing, it dawned on her where she'd felt this sensation before. When she'd been a kid, her parents had regularly taken her brother and her to the closest adventure park. Longley Valley – a fantastic area of woodland where they could cycle, climb on the numerous purpose-built play structures and generally spend time outside, mucking about and letting off steam. It was a forty-minute drive from their home, and once her parents had begun to add foster children to the brood, her dad had managed to get hold of a people-carrier to fit them all in. She and Jay always bagged the back row of seats, claiming priority status, and she'd resolutely travelled in that seat every time, even though she'd ended up with exactly this sensation – and she'd usually thrown up the moment they arrived at the park.

Bella gripped at the handrail as the roiling in her stomach intensified. This had not been part of the plan. Sailing around the Med was supposed to be an exciting way to spend the summer, a way to prove her ability to self-fund her travel plans. It hadn't ever occurred to her that the sailing itself might be a problem.

Praying the yacht wouldn't take too long to get to its next anchor point, Bella turned her back on the view and closed her eyes, then opened them again when she realised that felt worse.

Perhaps Tobias would have some anti-seasickness medication – she definitely wasn't going to ask, or tell, any of the others. In the meantime, she would spend as much time in the fresh air as possible and avoid food. As far as that was practical on a yacht where her primary role was to serve food and drink.

Pulling her mobile from her pocket, she messaged Jay.

'*Yacht awesome. Scenery wonderful. But I'm seasick*'

She added an image of an unhappy face and pressed send. A message plinked instantly – no words, just a line of laughing emojis and a final one projectile vomiting. Helpful, especially from a doctor.

Bella huffed a laugh. This was perfect.

When Bella returned below deck, Tobias was stacking the dishwasher.

'I assumed you didn't want any of the food,' he said, gesturing towards the empty dishes. 'I can always find you something else, if you like?'

She shook her head.

He straightened, studying her more closely. 'Are you OK? You look a bit pale.'

Resting her hands palm-down on the stainless steel of the counter, Bella paused as her stomach gave another roll. 'Feeling a bit seasick, if I'm honest.'

Tobias began to laugh. It started off gently enough, then grew louder as he stared at her, and tipped over into near-hysteria when she asked him if he had any anti-seasickness medication. He wrapped his arms around his sides as if she'd delivered the killer punchline to a joke she'd been cultivating for hours.

'Don't,' she pleaded. 'It's not funny.'

It didn't matter what she said, though, he just laughed harder, eventually wiping the tears from his face. 'Oh, God. That's too much. You're too much. A seasick first stewardess . . . That's a new one on me.'

'Don't laugh at me. It's not bloody funny.' The anger she felt bubbling actually went some way to counteracting the nausea. Perhaps she'd have to make sure she spent the entire cruise being annoyed by something.

'Well, don't hurl in my galley.' Tobias stacked more dishes. 'Or over the side. Deck crew don't want to be cleaning it off the yacht's hull.'

'You're full of compassion.'

'I'm full of something,' he said. 'Or so I keep being told, but it's not compassion, sorry. I haven't got anything – any anti-puke stuff, I mean.' He chuckled again. 'I can't believe you didn't know you'd need it. Have you literally never been on a boat before? At all?'

It probably sounded ridiculous, but she hadn't. When they were kids, holidays had always involved plenty of time on beaches, messing around in the shallow water and building sandcastles. Or outdoorsy destinations with stunning scenery and a countryside that needed to be attacked with a good pair of walking boots, possibly even ropes and crampons. And when she'd got the job at the hotel in St Austell, she'd still never been on board a boat, even if her vista was dominated by small craft bobbing and clinking in the harbour.

It hadn't occurred to her that this might happen.

Tobias's tone softened; the amusement flickered and faded away. 'There'll be something in the on-board pharmacy. We keep stocked up with quite a few over-the-counter medications, painkillers, headache pills, insect bite cream – that sort of thing. Also, some heavier-duty stuff, just in case. Which is why you'll need to sign for any medication you take, and explain who it's for.'

That sounded promising. 'OK. Who do I need to see for that?'

'Captain Kirque. He's the only one with a key.'

Bella shook her head. The last thing she wanted to do was tell the captain she was feeling seasick. 'I don't want him to know. How unprofessional am I? Day one of the charter and I'm already ill . . .'

Tobias rubbed at his chin. 'Well, why don't you see if you can go ashore when we anchor at Camogli – see if you can find a pharmacy?'

'You won't tell anyone, will you?'

He laughed again, then pressed a finger to his lips. 'Won't tell a soul.'

As she thanked him, Tobias picked up the sausage tray from earlier, tipping it towards her. She glanced inside before she realised it still contained a couple of stragglers that rolled across the congealed, clinging streaks of caramelised browns, and white globules of fat at the bottom.

'Are you sure I can't tempt you?' he said.

Recoiling, she shoved a hand across her mouth. 'You bastard,' she squealed, which only made Tobias laugh harder.

'Get out in the fresh air,' he said, as he tipped the remnants into the bin. 'Stay there for as long as you can. And get yourself on that shore tender. Failing that, I have some mint tea. Or ginger. You can chew on that.'

Chapter Four

By the time Jean-Philippe was issuing instructions about their mooring spot for the evening, Bella had done as Tobias suggested and stayed above deck as much as possible. She'd pasted a smile on her face as she assisted the guests with their requests.

But the broiling in her stomach didn't let up, and Bella had to grit her teeth as Felicia asked for bottled water – a brand she'd specifically requested be available. Breathing deliberately, Bella did her best to listen patiently as Felicia explained how this particular brand of water was harvested from melting slabs of icebergs. The husband – Nikolai – asked in very precise language about the internet connectivity while they were aboard the yacht. Patti Prior wanted a sun lounger to be moved so she could better watch the coastline as it passed by, and Hannah requested another bottle of champagne.

Thankful for small mercies, Bella noticed that Leo didn't ask for anything and spent most of his time at the back of the boat – stern, she reminded herself, it was called the stern – sitting on the steps leading down to the swimming platform with one leg stretched out, a livid scar running the length of his knee joint, while he watched the foamy water churning from the back of the ship.

At least, that's what Bella assumed was filling his vision – she couldn't bring herself to look too closely at anything that moved with that kind of a motion; there was enough turbulence inside her stomach. She hadn't eaten anything all day, and as the afternoon pulled on, and the requests kept her running up and down the steps into and back out from the galley or the guest suites, she wondered if that had been a sensible decision. Whether, in fact, her stomach acid was churning around on itself, making her situation even worse. Either way, she didn't plan on consuming anything but water – ordinary crew water rather than the hundred euro a bottle type – until her nausea was under control.

'*All crew, all crew.*' Jean-Philippe's words sounded in her ear, a disembodied voice shaking her out of her own thoughts. '*Time to anchor, forty minutes. Stewardesses, please be making sure our guests are aware. Yannis, Dimitri – tender checks completed within the next ten minutes, then ready with the anchor. That is all.*'

Bella flicked her finger against her two-way radio, and her voice sounded tinny and distant in her own ear. 'I'm with the guests and will ready them. Mel and Jessica, can you ensure all the supplies are organised for going ashore?'

Anything to stay above deck, to avoid spending more time than was necessary in the bowels of the ship. She received an immediate acknowledgement from Jessica, but no response from Mel.

She tried again. 'Mel, copy please. Can you and Jessica ready supplies for going ashore?'

Footsteps behind her had her turning. It was Mel.

'I heard you the first time,' she said, voice lowered but with a coldness it was hard not to notice prickling at the edges of every word. 'And I certainly don't need to be told twice. I know exactly what *I'm* doing.'

Pushing past Bella, Mel slipped down the steps and onto the swimming platform, something swinging from her left hand. Bella couldn't hear the conversation Mel had with Leo, but he took the neoprene support wrap with a nod and fixed it around his damaged knee, pulling the flesh-coloured Velcro attachments tight against the warm tone of his skin.

Mel pushed back past her, cocking an eyebrow at her expression. 'Just keeping the guests happy. Now I'll go and count towels, shall I?'

'That's not what . . .'

Before she had finished her sentence, Mel was gone. Bella

puffed air into her cheeks, allowing it out between tight lips in a soft whistle. It was hard to understand where Mel's irritation was coming from, but there was no mistaking it. Once Bella had managed to get her seasickness under control, she needed to work out what Mel's problem was and try to dispel the aggravation. It would have to wait, though, as Bella informed the guests of the plans for dinner in a small restaurant in an unspoilt Ligurian resort, and the opportunity to wander the streets of the picturesque town.

It was possible that the journey to shore on the tender was even worse than being on the yacht. Bella sat at the back, her smile as rictus-tight on her face as her hands were on the edges of the support craft. Her phone, stuffed with euros, was fastened into a pocket in the hope that she would be able to dart away and search for a chemist shop.

Yannis was in charge of the tender, but Mel was making the trip, too. Which could work to Bella's advantage, she decided – surely Mel would enjoy having sole charge of the guests for a while. Put her centre stage for long enough for Bella to complete her search for a pharmacy. Perhaps that was all Mel wanted – to be more involved with the guests.

Jean-Philippe had chosen their mooring well. Camogli's harbour wasn't suitable for the dimensions of the yacht, so they dropped anchor as close to shore as was practicable and took the smaller boat in. The quay to which Yannis tied the tender was rustic, but well maintained. The town, with its castle and church overlooking the harbour, nestled between the coastline and the surrounding verdant hills, the amber-and-gold-painted buildings decorated with intriguing frescoes. There were even some traditional fishermen's nets hanging out to dry, and ancient ankle-twisting cobbles.

A man of few words, but with an impressive frame and a wonderful broad grin that dimpled his cheeks, Yannis helped each guest from the boat with a firm grip. Bella didn't realise how firm his grip was until it was her turn, and he all but lifted her bodily from the edge of the boat.

'You're going back to *Blue Sky?*' she asked.

'Yes. You tell me when to return. Radio the yacht. I'll be here in a few minutes.'

She watched him steer the tender away from the dock, the turquoise blue of his crew polo shirt fading against the blue of the water as he headed towards the yacht, the motion of the water still pulsing through her own body even though she was now on dry land.

Pulling a small piece of folded paper from her pocket, on which was drawn a crude map and the name of the restaurant, Bella headed off the jetty and away from the quaint harbour, with what she hoped looked like confidence. The town proved to be more of a maze than the map indicated, and she heaved an internal sigh of relief when she located the restaurant. Set back from the shoreline, down one of the many darkly twisting *caruggi*, it opened out onto a wooden platform where the owner stood ready to welcome them – all beaming smiles and a promise of an evening unlike any other.

That could go either way, Bella mused. But the menu – presented with a flourish – boasted an astounding list of freshly caught fish and when she heard Felicia describe the spot as 'magical', she began to relax.

'One of us should wait with them, in case there are any issues,' Bella said to Mel. 'Would you stay for now? I'd like to take a look around the town, if that's OK. If you need me just call.'

'I'll be fine.' Mel's eyes narrowed as she replied. 'It's not as if this is my first rodeo. I'll see you later.'

As Bella headed uphill towards where she thought the main street was, it occurred to her that it might take a while to find what she was searching for – and if she did, the shop might already have closed. Her Italian wasn't up to much. In fact, it wasn't up to anything, past *ciao* and *bella* – which was ironic – so she would have to eliminate streets and shops until she stumbled on the right one or ask for help using some sort of pidgin sign language.

Plenty of people passed by, locals and tourists alike, every one of them filled with a sense of purpose. Eventually, she stopped a couple talking loudly enough for her to identify them as Americans, who thought there might be a pharmacy further down the street.

At last, she saw a green cross on a white background and a large picture window holding displays of suntan lotions and toiletries. Inside, she threaded her way along the shelving, a frown gaining traction as she glanced around. Where were the medicines? All she could see were beautifully gift-wrapped toiletries and more skincare products. How was she going to find what she needed?

She lifted a few packets she thought might contain medicine, turning them over to see if she could glean a clue from the back of the box. Pulling out her phone, she searched for Google Translate, when a voice behind her made her pause.

'Oh, hi there. I didn't realise you were in here.'

Leo Kennedy-Edge looked embarrassed. Almost as embarrassed as Bella felt at being caught in a shop, when she should be with her guests.

'Is everything all right?' she said, automatically resuming her role as crew member.

'Yes. Totally. I just needed to . . .' He glanced at the shelves by which they both stood. 'I just want some . . .' He sighed, his gaze dropping to his knee. 'Painkillers. That's all.'

'For your knee?' she asked – a flustered question, with an obvious answer, but he'd surprised her. The last thing she'd expected was to come face to face with the toned perfection of Leo Kennedy-Edge while she was scrabbling around looking for medication. Glancing at the packet in her hand, she hoped it wasn't for something like cystitis.

'Yes.' A momentary arch of his eyebrows was replaced by a shake of his head, as if he were trying to banish a thought, or a memory.

'What happened to it?'

'Oh, God. Such a stupid accident.' He shrugged. 'But then, isn't that always the way? It was supposed to be a gentle hack – just Pannacotta and me, rather than taking out a string. I still can't believe I ended up needing surgery.'

Bella's confusion must have shown.

'Sorry – I should explain. I play polo.'

'Polo?' Bella already knew what he did – it was on the guest manifest – but she didn't know anything more about the sport past the fact that it involved horses.

'We use a mallet – like for croquet, but with a longer handle.'

'Croquet?'

He grinned. 'OK. Ignore that comparison. It's sort of like hockey . . .' Pausing, he waited for her nod of recognition. 'Except the stick is shaped like a mallet, not a hook, and has an extended handle because you play it from horseback. But the idea is principally the same – team game, get the ball into the opponent's goal. Most points scored wins the game.'

'I understand the principle of a scoring system,' she said, wondering if he'd notice the rise in her eyebrows.

'Of course. Excellent.'

'How does *panna cotta* fit into you needing knee surgery? That's a dessert.'

'And also the name of one of my horses – strictly speaking she's called a pony, although she's horse-sized. A small horse.' He appeared more confused by his own explanation than she was.

She smiled through her incomprehension. This had to figure on her top ten most bizarre conversations to be having in an aisle of a pharmacy. Top five. Actually, scrap that. It was easily the most bizarre conversation she'd ever had, anywhere.

For clarification, Leo pulled out his phone, scrolling through photos before he turned the screen in her direction. Four horses stood side by side, each one carrying a man wearing a daffodil-yellow shirt slashed through with a blue band, white trousers and long boots with huge leather knee pads. Sticks were upended over their shoulders, and each wore a strange helmet alongside a huge grin for the camera. Leo was the one at the end, closest to the person taking the photo, his expression brighter and more engaged than the others, his upright posture and casual confidence clear even in the tiny image.

Leo pushed at the screen with a couple of fingers, enlarging the image until it was dominated by the white horse on which he was sitting.

'That's Pannacotta, at Cowdray Park last year.'

'She's very beautiful.'

'And she knows it.' His smile held genuine affection. 'She's also a bit of a handful. Do you know much about horses?' Swiping at the screen again, he pocketed the phone.

Bella laughed. 'They have four feet, a head and tail. And they kick. That's about the extent of it.'

'Four hooves, if we're being precise, not feet,' he said, with a shrug. 'Pannacotta has bucketloads of attitude. Feisty as hell, you might say. It makes her an excellent polo pony – she really loves the job. But trying to take her for a gentle canter around the countryside? Totally different proposition. Long story short, she took exception to a tractor working in a field and dumped me. To add injury to insult she also managed to stamp on my knee.' The grin faded. 'The impact broke my kneecap. Incredibly rare accident, apparently. They had to wire it back together.'

'Ouch.' Bella pulled a face. 'Painful.'

'It was – still is some of the time.'

'Will it heal completely?' she asked. 'Will you be able to get back on Pannacotta?'

'Try and stop me. All I need to do is work on some more strengthening exercises, and I'll be good to go.' Glancing at the shelves, he randomly picked up boxes of soap, frowning at them before shoving them back. 'But more importantly right now, we should get back to the restaurant for a cocktail. I'm thinking maybe a negroni.'

'Good choice.'

'When in Rome, and all that,' he said. 'Where are the painkillers?' He glanced around. 'Do you think they keep them behind the counter?'

'I have no idea. I'm looking for something else.'

'Oh. OK. Sorry. I'll let you get on.' He cast around again. 'There must be a pharmacist here somewhere. Do you want me to ask for you, too?'

Bella dithered over what to say, then pulled in a deep breath. 'It's a bit embarrassing, to be honest, but I'm searching for seasickness tablets. I didn't know I'd need anything . . .'

Almost immediately she wondered why she'd told him. His expression was unreadable. For a moment she thought he was going to laugh at her, like Tobias. Then he pinged a band on his arm, turning it to show her the plastic stud burrowing into the soft, pale skin of his inner wrist.

'You should try one of these,' Leo said. 'It presses on an acupuncture point, solves the problem. I never go near a boat without one. I'm a terrible sailor, wouldn't be able to survive without this. Actually, I've got a spare, if you want to try it.'

'That would be fantastic, if you don't mind.'

'Of course. I've also got some medication, back on board – if the band doesn't work. I remembered to bring that but totally forgot ibuprofen. Go figure.'

'We've got plenty of painkillers on *Blue Sky* – I'll get someone to put a box in your suite.'

Leaving the shop empty-handed, they fell into step and headed back towards the restaurant. It was quieter now, casual tourists done for the day or already seated at a restaurant, locals relaxing at home.

'Do you mind my asking, why did you decide to come on a cruise with your aunt if you're not comfortable on board boats?' Bella glanced up at him as they walked. In fact, she'd done little else than steal glances at him – it was hard not to. She had to force herself to look at some of the other scenery, as well as keep half an eye on the uneven pavement. Tripping over would only compound her feelings of non-professionalism.

A beat of time passed, and a complicated expression flickered and hardened, before he finally said, 'Because she invited me.'

*

In truth it was far easier for Leo to give a non-committal response to Bella's curiosity than to try to explain. He supposed the situation might appear unusual to someone on the outside – a rag-tag collection of individuals, his decision to willingly spend a week with the threat of nausea looming at any moment. A flippant response to quickly bring an end to the conversation would be to say that he needed a holiday, or that time spent saltwater swimming would help with the rehab of his knee. That he'd always wanted to explore the coastline and islands of the Ligurian Sea, or that you couldn't get a better negroni than one made in its country of origin.

And anyway, who in their right mind would turn down the opportunity of an all-expenses-paid week on a superyacht? In comparison, wearing a band on his wrist night and day was nothing more than a minor inconvenience.

But Leo didn't want to end the conversation, even if it did tug at complicated emotions. He couldn't explain it, but somehow Bella had caught his attention the moment he stepped on board. And though he'd had only the most basic of conversations with her, she'd already managed to burrow into the fabric of his family dynamics without trying. Simply by asking a straightforward, bland question.

'It must be nice to have an aunt who invites you on such wonderful holidays,' Bella said.

'It is. She's very generous.' Leo noticed the way the corners of Bella's mouth crinkled upwards as he talked, the openness of her expression. He wondered if her family was as complicated as his – somehow, he doubted it. 'I'm very lucky.'

The fact that relations between his family and Felicia were complicated was no exaggeration, nor was it anything new. Sometimes Leo felt like a pawn in a chess game he'd never fully understood. His mother and Felicia spoke every few months. Their sisterly bond had remained strong enough to allow Leo and his aunt to spend time together even though, to Leo's knowledge, his father and Felicia had never got on well and rarely communicated. His mother never had fully explained but apparently their clash of personalities had resulted in a massive argument, one they'd never recovered from.

When he was a child, Felicia had lavished attention on Leo, offering him unparalleled experiences and much of the time she seemed to treat him as though he was her son. As a kid, Leo had lapped it up – he'd got double everything. Two summer holidays, two ski trips, lavish presents for birthdays and Christmas. But there was always an accompanying undercurrent from his father. Time spent with his aunt would result in an even firmer hand when Leo returned home.

In his teenage years Leo became serious about the horses and time with Felicia dwindled. On the rare occasions that the Kennedy clan got together en masse, it was always on neutral territory. A place where civility was easy to uphold. A ski lodge with some extra friends to dilute the atmosphere. A hotel on Grace Bay in Turks and Caicos where everyone spread themselves around on loungers and soaked up the sun, with little need to communicate.

Although the trips and time spent together may have become sparse, Leo loved his aunt. Maybe he should have baulked at the idea of a week in her company – maybe he should have refused her invitation in favour of getting back to work. Riding would strengthen his knee as well as any swimming could. Except that there had been something in the way she'd asked, something in the request that wasn't a request at all. Felicia had made it sound as if it were important that he join the charter. That without him, the whole thing was a waste of time. Which seemed ridiculous now he was here, nothing more than a spare cog in the wheel of the Felicia Kennedy Show.

There was no way to crystallise his thoughts into something succinct, so Leo kept his reply bland. No doubt Bella was only asking to be polite, anyway. There was no reason for her to be interested past it being a way to make conversation as they headed down the twisty, narrow streets. He concentrated on not jolting his knee on the uneven stones underfoot.

The sounds of laughter and the bubbling of conversation greeted them long before they rounded the corner to the restaurant. Vines growing around the framework of the outside seating area glinted with strings of fairy lights now clearly visible in the failing light. Bella headed for a small table in the corner, at which the other stewardess was already seated, and Leo ran a hand through his hair, pinning his trademark smile to his face as he joined his aunt's group.

Two negronis later and with starters eaten and main courses in front of them, Leo had settled into the evening. The conversation flowed more easily as each fresh round of cocktails appeared, and it wasn't long before talk turned to Felicia's television series: *Murder in Mayfair*.

'It's not general knowledge yet, but the producers want to go again,' Patti said, eyes gleaming in the semi-darkness. 'Season fourteen. Can you believe it? I thought I was only signing up for the pilot, maybe the first season, but I'm still here.'

'You certainly are,' Felicia said. 'And it's a *series*, darling. I keep telling you, it's set in London, it's filmed in England, the writers are British . . . It's made by the BBC, for God's sake – so it's a series, not a season.'

Patti barrelled on. 'I don't envy the writers. How on earth they manage to come up with fresh storylines every year is amazing to me.'

'If I agree to do another series, that is,' Felicia said.

'Oh my Lord, Felicia. If I've heard you say that once, I've heard you say it, like, a hundred times. Of course you'll do another season.'

'Series.'

'Whatever. You'd be crazy not to. Talking of crazy, do you remember a few years ago, that storyline with the sous chef and the magician and the poisoned spoon?'

'No.'

'Yes, you do. They got that beautiful young actor to play the magician – what was his name?'

'It was Matthew Lewis.'

'You see, you do remember. Such a pity he was dead inside of twenty minutes. He had a part in the Harry Potter films, too.'

'Who hasn't?'

Felicia might be feigning boredom – the signs were obvious, overplayed – but for all that, Leo recognised that she was engaged in the conversation. Her knowledge of the series she and Patti had driven to the top of the ratings was encyclopaedic, her self-deprecation about the other roles she'd played over the years only partly an affectation.

Conversation moved on, dominated by the gentle bickering between the two women, and as the natural light continued to fade and the sounds of insects grew louder all around them, Leo allowed his gaze to wander across to the table occupied by Bella and the other stewardess. He wondered if they were friends. It didn't look likely, based on their body language. They weren't talking. Bella seemed preoccupied by her phone; the other woman leaned back in her chair, arms folded and ankles crossed as she stared into the middle distance, deep in thought.

The blue of the crew shirts was a perfect match to the logo and some of the accessories aboard *Blue Sky*; he supposed it was a livery of sorts – and far more practical than the white uniform shirts in which they had greeted them earlier in the day. The turquoise blue was also a great colour for Bella; it brought out the rich chestnut of her hair, made her brown eyes seem even deeper in tone.

A group of musicians had set up in the corner behind the stewardesses' table, tuning their instruments efficiently before they played a medley of tunes, some he thought he recognised, others he didn't. It gave him the perfect excuse to rest his gaze on Bella, as he wondered what had led her to this moment in her life, what sequence of events had coincided to bring her aboard *Blue Sky*. Especially as it seemed she wasn't a natural sailor. He found himself huffing a sympathetic laugh under his breath as he reached for his drink.

*

Mel pinched at the bridge of her nose, annoyed that the band had decided to set up right behind her. The last thing she needed was to end the evening with a cracking headache. Even if the guests viewed their arrival back on the yacht as the conclusion to the day's events, the crew still had plenty to prepare for the following day. They still had to sail to their night mooring outside Portofino, with all that entailed. And who was to say the guests wouldn't want to continue with their evening once they were back on board? They didn't generally take early nights aboard a superyacht. Late-night hot tub sessions were more usual, with requests for cocktails, or snacks or whatever else they required continuing into the early hours.

She glanced across at the brightness of Bella's phone screen. In the half-light, it was easy to see what she was looking at. She was busy Googling *Leo Kennedy-Edge – polo*, scrolling through photos of the bloke dressed in all the gear, standing next to horses, sat on top of horses, travelling so fast on a horse that the whole animal was cornering like a MotoGP bike taking a chicane. There were photos of him standing with his teammates, holding aloft an enormous silver cup with ribbons dangling from the handles. It wasn't long before the scrolling brought up a picture of him shaking hands with Prince Harry, a smiling Prince Charles – as he was then – in the background. That must have been taken a few years ago, Mel thought.

It was on the tip of her tongue to suggest that Bella should also do a search for *Leo Kennedy-Edge – girlfriends*. The results for that might take even longer to scroll through. The guy was bound to be a player – and not only on the polo field. One look at him was enough to make that assumption. Tall and lean, with tousled nutty-brown hair, an oh-so up-to-the-minute designer beard and dark eyes whirlpooling with depth, he had to know his own appeal. Men like him always did. Add to that the clues to his obvious wealth – clue number one being that he was a guest aboard a superyacht. Clue number two – horses were mega-expensive to own, even Mel knew that, and she'd only had a fleeting acquaintance with the animals. On a day trip to the New Forest as a kid she'd tried to pat one; it nipped her hand, and she'd spent the entire car journey home sneezing because nobody'd realised – until that day – that she was wildly allergic to them.

As far as Mel was concerned, men like Leo Kennedy-Edge were always dripping in two things. Money – obviously, and Barbie-perfect blonde women with aspirations larger than their IQs. If she'd seen it once in her five years aboard *Blue Sky*, she'd seen it a dozen times. And even though there wasn't a blonde in tow at this moment in time, it wouldn't take him long to find one. Or a brunette, or a redhead. Come to think of it, he was probably banging the American actress's daughter – Hannah Prior.

Mel leaned across, making the movement obvious enough to gain Bella's attention.

'Word of advice,' she said. 'You're deluded if you think he'll be interested in you for anything other than the obvious. And you wouldn't be the first to fall for the charms of someone like him. I'd steer clear if I were you.'

'I wasn't . . .' Bella glanced at the screen of her phone, then shut it off, placing the handset face down on the table. 'I was getting some background information, that's all.'

'If you say so,' Mel said. 'Just bear in mind you won't increase your percentage of the week's tip by spending your time on your back. *That* sort of fraternising with the clientele is frowned on. Anyway, we've agencies we contact if the charter guests require that kind of amusement. Professionals.' The shocked expression on Bella's face had Mel finally cracking a smirk. 'You've got so much to learn, haven't you? The stories I could tell you . . . How much longer do you think they're going to be? I'm bloody knackered.' She checked her watch. It was barely ten o'clock – they could be hours yet.

Perhaps she should have stayed aboard *Blue Sky*, used this opportunity to speak to J-P. But what exactly was she going to say to him? She took a breath, finding each glinting constellation in the night sky as she settled back against her chair to wait.

Chapter Five

The tender party hadn't long been back on board *Blue Sky* before Bella heard shouting. It was coming from the guest suites and, as she headed that way, it became easy to distinguish a woman's voice, raised in anger but still retaining its elegant vowels. Felicia was in her suite, with the doors flung wide and her fisted hands resting on her hips.

'How difficult is it for people to follow simple instructions?' She was screaming now, waving a hand at . . . Oh God, from the open doorway Bella could see what she was gesturing towards. The flower arrangements. They were still in situ, the large arrangement on the table between the cream leather chairs; the smaller one, packed with blooms, on the occasional table by the door to the en suite. They should have been moved a couple of hours ago. She'd read the request on the guest manifest; it had stuck in her mind because it seemed strange. Hadn't she asked Jessica to move them while they were on shore? In the heat of the moment, she couldn't be sure.

Nikolai was first to notice her in the doorway, his expression taut.

'Felicia, that's enough. Stop it now,' he said, his voice retaining its quiet calm amidst the onslaught.

'Ms Kennedy, I can only apologise.'

Felicia swung around at the sound of her voice, her features twisted in anger.

'Why are these flowers still in my room? I gave very clear instructions – how difficult can it be to follow a set of simple instructions?' Every word was enunciated clearly, despite her rage.

'I'm so sorry, I'll have them removed immediately.' Bella

advanced into the room, the space she left in the doorway quickly filling with other figures. Third stew Jessica appeared at her elbow and Bella hissed at her to grab the small arrangement.

'What the hell's all the noise about?' Patti directed her question at the room in general, as she scanned the scene. 'Oh, God damn. The flowers?'

Nikolai nodded.

'Felicia, get a grip. They're only flowers for Christ's sake.'

'Patti, quite frankly you can bugger off. Nobody asked your opinion.' Felicia turned her white-hot rage in Patti's direction long enough for Bella and Jessica to grab both vases and exit the suite. Nikolai followed them.

In the corridor, Bella was about to apologise again, but was beaten to it by Nikolai.

'You must understand the importance of my wife's request,' he said. 'You may believe her to have overreacted, but her instructions were perfectly clear, were they not?'

'I can only apologise, Mr Bjerregaard. It won't happen again, I personally guarantee it,' Bella said. 'If you and Ms Kennedy would like to head up to the sun deck, perhaps? We are sailing past the beautiful San Fruttuoso abbey shortly. I'm told it looks stunning in the moonlight, and it would give us a chance to sort out your rooms for you. Bring you coffee, perhaps?'

Nikolai nodded; a chink of a smile appeared. 'I will suggest that to Felicia.'

'Is there anything else we can do to calm the situation?'

'No. I will deal with things, now.' He headed back into the suite and closed the doors. They could still hear voices – Felicia's remained loud and high-pitched, Patti's edged with humour, Nikolai's deep and gruff, but calm.

'I'm so sorry,' Jessica whispered, the words hitching in her throat as she did her best to hold back tears. 'I totally forgot. It's my fault.'

Bella shook her head. 'Honestly, don't worry about it – I forgot to remind you. I'm equally to blame.' She grimaced. 'Well, one thing's for sure: we won't forget again.'

'Christ, no.' Jessica let out a prolonged, ragged breath and escaped down the staircase to the crew area. Bella was about to follow when she heard another voice.

'What's going on?' Leo rounded the corner from the guest suites situated further back on the yacht. 'I heard yelling.' He took in the vase full of flowers in her arms and the discussion still audible from the suite and pulled a face. 'Oops,' he said.

'It was an oversight,' Bella said, gripping the slick glass of the vase with trembling fingers. 'I'm so sorry it made her that angry.'

The lift of Leo's eyebrows suggested it was a situation he had come across before. 'What I've never understood,' he said, 'is that if she's got such a thing about having flowers in her room overnight – why does she insist on them being there during the day? Why have them there at all?'

'I couldn't say. I suppose because they're beautiful?'

'Where are you going to put them?'

'In the galley, I think.'

'Can I assist?'

Bella wrinkled her nose. 'That's really not necessary. The galley's not the most elegant part of the yacht.'

'OK, I'll put it another way. I'm terrifically nosy – and I'd love to take a look, if that's all right?'

'I suppose so, if you want to. The yacht is yours for the week – you can do what you like on it.'

'Within reason, I imagine.' His eyebrows hitched as he held out his hands for the vase.

Shrugging, she said, 'I think there's a fairly wide remit for guests, to be honest.'

'Excellent. In that case, lead on.'

The galley lay behind the formal dining room, one flight down from the guest suites and one flight up from the rest of the crew quarters and the engine room. It was positioned to enable speedy serving of the meals to either the dining room itself, or the sun deck at the very top of the yacht – or indeed for any room service requests.

Bella took Leo down the guest staircase from the suites, the wide curve of the treads graced by a turned wooden banister polished to such a high shine she could see her face in it. The rounded wall held some long, narrow paintings, framed to match the shape of the curvature. Bella hadn't taken much notice of them up to this point; every time she'd taken these stairs before the cruise began had been at speed, rushing around in preparation for the guests' arrival. Right now she was paying more attention to the vase full of flowers in Leo's hands as she led the way down the steps.

'Interesting pieces of art,' Leo said, as he kept pace with her.

A closer inspection of the narrow paintings had her falter on the step. Bella stumbled and jerked at the banister to regain her balance. The paintings were all depictions of ancient Greek or maybe Roman couples in a party setting. She hadn't noticed that as the paintings curved up and around the staircase, they altered from a polite and formal feast into something totally different. Figures already scantily clad were ripping togas from one another's shoulders and shoving fabric away from thighs as the action intensified throughout the series of pictures. Bowls of grapes fell to the floor and goblets spilled in the final painting as food was forgotten in favour of far more intimate activities.

Bella swallowed. How hadn't she noticed the subject matter before this moment, and why did it have to be Leo who pointed it out to her? Suave, desperately attractive and definitely off-limits Leo.

Doing her best to appear unfazed, she attempted a grin. 'The owner clearly has singular tastes.'

'Clearly,' Leo replied.

Was that a hint of sarcasm in his voice, or amusement? Bella chose not to say anything further on the subject, wondering what else she hadn't noticed on board *Blue Sky*. A glance at the vase in his hands reassured her that at least she hadn't handed him something that resembled a giant phallus.

Once through the formal dining room, she pushed open the panelled door leading to the galley and gestured for him to slot the vase of flowers into a sink. Tobias would have to move them in the morning; she'd worry about explaining then.

'Here it is,' she said. 'The hub of the yacht. Or at least, that's what the chef would have you believe.'

'What's on the menu for breakfast?' Leo moved through the space, stopping short of opening cupboards, but seemingly fascinated by the range of ovens.

'What would you like?' She hoped the question wouldn't prompt a long conversation about food. Although the sea had become dead calm, and the yacht's motion wasn't anything like as bad as it had been while they were under motor, she could still feel the roll in her stomach.

'No idea. But nothing too rich for me.' He patted at his belly. 'Even with my wristband, that's a step too far first thing. Actually, that reminds me.' A hand darted into a pocket, and he pulled out a small cardboard box, as well as a band similar to the one encircling his wrist. 'This is for you to try.'

Lodging the box of anti-seasickness pills onto the counter, he gestured for her hand. 'It has to go in the right place to work, though.'

His touch was warm, his fingers surprisingly gentle as he turned her hand and stretched the band to fit over the widest part of her palm and on to her wrist. He edged closer, and she could smell oranges and faint traces of alcohol and salt. There was a wrinkle of concentration between his eyes as he focused his attention on twisting until the hard plastic disc sat against the blood vessels of her inner wrist. She found herself staring at the dip between his collarbones, where the open neck of his shirt gave the merest hint at the dark colour of the hair beneath, his proximity accentuating the broadness of his chest. It took Bella a few moments to realise he had finished twisting the band, and also that she was holding her breath.

'There,' he said. 'You might have to adjust it a bit if nothing happens. But that's the sweet spot for mine.'

Leo took a fraction longer than was necessary to release her hand, his thumb passing one more time across the sensitive skin of her wrist before he let her go. Or was that her imagination? What she wanted to believe, rather than actual events?

Taking a step back, she forced some air into her lungs. 'Thank you,' she said.

'Let me know if it works.' He pointed to the box on the counter. 'And if all else fails, you can always take some of these. But you don't really want to be taking medication all summer.'

Shifting away from her, he continued his recce of the space. 'I've always been fascinated by what goes on behind the scenes. You know, how things work – how they come to appear so seamless, and the effort involved in making it appear so.'

'The swan effect, you mean?'

'That's a good way to describe it, I suppose. Serene and effortless above the water, paddling like fury below.'

'Exactly. In essence that's how every place I've ever worked operates.'

'Where have you worked?'

She gave him the potted version. 'Lots of five-star hotels, mostly front of house – I did my fair share of waitressing, then began to take on more managerial roles. At least, that's what the job titles usually included. In truth, there was a lot of solving staffing issues, stepping in when needed, making everything appear perfect, rather than being "management". It's one of the reasons I got this job, actually. I became quite the expert at making sure that even if a brawl's broken out between chefs in the kitchens, or the laundry's on fire, or members of the SAS are parachuting into the grounds – or all three simultaneously for that matter – the guests never know about any of it. Not that I manage to look as serene as a swan – but that's the aim.'

'Not a million miles away from what my aunt does, then?'

His comment surprised her. 'What do you mean?'

'You're playing a role. Making sure that your audience sees one thing, an illusion of perfection, while the reality could be something else entirely.'

'I suppose so. Sort of. But I'm no actress.'

'I think we're all much better at acting than we think.' He

turned away, studying Tobias's racks of spices, held secure behind rails of wood. 'Do you think you could arrange for me to see the engine room?'

When Felicia woke the following morning, it took her a while to assimilate her surroundings. The bed was comfortable, but it wasn't hers. Nikolai was with her. He was still asleep – she could tell from his rhythmic, relaxed breathing. His presence meant she wasn't on location, wasn't in some random hotel room booked by a production company. It was quiet. Extremely quiet – and in this room, this unfamiliar room, the walls were curved. Everything felt fluid, as if they were moving. Taking a deep breath, she realised they were aboard the yacht. Remembered. Perhaps that was a better word. They were spending a week aboard *Blue Sky*, sailing around the Ligurian Sea. For Nicki's birthday.

Closing her eyes, she waited for the tight band of headache to make its presence felt. When it didn't, she smiled. It was one thing, putting on a brave face when she didn't feel a hundred per cent, gritting her teeth and giving the cameras what they wanted. She'd been doing that for years. It was quite another to be able to smile properly, freely, purely because she wanted to.

Shifting onto her side, she watched Nicki as he woke, the relaxed lines of his beautiful face taking on a more precise composition, a greater tautness as he blinked repeatedly and gazed at her.

'Good morning,' he said. 'Did you sleep well?'

'Like a hibernating bear,' she said.

'You couldn't be further from a hibernating bear if you tried,' he said, shuffling closer to her.

The exchange had begun as a joke – her joke – not long after they became involved. She'd picked the most ridiculous simile she could think of, the absolute opposite of the sexy temptress she hoped she resembled when she'd woken up in Nikolai Bjerregaard's bed for the very first time.

His comment, on that first morning all those years ago, had

stemmed more from confusion, a language barrier, than a grasp of her sense of humour. But without fail since that morning they'd greeted one another in the same way every time they woke together.

How was it possible that he still looked as good to her now as he had done back then? Those serious ice-blue eyes, the twinkle in them reserved solely for her. The strength in his jawline undiminished, while the chins of so many of his peers wobbled into weak flabbiness.

'I apologise,' she said, stretching out to run her fingers across his brow, pushing a strand of hair away from his eyes.

'What for?'

'You know what for. I lost my temper, last night. The flowers were the final straw, but those musicians. Do you think the owner arranged it on purpose – to have them play the theme tune from *Murder in Mayfair*?'

'I imagine so. You stir interest in people, wherever you go. Surely you realise that?'

'But why did they have to play that tune? I starred in over twenty Hollywood films, Nicki. Why didn't they play something from one of those films' musical scores?'

'Maybe because Patti was also present at the table?'

She sighed. Nikolai's logic was impeccable, as always, but she needed to explain her frustration. 'I don't want to be remembered for some fluffy nonsense television show, though. Especially one in which my character is the moody bitch and Patti's is the one who gets all the breakthrough revelations. I've played queens, Nicki. I've been an international assassin. A scientist who died to save the world from an apocalyptic virus. I've appeared on Broadway, and the West End. And yet *Murder in Mayfair* is what I seem to be most recognised for. What I'll be remembered for.'

The crease between his eyebrows deepened as he processed her words, a smile dancing across his lips. 'Are you trying to tell me you are considering stepping away from acting?'

It was what he had wanted for so long; she knew that. For her to immerse herself in his world, a place where the rest of the planet didn't intrude, where they could go unnoticed. She'd never quite been able to understand why, even though he was a wonderfully photogenic man, he had always shied away from the camera, from the press, from the life she lived in the spotlight. She could count on one hand the number of times he'd accompanied her to a red-carpet event, could feel his tension in the way he gripped her hand as he barely tolerated the flashing lights.

It wasn't something she would be able to give him, though. Not long-term, anyway. She smoothed her fingers through his hair.

'That wasn't what I meant. I wanted to apologise for losing my temper. To explain. The flowers tipped me over the edge. I'm sorry.'

'Flowers?' His eyebrow quirked as a hand sought out her waist, under the covers, his fingers featherlight against the silk of her nightdress. 'I do not remember any problem with flowers. It is already forgotten.'

They had both made choices, back at the start. Left things behind to move forward, together. Compromised some of their own separate visions of a perfect life in order to create one together. She hadn't regretted any of hers. It had seemed a small price to pay for the promise of a lifetime spent at the centre of this stunning man's attention. Lodging her arm around his neck, she encouraged him closer, the familiarity of his touch, their kiss, the way he grounded Felicia in the moment – this moment . . . It was really all that had ever mattered, the times like this – and she'd continued to make choices, precisely in order to guarantee the unspoiled moments, for as long as possible. But time was finite, for everybody. Had she made the right choices? Did anybody ever get to know whether a different path might have been better?

Nikolai must have felt her tears, or perhaps the trembling of her lips. He drew back, concern in his expression. 'What's wrong?'

'Nothing, my darling,' she said. 'Everything is perfect.'

*

Everyone was already seated in the dining room by the time she and Nicki were ready for breakfast. Patti was cradling a cup of black coffee, her daughter toyed with a small plate of cut fruits. Leo must have arrived moments before them; his napkin lay untouched in his place setting and his coffee cup was empty, and he bobbed back to his feet as Felicia approached the table.

'No need to stand on ceremony,' she said to him as Nicki held her chair. 'We're supposed to be on holiday.'

Nicki took the chair next to her, draping his arm casually across the back of her seat as the stewardess with the straight dark hair materialised at the table. It took Felicia a moment or two to realise her focus wasn't on either Nikolai, or herself. Instead, the girl – Bella – was delivering a beaming smile in Leo's direction. Felicia wondered what on earth Bella was so pleased about.

What had Leo been up to? He'd been on board less than twenty-four hours and already he had the staff fawning over him. He was a handsome young man, without question, but then most men in their twenties radiated appeal. An in-built evolutionary failsafe, the ability to attract and ensnare the opposite sex for long enough to keep the species procreating. In Leo's case, he had inherited all the glossiest of his father's qualities – the broad shoulders, the excellent facial bone structure, the charisma. The natural athleticism. Felicia just hoped he had managed to keep at bay some of her brother-in-law's less appealing character traits.

'Does it work?' Leo said quietly.

'Like a charm.' Bella beamed again, speaking in low tones as if the two of them were sharing a secret. 'I can't thank you enough.'

After the girl had taken their breakfast requests and headed for the kitchens, Felicia leaned across.

'What was that all about?'

'Oh, nothing important,' Leo said. 'How did you all sleep?'

It was a world-class deflection, but one Felicia spotted in an instant. She'd used similar techniques herself repeatedly over the last thirty-odd years. If she'd learned one thing about how to get what she wanted from the world of show business, it was that a very large percentage of the people involved desperately wanted to talk about themselves. She often wondered if it was part of the reason she had found Nikolai so attractive – because he was the opposite.

With the rest of the table discussing the pros and cons of a night aboard a yacht, Felicia couldn't help noticing how Leo's gaze strayed time and again to the door through to the galley. For her part, on her return, Bella's smile remained luminescent in its intensity, and focused on Leo. The girl did have great energy, that much Felicia had already noticed, but this morning it was as if she'd turned the dial all the way up.

Patti wasn't going to be best pleased, though. Her co-star's veneer-thin pretence that Hannah's appearance on this charter was anything other than a direct play for Leo's attention hadn't fooled her for a moment. An unlikely match, in Felicia's opinion – and, even if it did succeed, not destined to stay the course, if Leo's previous haphazard love life was anything to go by. An infatuation with a member of the yacht's crew was likely to be equally fleeting on his part.

But, she supposed, even the most glorious of butterflies would eventually settle on the nectar of a particular flower.

Arching her eyebrows and arming herself with a knife and fork, Felicia turned her attention to the bite-sized pieces of melon and pear, and the delicate wraps of prosciutto presented with exquisite attention to detail on the plate in front of her.

As she speared a piece of melon, Felicia decided it might be fun to see how that aspect of this cruise played out.

Chapter Six

Bella couldn't believe how a disc of plastic could have such an incredible impact on her whole body. She wanted to tell Leo he was a magician, that the difference in the way she felt this morning in comparison to the previous day was polar. In fact, throwing her arms around his neck and hugging him would have been her natural reaction, if it had been appropriate. She wanted him to know he might have saved her entire yachting season, which had looked in danger of sinking without trace before it had even begun.

Tobias passed no comment when she'd shown him the wristband, managing to hold his tongue when Bella explained where it had come from, even though she'd expected him to make a joke, or poke fun at her. To be honest, it might have been better if he had – that way she could have pigeonholed him as a comedian, someone out for a laugh, but also someone who would have her back if the need should arise. A person on board with whom she could confide, even if it meant being on the wrong end of the chef's dubious sense of humour on occasion. Instead, Tobias had remained unusually tight-lipped, and Bella swallowed her excitement while trying to ignore the realisation that adjusting to life on *Blue Sky* was going to take more than a nausea band and a packet of Stugeron.

With breakfast cleared away, and the guests relaxing with a final serving of strong Italian blend coffee, she headed back into the dining room a final time. The decision had already been made to stay on board, rather than taking the tender to Portofino itself. Apparently, when Felicia and Nikolai visited a few years previously, Nikolai had been unnerved by the number of bags Felicia had bought from the never-ending boutiques – at least, that was Patti's version of events. Whatever the truth, not having to organise a tender did take the pressure off the crew.

'Before we leave our mooring and head away from Portofino, would you like to spend some time on the water with the jet skis?' Bella asked.

'I would love to,' Nikolai said. 'Felicia, will you join me?'

Felicia shook her head. 'Not this morning, Nicki. I think I hear one of the sun loungers calling my name.'

'Very well. Leo?'

'I'll give it a go, definitely.'

'And Hannah's always wanted to try, haven't you?' Patti said, a touch too quickly. 'Maybe she could ride with you, Leo.'

'Of course.'

'Can I tempt you to join me, Patti?' Nikolai asked.

'Lord, no. Thanks for asking, but I think I'll join Felicia on the sun deck.'

'Oh, goody.'

Bella wasn't sure whether Felicia's comment was intended to be audible, but Patti seemed undaunted, rising to her feet and announcing she'd be out in five, once she'd changed her outfit.

'Can't wait, darling,' Felicia said. And although Patti seemed oblivious to it, this time there was no doubting the barb in her words.

As she cleared the table, Bella suggested the other three meet out on the swimming platform once they were ready, where they could be fitted with safety vests.

Yannis was waiting for them when Bella shot from the galley to the swimming platform. He lounged against the side railings of the boat, his demeanour one of total relaxation, his shades hiding his eyes from the strength of the bright sunshine. The pair of jet skis bobbed on the water, moored with a couple of black boating ropes.

'Are the guests on their way?' he said.

'I think so. Three of them – two are going to share. Where are the life vests?'

He nodded his head to indicate the pile of vests behind her, and as she bent to sort through the sizes, she heard the slap of bare feet descending the steps. When she looked up, Leo and Nikolai were waiting for her, Nikolai shirtless, in loose swimming shorts. On an otherwise trim and firm frame, the curl of grey chest hair was almost the only visible nod to his age. A stab of disappointment ran through Bella as she realised Leo had chosen to wear a T-shirt alongside his board shorts. Doing her best to disguise the confusion she felt about her reaction, she busied herself fitting the men with the flotation vests while Yannis explained the jet ski controls and auto cut-off system.

'Is it really that effective?' Leo said, as she zipped up his life vest.

'Yes. If you happen to come off the jet ski, it stops automatically,' Bella said.

'No, I didn't mean the jet ski – I know how they work.' He lowered his voice. 'I meant your wristband.' Shielding his eyes from the sun with a hand, he turned away from the others. 'They don't always have such a dramatic effect.'

'Well, it's definitely working for me. I feel fantastic. Thank you again.'

'No problem.'

He looked as if he was about to say something else, then stopped, his attention shifting as Hannah floated down the steps towards them. Wearing a blood-red bikini and a neat pair of shades, her hair slicked back into a tight ponytail, the contrast between her milky pale skin and the colour of her costume was breathtaking. As he moved to greet her, Leo sucked in a breath, reaching down for a life vest and helping her to fit it.

With Yannis hauling in the jet skis until they bobbed flush with the platform, and all the guests prepared, Bella felt sidelined. Shuffling out of the way, she heard Hannah ask Leo if he'd look after her. The earnest expression on his face as he assured her that he would had Bella feeling like a fool.

Mel's words at the taverna the previous evening floated into the forefront of her mind. These people weren't her friends, would never be. Bella just wished she wasn't so drawn to Leo.

'Have fun,' she said, grinning as she did her best to keep her tone upbeat. Taking the steps to the main deck she wondered if it might have been better to have taken a role as a second or third stewardess – it would have allowed her to spend more time with the rest of the crew, rather than the clientele. As she headed for the sun deck to find out if Felicia or Patti needed anything, she found herself envying Jessica, who right now was busy in the laundry, ironing sheets for the guests' suites, her favourite music playing. Or Mel, in the galley polishing the silver cutlery and having a coffee and a chat with Tobias.

Bella suddenly felt very alone.

Pasting a smile into place as she crested the stairs onto the sun deck, she found herself wondering if Leo had really been searching the pharmacy the previous evening for painkillers as he'd said. Maybe her being there had thrown him – at the time she'd noticed he appeared flustered to see her. Maybe he was in there for a supply of something completely different. Something he might need to have available if he and Hannah became more than mere acquaintances. Perhaps they already were. Although if that were the case, he would have come prepared, surely? Shaking her head at herself, Bella crossed to the sun loungers on which Felicia and Patti had already prostrated themselves and were deep in discussion about the music at the taverna.

'I thought it was cute that they played our *Murder in Mayfair* theme tune,' Patti said.

'You would. I thought it was attention-seeking. I mean, who asked them to do that?' Felicia draped an arm across her forehead. 'Did they expect a tip, or something?'

'Hello, ladies – sorry to interrupt. Can I get you anything?'

'Not for me,' Patti said.

'Yes,' said Felicia, patting the lounger beside hers. 'You can sit down and tell us what you thought of the music last night.'

'I recognised the theme tune when they played it, if that's what you mean. I love your show.' Bella eased herself onto the padded seat.

'Programme,' Felicia said. 'It's a programme, not a show.'

Patti snorted a laugh. 'Show, programme, who cares? The girl's a fan. That's all that matters.'

'I've seen every episode, I think,' Bella said. 'I started watching when I was a kid.'

Felicia's expression had her wishing she'd bitten back that last sentence. How to make your charter guests feel old in one easy step. Casting around for something to say to fix the blunder, she noticed the plumes of water issuing from the jet skis as they shot across the bay, Nikolai's machine streaking ahead of Leo's.

'Your husband looks as if he knows his way around a jet ski,' she said.

'He adores everything to do with the ocean,' Felicia replied, shifting on the sunbed to catch a glimpse. 'He'd live on the water given half a chance. And how are you finding it – life on a superyacht?'

Bella nodded. 'Good so far. Not that I have much to go on yet. Everyone has been very welcoming.' Not strictly true, but the guests weren't likely to be interested in below-deck backbiting.

'How's your family feel about you being away from home?'

'I think my parents are quite pleased to have me out of their hair. They've got their hands full with a couple of new foster kids.'

'Your parents foster?' Patti wriggled herself into a more upright position.

'They've done it for a while – they started when my brother and I were teenagers. Sometimes the kids stay a few months, sometimes longer.'

'And how did that land for you, having to share your home with strangers?'

'Most of the time I didn't mind. I mean, it wasn't always easy; I didn't get on with all of them. But it wasn't really my choice to make, and some of them had had a terrible time before Mum and Dad stepped in. I don't think my brother, Jay, found it as easy. He couldn't wait to get away to university. But the thing is we were both adopted and I've always kind of felt grateful that we came first, that my parents chose to have us permanently in their home.'

'How old were you when they adopted you?' Patti said, shielding her eyes with the flat of her hand.

'Oh, very little. I was a baby. Jay was three. He sometimes says he can remember glimpses from before, but I'm not sure he can.'

'I think that's a truly wonderful thing.' Patti rested her head back against the lounger. 'I couldn't imagine doing it. Could you, Felicia?'

'Well, Nikolai was never interested in having children, so it wasn't an option,' Felicia said, shoving a spare sun deck cushion behind her shoulders.

'Did you really never want children?' Patti asked.

Bella shuffled to her feet. Perhaps the conversation was straying into territory she shouldn't be involved in.

'My career has always kept me frantically busy. Between filming schedules and Nicki, I've never had time for anything else. You know that. I don't know why you're needling for answers to irrelevant questions.' Felicia's forehead creased behind the dark orbs of her glasses, and she pulled at the pillow, eventually holding it for Bella to take. 'Get rid of that, will you. I can't get comfortable.'

'I'm not needling you for answers, I'm having a conversation. I think it's interesting, that's all. I still remember how I felt when Hannah was born – I don't think you ever forget that rush of emotion.' Patti shifted her attention to Bella. 'Couldn't your parents conceive naturally?'

'Oh, God Almighty, Patti.' Felicia flashed with anger. 'It's none of your business. You really don't have a filter, do you? Crass and intrusive, as usual. Don't answer that question, Bella. It's none of her business, the nosy cow.'

'Pipe down, Felicia,' Patti said, laughter edging her words. She was completely unfazed by Felicia's outburst. 'Who died and made you queen of the conversation?'

'It's fine,' Bella said, keen to smooth the situation. 'I really don't mind.'

'Well, I do,' Felicia said with emphasis. 'Oh, God. I don't believe it.' She pressed fingers to her temples and began to massage them. 'My headache's back.'

'Can I get you something?' Bella asked.

Felicia explained where to find her bottle of headache pills and requested a segment of lime alongside some of her glacier water, and once Patti had decided she could take a margarita, Bella was happy to escape the tense heat of the sun deck in favour of the cool cabins.

Inside the suite, she unzipped the box as indicated by Felicia, only to find it stuffed full of jewellery. The suite door opened behind her, and Mel pushed in with an armful of fresh linen.

'What are you doing?' she said, unguarded suspicion in her eyes.

'Looking for some medication Felicia asked for. Is there another box like this one?'

With a jerk of her head, Mel dropped the sheets onto the stripped bed. 'In the bathroom.'

With the bottle of pills located, and the medicine box replaced on a bathroom shelf, Bella headed out of the suite.

'Are you sure you were looking for pills?' Mel said, as she smoothed a sheet into place.

'Of course. Felicia's on the sun deck with Patti, and she complained of a headache. Why, what are you suggesting?'

Mel shrugged. 'Nothing. But there's a lot of expensive jewellery in that box. You don't want people jumping to the wrong conclusion, do you?'

'There's no conclusion to jump to, Mel. I was looking for headache pills.' Bella pressed her lips tight together to prevent her from saying anything else and headed for the galley.

Mel slipped the goose feather pillows into their fresh linen cases and replaced the rest of the bedding. It couldn't have gone better. She'd rattled Bella, made her feel as though she was doing something wrong; and it had given her an idea.

Mel knew J-P preferred to sack crew members somewhere they could be evicted from the boat immediately; he would far rather get rid of someone from the boat before they left the main Italian coast and headed for the islands. They'd all heard stories on other boats of disgruntled crew causing hundreds of thousands of pounds worth of malicious damage before they were removed. On a yacht worth tens of millions, everything was expensive to replace. And nothing got a crew member ousted from a superyacht quicker than the smear of theft.

Riffling through the jewellery box Bella had mistaken for a pill case, Mel took a moment to marvel at some of the pieces. Randomly cracking open some of the smaller boxes held within, it took no time to identify diamond stud earrings whose stones had to weigh in at two, maybe three carats each alongside a gleaming diamond bracelet; emerald earrings set in burnished platinum; a string of huge opaque black pearls. In an old velvet pouch, there lay a huge vintage teardrop ruby necklace and matching earrings. Every piece screamed quality. Five years on board had provided Mel with plenty of opportunity to study the very best in jewellery – even if it was always against someone else's skin.

Nestled amongst some of the more ostentatious pieces lay a relatively discreet diamond pendant, on a fine platinum chain. The kind of item someone might think could go unmissed by its owner, especially in light of its stellar company. The kind of necklace a regular person might aspire to own, or a light-fingered stewardess might pocket to sell at the end of the season, to supplement her income.

It was also the kind of jewellery easily hidden in the crew quarters, while Mel began to sow seeds of doubt surrounding Bella.

It would serve J-P right if he had to deal with the fallout of a crew theft from such a high-profile guest this early in the season. After all, it had been his decision to take Bella on as chief stewardess.

She was still smarting from her conversation with J-P earlier.

While everyone else was occupied, she'd taken a large Americano to the bridge, where she knew he'd be taking the opportunity to relax, or to check charts before they continued along the coast of the Ligurian Sea, towards the gravity-defying villages of Cinque Terre.

'Can we talk?' she'd asked, recognising immediately the tensing in his shoulders, the pause before he gestured for her to sit.

'What is there to talk about?'

She was tempted to crash straight in, to ask him why he'd employed someone with absolutely no yachting experience over her head. Why he was crippling her career like this. Why he wanted so much for her to be gone. Why what had happened the previous season had been so very terrible. Because it hadn't seemed that way to her.

Instead, in an uncharacteristically conciliatory moment, she decided to offer him an olive branch.

'Is there a way to move forward, to put what happened behind us? After all, we're both adults.'

She watched as he twisted his wedding band around and around on his finger, his gaze fixed somewhere in the space behind her left ear.

'Look at me, J-P . . . Please . . .'

'Don't tell me what to do, Melanie.' At last, he'd brought his line of sight to her own, the use of her full name ricocheting through her body. He was the only person who ever called her Melanie. '*I* tell *you* what to do. More than that, I tell Bella what to do, and *she* tells you. This is how it must be. If you cannot handle this, then please, say the word. Now . . .' Then he'd risen to his feet, turned his back to her and absently picked up a pair of binoculars as he stared through the window. 'You will excuse me. I have the preparations to make.'

It had been the coldest of exchanges, colder even than she'd been expecting. Cold enough to send her scuttling to the laundry, telling Jessica that she would make up the guest beds and tidy the cabins. Anything to keep to herself for a while.

With Felicia's necklace now tucked safely into the pocket of her day uniform, Mel headed for the crew cabins, determined to plant the necklace at the very bottom of Bella's carry-on suitcase, somewhere she wouldn't happen across accidentally.

Telling herself she'd take no pleasure in what she was about to do, that it was simply a means to an end, she halted abruptly at the sound of movement. Logic told her that nobody could have seen what she had done, nobody knew she had the necklace in her pocket, and yet her breath quickened, and sweat prickled beneath her arms.

Suddenly the necklace burned hot against her fingers. Mel found herself glancing down to see if the diamond had gained special powers, was somehow glowing through the fabric of her skirt. It was a ridiculous thought, and yet her chest tightened at the possibility of being caught with the jewellery in her possession. Because she didn't doubt that J-P would have her removed from *Blue Sky* just as quickly as any other member of the crew. Her career would cease to exist. This spur-of-the-moment plan suddenly felt reckless.

With the sound of footsteps becoming louder, and Mel's nerve failing her, she fished out the necklace and burrowed it into a bowl of glass crystals on an occasional table until it was hidden from view. Smoothing the glass crystals over the top of the diamond, Mel shot to the staff staircase and headed for the galley.

Felicia had given up trying to enjoy the sunshine on the upper deck. She couldn't seem to persuade Patti to stop talking. The woman was being impossibly upbeat and cheerful, chatting on and on about Hannah and Leo and the promise of youth and, and, and . . . It was very draining.

Over the years Felicia had learned how obtuse Patti could become. The more it was suggested she might take one route, the more likely Patti was to follow a different path, literally or figuratively. At times it came as no surprise to Felicia that Patti's husband had left her. No, that was a cruel thing to think – Patti's husband had been truly awful, only with her for her money and a leg-up into the spotlight. The breakdown of her marriage had happened during filming of the second – or maybe third – series of *Murder in Mayfair*, and it had been the first time Felicia had felt anything other than irritated by the woman. They'd come a long way since then.

Even so, with no sign of Patti quietening down any time soon, Felicia had made a feeble excuse, heading downstairs on the pretence of grabbing a silk cover-up. All she really wanted was a little peace and quiet, a few moments alone to process their conversation with Bella, the frankness of her comments about adoption, and the foster children her family had welcomed. A life lived a million miles away from Felicia's own.

From the staircase she took the curving passageway from the rear cabins, the occasional mirrored panels allowing the passer-by a surreptitious glance at themselves, or – in this case – allowing Felicia a clear view of the rest of the corridor. Another of the stewardesses – the lean, blonde one – was there, lingering for no apparent reason, a hand in one pocket.

Something in her demeanour had Felicia pausing. Her eyebrows arched as she saw the stewardess, Mel, draw something out of her pocket and bury it in a bowl of glass chips before she headed for the crew area.

Felicia almost checked for cameras; the whole thing had the air of a scene from *Murder in Mayfair* about it. All thoughts of the shawl in her cabin faded to the back of her mind as she scattered bits of glass to the edges of the bowl to see if she could work out what the stewardess had been up to.

The necklace wasn't buried very deeply, Felicia found it in a matter of seconds and turned it in her fingers. It was one of hers – the platinum chain with the single-carat pear-shaped diamond. What a nasty little thief – and on a boat like this? Outrageous. Her immediate impulse was to tell Nicki, to cause an enormous fuss, but her initial burst of outrage tempered slightly as she considered the consequences. The charter would be ruined. Nicki's birthday would be ruined.

Swinging the necklace between her fingers for a few moments, Felicia made a decision and buried it back where she'd found it. Out of all the jewellery she'd brought with her for this trip, that piece was of negligible consequence. It wasn't worth making a terrible fuss over, not right now, anyway. Instead, she would keep a close watch on the rest of her jewellery, as well as a hawkish eye on that stewardess. Try to work out her motives. Maybe there was more to this than pure theft – why else would the girl dump the necklace here? A frisson of excitement coursed through Felicia – a real-life mystery to be solved. And maybe this time it would be Felicia who would solve it.

If need be, she would have a quiet word with the captain, but she would keep this to herself, for now.

Because she wasn't going to let anything spoil this trip.

Chapter Seven

Later that morning, with the anchors in their pockets and the yacht flowing smoothly down the Italian coastline, Bella did her best to relax and enjoy the beautiful scenery. Now that her seasickness was under control, she could settle into her role.

The secret was to stay calm and communicate – it was her job to make the interior of the yacht appear swan-like. She liked the analogy, and it reflected the way she needed to make everything appear for the guests. No request was too much trouble, nothing was impossible.

Behind the scenes could get as messy as it liked, so long as the guests were none the wiser. And Bella had dealt with tricky members of staff before. Tobias could continue all he liked with his double entendres and snarky comments so long as the food he produced remained excellent, and Mel could take all the time she needed to defrost if she remembered to appear charming when she was with the guests.

At least third stew Jessica seemed straightforward enough. Shy and happy to fill her time with the bulk of the laundry work and cleaning. The fact that she enjoyed listening to a heavy-duty rock band – apparently her boyfriend's all-time favourite – and had left the boyfriend and a labrador called Trevor at home was all Bella knew about her so far. She supposed there was plenty of time to find out more.

If her only problems were being needled by the chef and second stew, and having to remain disciplined enough to treat Leo as an upper-class bloke who happened to be devastatingly attractive but was probably a flaky bastard in real life, then Bella reckoned she was going to be able to sail through this charter.

She laughed at her own weak nautical joke as she pulled on some white cotton table-laying gloves.

The plan for today was to moor somewhere close to the Cinque Terre villages – apparently a group of five centuries-old settlements that gave the impression of having grown out of the coastal rocks of the Riviera. Surrounded by vineyards and picturesque, tiny harbours filled with fishing boats, it was a must-see according to the guests' itinerary.

While moored, lunch would be served – albeit a late one. Time had already taken on a nebulous quality aboard *Blue Sky* and although the guests had been remarkably early to bed the previous evening, none of them had been up with the lark today. Plus, Nikolai, Leo and Hannah had been out on the jet skis for ages, delaying their morning departure.

As far as Bella was aware, all the guests were up on the sun deck making the most of the sun loungers and easing jet-ski-pummelled muscles in the hot tub as they watched the Italian Riviera pass by.

Bella was also taking every opportunity to steal glances at the coastline – it was simply stunning. Even quick looks as she gave each piece of cutlery a final polish were enough to have her wanting to pinch herself, to check she wasn't dreaming. Heading back into the main salon, she lifted the tray of glasses and took them to the table. Once they were in position, she gave the table a final once-over. Across its centre she'd draped a length of turquoise voile, dotting it with exotic seashells and votive LED candles in crystal glass holders, leading the eye to the main focal point, a huge conch shell with a posy of flowers spilling from its open neck. This might only be lunch, but lunch on a superyacht wasn't ever going to be a serve-yourself buffet.

Stripping off the gloves, she headed up to the sun deck. As she walked, she radioed Jean-Philippe for an ETA on the mooring point. There was enough time for a final drinks run, and the offer of some snacks before their arrival. Plus, she needed to double-check the guests were happy with the plan before Tobias started cooking any of the langoustine.

With her front-of-house smile installed, Bella crested the staircase and assessed the scene. Patti and Felicia were still reclining on sun loungers, but they had relocated them under the canopy for some shade, and a better view. Hannah was face down on the padded area surrounding the hot tub, the delicate strings on her bikini unfastened to allow the sun – and maybe Leo – a full visual of her flawless skin.

Nikolai reclined in the water, leaning against the side of the tub, the picture of relaxation, and Leo – Bella had to pause and take a breath – Leo chose precisely that moment to step out from the hot tub, onto the wooden slats of the decking. Rivulets of the steaming water coursed their way down his upper chest, bumping their way over the musculature of his torso before trickling down his navel and soaking into the sodden material of his swimming shorts. He reached haphazardly for a towel, rubbing at his head as he gazed out to sea, the muscles in his arms flexing and bunching as he scrubbed away most of the moisture from the crown of his head, then settled the towelling square around his neck.

Bella couldn't stop herself from moistening her lips, couldn't ignore the quickening in her heart rate. Nobody else seemed the slightest bit interested in what Leo was doing, but she didn't seem capable of dragging her gaze away.

Eventually she re-established a connection between brain and feet and got moving, announcing her presence as she drew closer.

'Can I get anyone anything before lunch?' she asked. 'A drink? Some nibbles, perhaps.'

With a list of requirements committed to memory and having given the guests a rundown on what Tobias was preparing for lunch, she descended the stairs, unaware that Leo was right behind her until she heard his footsteps, the bare slaps of wet feet against the wood of the decking.

'Bella, can I ask you something?'

'Of course.'

It was difficult to concentrate as he continued to dry himself, patting at his arms, then his torso with the towel as he said, 'I wanted to make sure you're aware it's my uncle's birthday at the end of the week.'

She nodded, sidling back to allow herself some air, only to bump against the rigid curve of the wall. 'Yes.'

'Can I add something to the requirements list? Or at least check if it's already been noted.'

'Of course.' At this proximity, not only was Bella's brain beginning to steam, but her tongue was becoming equally uncooperative. Best to keep her answers short, she decided, so she didn't fall over her words.

'Felicia doesn't like Nikolai to smoke them, but he absolutely adores the occasional Cuban cigar. Is there any way he could have one on his birthday? Or is that a problem on board – a safety issue?'

'I'm sure we can sort something out,' she said. 'Inside the vessel, smoking is completely prohibited . . .' She gave herself a virtual high five at managing to get the words out in some semblance of order.

'Yes, absolutely. I understand.'

Leo continued to work the towel across his body; it was all Bella could do to stop herself from asking him if he needed some help. Instead, she said, 'But we do have areas where he would be welcome to enjoy a cigar. Or we can make sure they are available at any time when we go ashore.'

Leo nodded. 'That's a great idea. I bought him a box as a gift, and then it struck me it was probably the stupidest thing I could possibly have brought onto a yacht.'

'We can make it work, don't worry.'

'You're amazing, thank you.' A crinkle marred the skin between his eyes as he stared at her. Then he shook his head, and perfection was restored. 'We haven't met somewhere before, have we?'

'No. I definitely would have remembered meeting you.' Bella hoped the heat flaring in her cheeks wasn't too visible.

'It's just that I keep thinking I know you from somewhere. You must remind me of someone,' he said. 'I wish I could work out who it is.'

'Someone nice?' She was pushing her luck, stepping outside her remit of conversation with a guest, but the words were out before she could stop them.

The towel stopped, mid pat, and he stared at her. She waited for him to break eye contact, step away and release the tension from the moment, but he didn't. If anything, the moment intensified.

Then he smiled, and his eyes crinkled and glittered for an instant before he walked away.

Leo was breathing hard by the time he reached his cabin. This was crazy.

He had absolutely no idea why she reminded him of someone, but he'd stopped wondering who it was when she'd asked if it was someone nice. Because there was no doubting that Bella fell very neatly into the category of 'much more than nice'.

It had been on the tip of his tongue; he'd almost said as much in reply to her question, but had stopped himself by walking away. He'd spent next to no time in this woman's company, and yet he was desperate for Bella to notice him. Really notice him. It had been no accident that he'd pulled himself from the hot tub at that moment, when he'd seen the crown of her dark hair appearing up the sun deck steps. Stood there like a prize bull in a show ring, hoping she'd look at him.

He'd never felt the need to pimp himself before, wasn't even sure why he was doing it now. Except perhaps that to the casual observer he had a perfectly choreographed companion for the week, currently lying practically butt-naked on the sun deck. And he didn't want that casual observer to misinterpret.

There was no point pretending the promise of casual sex hadn't dominated his early twenties – back then everything had been fast-paced and easy – although Leo hadn't necessarily played the field with quite the same determination as many of his compatriots. The horses, the polo, the women, and the tempo of his entire existence had been ultrasonic; the upward spiral of his life had seemed without limit. But there were limits – he just hadn't seen them coming.

Lying in the mud while Pannacotta did a number on his kneecap had caused him to reflect on his life choices in a way he hadn't previously. Had caused him to re-evaluate.

It had occurred to Leo, for possibly the first time, that he wasn't invincible. He was no longer twenty-one, with his star rising. And months on from the injury, his knee still hurt, remained stiff and weak. In the quiet moments, when he'd levered himself out on crutches time and again to check the young stock, it had dawned on Leo that what had fuelled the fast pace of his existence up until recently wouldn't be sustainable, not forever. More than that, it struck him it wasn't even desirable, not long-term.

It occurred to him that seducing a woman for a quick shag might no longer satisfy the brief, and that if his interest in a woman was driven purely by his libido – and vice versa – then maybe it wasn't enough. He needed something more.

As he stripped off and stepped into the shower, he frowned. Because none of that went any way towards explaining the irrational attraction he felt to *Blue Sky*'s chief stewardess.

Chapter Eight

Felicia doubled up on her headache medication. She was completely aware it wasn't a great idea, but as the last of the lunchtime crockery was being cleared, she slipped another couple of pills into her mouth, swigging at her glass of water and swallowing as unobtrusively as she could.

'It looks like the buildings have been carved out of the rocks, don't you think?' Patti said.

'Absolutely. And those colours. So authentically Mediterranean.' Nicki took a hold of Felicia's hand. 'Can you see the church, at the very top of the cliffs?'

She nodded. The backdrop was simply stunning. She had to hand it to the captain – he was ticking every box on the wish list so far.

'It's a shame we're not staying here longer. I'd love to explore,' Hannah said.

'Me too,' Patti said. 'And I'll bet Leo would love an excuse to stretch his legs.'

'Perhaps.'

Leo's reply sounded cagey. It reminded Felicia of his father. Non-committal. Retaining the upper hand by being secretive with his thoughts. Or perhaps it was more straightforward; maybe Leo didn't desperately want to trudge up and down the narrow – and probably near vertical – streets of the fishing village. 'How is your knee?' she asked.

'Oh, you know. Getting there.'

When Bella reappeared, Patti asked if it would be possible to take the tender across to Riomaggiore. Perhaps spend a couple of hours exploring. As Bella set the request in motion, Felicia took the opportunity to head back to the suite.

Nicki arrived a few moments later and began shuffling through racks of shoes.

'Have you seen my walking boots?' he said, his voice muffled by the confines of the cupboard.

'Did you bring walking boots?' Felicia perched on the edge of the bed, then eased herself back against the pillows.

'I am sure I asked Mrs Davies to pack them. Where are they?'

Felicia closed her eyes. Nicki's accent became stronger the more ruffled he became, and she smiled as she heard him utter an under-his-breath Danish oath.

'*Fandens*. Felicia, I cannot find them.'

'Your boating shoes will be fine, won't they? You're not scaling mountains, after all.'

'You are coming too. Perhaps you should find some suitable footwear also?'

She groaned. 'Do I have to, Nicki? Couldn't I rest here for a few hours instead? You'll have plenty of fun without me.'

'I do not want to have fun without you,' he replied, emerging from the cupboard with his boating shoes in one hand. 'You are coming with me. I insist.'

'And in turn, I insist we're not walking all the way up to that church.'

'Very well.' Perching on one of the chairs, Nikolai pulled at the leather laces on the shoes. 'Are you changing?'

'Do I need to?'

'Of course not, you are *passende* as you are. Absolutely perfect.' He cocked an eyebrow. 'Apart from needing some shoes.'

With suitable footwear in one hand and a supply of headache medication in a small shoulder bag, Felicia headed out to the tender point, where one of the deck crew was ready with a steady arm to assist her onto the smaller boat, and Bella, although she was remaining aboard *Blue Sky*, was checking the guests had everything they needed. Once the entire charter group was on board, they were joined by another stewardess – Felicia was glad to see it was the lean, blonde one; it would give her less opportunity to tinker with anyone's belongings – and a deckhand to pilot the tender.

'Oh – Bella. I almost forgot,' Felicia called, as ropes were cast off and the tender drifted away from the yacht's hull. 'We would very much like Captain Kirque to join us for dinner tonight. Can you make that happen?'

Bella's reply was whipped away by the breeze, obscured by the growl from the tender's engine.

'What did she say?' Felicia asked.

'I think she said she's going to *"make it so"*,' Patti said with a grin.

'Did she? How very droll.'

For the first time since the charter began, Bella felt properly off duty. She'd sent Jessica on a well-earned break, to get a few hours' sleep, and Mel was on shore with the guests. They weren't due back for a few hours and everything on board was ready for their return. Bella had made the captain aware of the request for him to join the charter guests for dinner. This was the moment when, if she smoked, she'd be taking a cigarette break. A 'behind the bins out the back of the kitchen' quiet moment.

But she was on a superyacht, off the coastline of the Italian Riviera. Now was not the moment for cigarettes, or bins for that matter. No. Bella knew exactly what she wanted to do.

Back in her cabin, she stripped then pulled on her bikini. While it wasn't scarlet and stringy, like Hannah's, it was a great shade of peacock blue and she loved the way it was cut high at the sides, making her legs appear slightly longer than they really were. Not that it mattered a whole lot, nobody was going to see her.

She grabbed a towel and headed for a secluded area, rubbed in some factor-20 sunscreen, and settled herself, the warmth from the mid-afternoon sun penetrating her skin the moment she lay down. Lodging her shades up into her hair, and with eyes closed against the glare, she ran through a relaxation routine she'd picked up a few years ago, when there'd been a yoga retreat in the hotel she'd been working at. Starting with her face, she screwed up and then relaxed the muscles, releasing as much tension as possible. It probably looked a bit weird, but it was surprisingly effective. By the time she'd worked her way down to her feet, her breath was oozing in and out of her lungs, and her whole body had melted into the fluffiness of the towel beneath her. Bliss.

The gentle lapping of water against the hull, the distant screaming of gulls whirling high above, and the occasional buzz of a motor from a fishing boat or another yacht were the only sounds, and it was possible she dozed off. She certainly didn't hear the return of the tender, wasn't aware that anyone had returned to the yacht until she heard his voice.

'Bella? Sorry to disturb you.'

His frame blocked the majority of the glare from the sun, but she was still momentarily blinded as she scrabbled for her dark glasses and tried to wrap the towel across herself. 'You're back?' She knew she sounded confused – she *was* confused. Leo shouldn't be back until much later. What was the time? In a panic, she twisted her wrist to glance at her watch. Perhaps she'd fallen hard asleep, perhaps everyone was already on board, and she was completely on the back foot.

'I brought my aunt back early. She says she's not feeling too well. She's asking for a bottle of her iceberg water. Can you tell me where to find them?'

Bella scrambled to get up. 'I'll fetch one for you.'

'No. I can get it – I just need to know where to look.' Leo frowned. 'Please stay put. You're not our servant.'

That's exactly what I am, she thought.

'It's no problem.' Standing, she wrapped the towel around herself. 'It's my job to look after you.'

'Not while you're on a break, it isn't. I insist you tell me where the water is. I'm a grown-ass man, and while that doesn't necessarily equip me to do much, it might surprise you to learn that I *can* carry a bottle of water completely unaided.' He paused for a beat. '*And* I can give you the dictionary definition of sarcasm. Multi-skilled, see?'

Bella grinned and explained where she'd stacked the bottles of Svalbardi in the galley's cold room.

'Does your aunt need anything else?'

'No, thanks. I think she's tired. A couple of hours' rest and I'm sure she'll be back to her normal, acerbic self.'

'Well, if you need anything else, let me know.'

'I will.' He turned to go, then doubled back on himself. 'How much longer does your break last?'

'I'm finished with it, now some of you are back on board. I'll go and get changed.'

The smile slipped from his face, replaced by the crinkle between his eyes. 'Oh, that's a shame.'

Her frown matched his. 'What do you mean?'

'I felt like swimming from the boat while nobody else is around. I wondered if you would join me. Do you swim?'

'Yes, but . . .'

'Perfect. Give me five minutes and I'll be back.'

'No, I swim but—' Before she could get the rest of the sentence out, he was gone.

There was no way swimming with the guests would fall under her terms of employment, would it? And he'd misunderstood, hadn't waited for her to explain. Unsure what to do, she wrapped the towel more tightly around herself and headed for the interior of the yacht, determined to slip down into the crew quarters before Leo returned.

Halfway down the stairs, Bella paused. Was she overthinking this? Was she allowing the attraction she felt for this man to cloud her judgement? Nobody need ever know how she felt about him – she didn't even know how she felt. It was probably nothing more than a massive crush, a throwback to when she'd got her first hotel job as a naïve eighteen-year-old and fallen madly in love with the night manager, Paul. She just needed to separate the emotion from the job. She'd done it before – she'd learned hard and fast, when it had transpired that what she thought was a relationship with Paul was actually nothing more than an older man screwing someone who wasn't his wife. She'd learned her lesson.

The bottom line was always that if a guest asked for something, and it was within the realms of possibility and propriety, then it was her job to provide it. So the situation could become a problem exactly because she *didn't* agree to take a swim with Leo. And where would she stand if he took a swim alone and got into difficulty out on the water with nobody to help him?

Heading back up the stairs, she laughed at herself. That was stretching logic a bit far, but it did make sense for someone to be on hand. By the time she'd headed out to the swimming platform, Leo was already there.

'I thought you might have changed your mind.'

He lounged against the side of the platform, shades in one hand as he ran a hand through his hair. Why did he have to keep doing things that accentuated the best bits of his body? She dragged her gaze away from his tautness and dumped the towels she'd scooped up on her way onto the wooden decking.

'Needed to get some fresh towels.'

'Are you ready?'

When she nodded, he dropped his shades and took a running dive from the edge, surfacing a short distance from the boat. His reaction was instant, and positive. 'Wow. Come on in – it's fantastic.'

Bella hovered on the edge of the platform, a final few seconds of indecision before she too dived in.

Although the water was cool on her skin in comparison to the pummelling of the sun's rays, it wasn't cold. She surfaced, taking a second or two to orientate herself. Everything looked much bigger from the sea. The yacht towered above her, and the coastline appeared both further away and more imposing. She bobbed, clearing water from her eyes as Leo swam across.

With her arms flowing back and forth below the surface to

keep herself steady, she trod water until he reached her. 'You're right. This is fantastic.'

'It really is. Very refreshing after those dusty streets.'

'Are the rest planning on climbing all the way up to that church?'

'I think so. Nikolai loves that kind of stuff.'

'From here it looks as though it's perched on the highest possible part of the cliffs.'

'As close to God as they could build it, I suppose.'

Scraping her soaking hair back from her forehead, Bella glanced around. 'Shall we swim around that buoy and back?'

'Race you?'

'You're on.'

Unless he was a hopeless swimmer, there was no chance Bella would win this race. She enjoyed swimming well enough, but not in a competitive way. She wondered how deeply Leo's natural desire to win ran. Anyone who competed for a living must be hardwired to want success – and as he struck off through the water, she realised she wasn't wrong.

Kicking off, she did her best to catch him, slicing her way through the water and keeping her focus on the target buoy. Rounding it, she set her sights on the yacht and worked her legs as hard as she could, seeing the swing of his arms, or the spray from his kick, always out in front of her. As they neared the boat, he slowed, and she caught up to him, puffing from the exertion.

'You're quick,' she said.

'I've been doing a lot of swimming – it's good for my knee.'

He was barely out of breath, and she did her best to cover her own demands for oxygen. At a slower pace, they swam to the edge of the yacht, each resting an elbow on the platform. It was good to allow her tired legs to dangle in the cool water, while her face and shoulders warmed in the sunshine.

'I could stay here forever,' Leo said.

She didn't disagree, allowing herself to enjoy the moment. Neither of them spoke for a while, Leo rested quietly against the side of the yacht, eyes closed, and she did the same, except watching him.

Eventually, her line of sight moved past him, settling instead on the water. After a while she blinked, checking she hadn't imagined it. Two sleek fins, on equally sleek grey backs, slicing through and curving above the water, then disappearing.

Without thinking, she reached across and wrapped a hand across his shoulder.

'Leo, over there.' She spoke quietly, not wanting to frighten the creatures as they crested the water again and she pointed. 'Dolphins.'

They watched silently as the pair broke the surface three, four more times, before they were gone. Her hand still rested on his shoulder, and when it was clear the dolphins had moved away, she withdrew it, noticing how closely he watched her actions.

'I'm sorry,' she said.

'Why? That was magic. I love dolphins.'

'I don't mean them. You know why. That was unprofessional of me, and I want to apologise.'

Leo studied her, a frown etched into his forehead. 'I presume you mean you have rules about not mauling the guests?'

'Mauling?' Panic edged into her voice as Bella shook her head – maybe she shouldn't have got into the water with him, after all.

Before she could make her excuses and climb back onto the boat, Leo's expression morphed into concern. 'Whoa there – I was joking. I'm not that much of a knob. I invited you for a swim, we swam, we saw dolphins. Where's the harm?'

It was all right for him. He wasn't doing a job, had nothing riding on any of his actions. Whereas Bella should be more circumspect. Tricky when the touch of her hand against his naked shoulder had sent bolts of something akin to lightning through her body, and she'd had to drag her fingers away from him.

'Don't feel the need to apologise. I get it, I've lived my

whole life with other people's perceptions that I must be an overprivileged dick. That it's only a matter of time before I throw my weight around and get all overbearing.' He paused. 'I guess I am overprivileged, but I'm not a dick. At least, I try not to be. And the thing is, if I want to spend time with somebody, it's because I want to spend time with them, you know? Not because I have some inbuilt perception of what the world around me should provide, or how I should be treated.' He paused, as if he was about to say something else, but stopped himself. Gazing out to sea, he sighed.

Bella wasn't sure if he wanted her to reply, wasn't sure what to say. She opted to stay put but say nothing, instead concentrating on the cool water as it eddied around her feet.

Eventually, Leo pulled in a deep breath. 'Now I'm going to apologise.'

'What for?'

'For being a buzzkill in such beautiful surroundings. The last thing you want is my tedious interpretation of my life. OK, let's lighten the mood. Tell me one totally inconsequential thing about yourself, Chief Stewardess Bella Mason.'

It was impossible to ignore the crinkle at the edges of his eyes, the way his grin lit up the whole of his face, and Bella found herself smiling through her concentration as she considered what to say. 'Um, I wanted a hamster so badly when I was a kid that I made one from an old ball of wool and called it Edgar.'

'Edgar?'

'Yeah. Something wrong with my choice of name?' She tilted her chin and set her expression to neutral.

He laughed, a sudden explosion of noise. 'Nope. Nothing wrong with the name. It's quite cute, actually. It's more that I'm trying to get my head around the idea that you made a wool hamster. Did you ever get a real one?'

'No. Which was probably just as well to be honest, because I managed to lose Edgar and he was inanimate, so . . .' She shrugged. 'How about you? What's your inconsequential fact?'

'Oh, that's easy,' he said. 'I absolutely adore Haribo sweets.'

Her reaction was spontaneous. 'Me too. Any in particular?'

'All of them, but especially the sour cherries. My guilty pleasure.'

'Did you note it on your preference sheet?' She knew he hadn't – she'd committed them all to memory.

'No. Because that would land me firmly in the overprivileged dick category. Do you get many requests for trivial things like that?'

'Aboard a yacht – I'm not sure. Probably.' She decided to keep her conversation with Mel at the restaurant to herself. Not all the requests were trivial. 'In hotels . . . you wouldn't believe some of the things ordered via room service.'

He raised his eyebrows. 'You've never seen my father in action. No request is too petty for him to make.'

'OK, so maybe you would. But put it this way, you're on safe ground if all you want are sour cherry sweets.'

'Well, either way you don't need to worry – I brought a few with me.' Swinging himself around until he faced her, his expression became serious again. 'Bella, can I ask you something?'

'Of course.'

'What would you think if—'

Leo didn't get to finish the question; instead their attention was taken by another male voice, loud and directly above them on the swimming platform. The captain's voice, asking Leo if he could spare the chief stewardess for a meeting – a meeting Bella knew wasn't scheduled, but from the hard edges of the captain's expression had moved to the top of the agenda.

'I'd better go,' she said, pulling herself out of the water and wrapping up in a towel, aware of the captain scrutinising her every move.

'I wish to see you on the bridge in ten minutes, Miss Mason.'

Chapter Nine

Mel had no idea why Bella was meeting with J-P, nor why she looked so stony-faced as she left the bridge afterwards, but was keen to find out. Could it be that the girl was playing into her hands without Mel having to do a thing?

'Hi, J-P. Could I grab a word with you?' She beamed a wide, non-confrontational smile at him and perched on the casing to the side of the vast array of control panels, levering her feet up onto the edge of the bridge steps wall. Sitting here, and like this, would make it very difficult for J-P to ignore her, even if he pretended to check instruments, or be completely absorbed by course-setting or weather forecasts.

'What is it, Melanie?' His focus appeared to remain steadfastly beyond the glass of the panoramic windows.

She shifted her position, stretching her legs a little further before replying. 'I don't know if you are aware that part of the charter group came back to the boat early.'

He stiffened, pulling in what sounded like an irritated breath. 'I am fully aware.'

Mel knew J-P well enough to decipher a connection between the tender's early return trip and his meeting with Bella. Oh, good. Bella had stuffed up somehow. Mel put that on the backburner; she'd come to it in due course.

'Well, once Felicia had returned to the boat, the rest of the group were talking about her. I imagine that happens a lot. But what was interesting was the chat was mostly about her time in Hollywood. The films she made back then and how she's referring more and more to that time in her life.' She paused, wondering how J-P would react to her suggestion. 'I was wondering if it might be a nice idea to find out which were her favourites out of the films she made, and then have a movie night? Maybe even with movie-themed cocktails. I've looked up recipes; I'm sure we've got most of the ingredients and I could source the rest. We could have chocolates and sweets, some nibbles. Then a late dinner – maybe even put down the red carpet. The full works. What do you think?'

At last, she had his attention and he'd lost some of the tension from his frame.

'I like it. This is a good idea.'

'Thank you.' A beat of time passed, a moment in which she saw it, the dip in his eyeline, the glance at her legs. Wondered if she'd imagined it as he focused his attention to some distant point far out to sea. 'I should never have done it, J-P. Those things I said last season – I was asking for too much. I realise that, now.' Shifting again, she reclaimed his attention. The intensity of his stare triggered a tremor deep inside herself as she stared back at him, just as hard. 'Can we start again?'

The question, her confession – she could tell she'd wrong-footed him. Surprised him with an apology, rather than an attack. She realised that had been her mistake. J-P was the kind of man who needed to feel in command, to have control of every situation. It was what made him an excellent captain and had been a large factor in her attraction to him in the first place.

'Start again?'

'Maybe not completely, but you know how well we work together. You know how good I am at my job. Let me show you what I can do, J-P.'

'You ask a lot.'

'Maybe. But you expect a lot, too. I know I can give you what you need.' She chose her words with precision, knew she'd hit the mark when his breathing tightened, and his gaze dipped to her bare thighs again. 'I've always known what you need.'

There was a saying in yachting – what happens on charter stays on charter. That had been the root of her mistake, the previous season. Bringing the outside world crashing in where it wasn't welcome, moving too fast. Lesson learned. She wouldn't make that mistake again – would bide her time more carefully this summer.

'What was your meeting with Bella about?' Her change of pace had him on the back foot again, as she slid from her perch and stood eye to eye with him, smoothing her shorts with a latent smile on her lips. She could do non-combative and sweet when she wanted to. Maybe it was time to remind him.

'She has much to learn about the world of yachting,' J-P said.

Cryptic, but she presumed it had something to do with the delicious Leo Kennedy-Edge. It didn't take a psychic to work out what Bella thought of him; one look at her when he was around said it all. Still, Mel itched to ask what J-P meant, to probe him for information about how badly his brand-new chief stew had fucked up. Ached to tell him that whatever the mistakes were, there was no way *she* would have made them if he'd given her the role instead of Bella. Instead, Mel edged close enough to be able to breathe in J-P's distinctive sharp body spray, to know he'd recently had a black coffee from the lilt of it on his breath.

'I'm sure she'll pick it up eventually,' she said. 'I'm doing my best to help her.'

It would have been so easy to have reached out and touched him. Easier, perhaps, than turning away. But Mel needed to stick to her plan, to play the long game – a game that, if she played it correctly, could see her wind up with everything she still held on her wish list. The perfect job, and the relationship she wanted, too.

'Do I have your permission to go ahead with the movie night?' she asked.

J-P nodded. 'Perhaps have a word with the husband, or the American friend, to be sure it would be appreciated. Then I will leave it to you to discuss with Tobias the dinner, and to organise everything else.'

'Perfect. Thank you, J-P.' It really was perfect – he hadn't mentioned Bella at all. Perhaps she could lever Bella out by simply being better than her. 'Can I get you a fresh coffee before I go?'

'I would like that. Thank you, Melanie.'

As she headed down the steps, she risked a final glance in his direction, fully expecting his attention to already be on the engine control board, or weather radar. To her delight, his gaze was firmly fixed on her – she recognised the look in his eye, and it made her stomach contract. Until that moment, she hadn't realised how much she wanted this, or how far she'd go to get it – and him – back.

Bella knew she hadn't handled the meeting with the captain as well as she might. Perhaps it wasn't surprising. She'd been caught completely off guard, had been utterly focused on what Leo was about to say when Jean-Philippe loomed dark above them like a storm cloud. In her scrabble to get dressed she'd run through every scenario she could think of – from the meeting being completely unrelated to her swimming with Leo, which she felt was unlikely, all the way up to a summary dismissal. As she'd headed for the bridge, she was wondering how she would get back to the UK, if she was removed from *Blue Sky* with immediate effect. What she would say to her family in explanation.

Her hands were shaking by the time she rapped her knuckles on the wall at the top of the bridge stairs, her mouth dry as she took the final steps.

'Bella, come in.' The captain was at his desk – a large table set back from the control panel with banquette seating on three sides – an open laptop and an insulated cup of coffee in front of him. He gestured for her to join him, closing the laptop as she took a seat.

'No one is more aware than me that you are new to life on board a charter yacht, and I know it takes a while to settle in. But I think now would be a good time to clarify how things are done on *my* charters. Before too many mistakes are made.'

'I would appreciate that, Captain.' Bella clasped one hand within the other out of sight beneath the table.

'From time to time we have guests who, for whatever reason, generate a level of interest for a member of the crew, one which is above the normal. Sometimes the attraction is mutual. And while this is not to be encouraged, we are no longer living in strait-laced times, either.' He cocked an eyebrow. 'On occasion it can be an advantage, to catch the eye of a good-looking man, don't you think?'

'I wasn't trying to . . . He simply asked if I wanted to swim with him. I thought it would be rude to refuse.' It sounded a bit lame, saying it out loud, and the captain seemed to agree with her, if his stifled laugh was any gauge.

'Bella, we have a long season ahead of us. These attractions happen – many of our guests will be *très charmants*, very charming. You need to understand the mechanics, that's all. I have no interest in what happens between the two of you – but of concern to me is how it impacts my reputation and the reputation of *Blue Sky*. I have to make my report to the owners of this yacht; this is not to be forgotten. Also, the guests' enjoyment of their charter is of the greatest importance. In essence, don't promise him anything you aren't willing to give, and don't think for a moment he's going to do anything other than walk away at the end of the charter. It will be of no importance to the rest of his life. This may sound harsh, but I do not need a lovesick puppy for a chief stewardess.'

'I swam around a buoy and back with him, that's all.' Her hands were no longer shaking with nerves; anger was building instead. 'I'm only trying to do my job.'

'And I've heard it all before.'

He lifted the coffee to his lips and Bella had to squash a desire to bat it out of his hand. How dare he treat her as though she was seventeen, and as naïve as hell. 'I think you underestimate me, Captain.'

This time he laughed out loud. 'Maybe I do. Time will tell. But you need to know that if something you do impacts on *Blue Sky* in any negative way, you are easily replaced. Very few people on this yacht are indispensable. And while this may sound harsh, it is the way this profession works.'

The conversation was spiralling – as were Bella's emotions. She needed to get a grip, put things into perspective. Focus on what was important. Her parents had thought her mad to quit her job at The Magnolia in favour of a few months in the Med, saw it as Bella jacking in her entire career for a completely unknown outcome. 'Risk-averse' was probably a bit harsh – they'd taken and continued to take huge gambles with the children they invited into their home – but her parents favoured a well-trodden career path, the safety of regular paycheques. A fixed-rate mortgage. Manageable car repayments. Couldn't understand her wish to travel and see the world, intimating that they thought she was being immature and frivolous.

If Bella failed in her role on *Blue Sky*, if she fell short of the standards expected and had to travel home early, with her tail between her legs, she wasn't sure she'd get another chance as good as this. Earning money while travelling in such a glamorous way – the only similar option she'd come up with was becoming cabin crew for an airline, but figured doing that wouldn't show her much more than airports and hotel rooms.

The captain drew a breath, the flicker of a frown crossing his brow. 'I do not want to be speaking like this so early in the season, but you need to be careful, Bella. Focus on what is important to you. Do you understand? You're the chief stewardess aboard *Blue Sky* – remember you need to lead by example.'

'I will certainly do my best.' She squeezed one hand inside the other, annoyance still bubbling at his inference, even though she should perhaps be relieved the reprimand hadn't been worse.

'Oh, and for the record the part of the aft deck you chose for your sunbathing isn't perhaps as private as you had hoped.' The captain pointed to a screen on the control desk, split into four images of various parts of the ship, the pictures flickering and swapping between views. 'The cameras cover the majority of everything topside. And your swimwear?' He bunched his fingers together and brought them to his lips, exploding them out as he said, '*Magnifique*. You will catch many glances this summer, Bella. Just remember that.'

She was still stinging with embarrassment and hot with anger by the time she reached the galley.

'I'm thinking French onion soup for our starter tonight,' Tobias said, knife busy as he peeled and chopped white onions. 'In honour of J-P joining the guests.'

Bella's snorted huff was enough to garner a glance from the chef.

'Everything OK?'

'Everything's awesome.' She rattled at the kettle, then flicked on the switch. Surely there were rules about comments like the one the captain had made about her swimsuit, weren't there?

'Good. Then I'm thinking monkfish for main course. Maybe with crispy pancetta, or a lemon dressing. It might pair well with the *Pouilly-Fumé* – the Loire Valley one. We've got loads of that, and it's another nod to our esteemed leader.'

'Sounds wonderful. And dessert? How about *tarte Tatin*?' She hoped the catch in her throat wasn't audible. It wasn't as if Bella was a stranger to sexual harassment – she'd worked in hotels for years, for God's sake – but had that been what Jean-Philippe was inferring? 'They could have it with Chantilly cream.'

Oblivious to her emotions, Tobias shook his head. 'Too late. I've made *panna cotta*.' He set the knife on the board, wiping his hands in a cloth as he studied her more closely. 'Is everything really OK?'

Unable to quash her tumble of thoughts any longer, she said, 'Did you know everywhere on the boat is covered by cameras?'

'It's not everywhere. None of the cabins have cameras, obviously. It's mostly topside. For safety reasons.'

'I didn't realise.' Now she did sound naïve.

'Why does it matter?'

'I thought that while the guests were exploring Riomaggiore, I might take a bit of downtime, do a bit of sunbathing on the aft deck.'

'Ah.'

'If I'd known there were cameras, there's no way I would have . . .'

'Topless?'

'No!' From the amused arch in Tobias's eyebrows, she could tell he was enjoying this a bit too much. 'But the captain saw me.'

'And?'

'I wish he hadn't.'

Tobias shook his head. 'You're OK with J-P.'

'Are you sure?' The swimsuit comment hadn't seemed in the least bit innocent.

'He probably wanted to give you the heads-up, that's all.'

'Well, I wish he'd done so *beforehand*.' She sighed, deciding against telling Tobias the rest of it. 'I feel a bit stupid, I suppose.'

Tobias tilted one hand into a near-vertical angle. 'Learning curve on a yacht looks something like this. And from where I'm standing, you're doing a pretty impressive job of keeping a grip on everything so far.' Restarting his chopping, he added, 'Don't let the buggers grind you down.' He waved the knife in her general direction. 'And next time you decide to go sunbathing, either choose the swimming platform, where there aren't any cameras, or give *me* the heads-up. I'm only too willing to come and hold your towel for you. I could be your personal shield, if you like.'

'That's a kind offer, but it won't be necessary,' she said, grinning at the exaggerated downturn in his expression.

With setting the dinner table delegated to a surprisingly enthusiastic Mel, Bella headed around the yacht to check in with the guests. Patti and Hannah were on the sun deck, relaxing in the shade. By the sounds of the conversation, Patti was trying to encourage her daughter to join Leo in the gym. Hannah wasn't having any of it, and to be fair she did look wonderfully comfortable on her lounger.

Darting back to the galley to grab a couple of bottles of standard non-iceberg water for them, Bella came face to face with Leo at the entrance to the gym.

Wondering if she radiated the awkwardness she felt, she took a step back, which only served to make it easier to look at him properly, loose shorts and a pale grey tee framing his toned physique, a small towel looped around his neck. He was sweating, had clearly completed a rigorous workout as he caught an edge of the towel in his hand and rubbed it around the back of his neck.

'Hi.'

'Hello.'

Awkward as hell. Or perhaps that was her interpretation. Her conversation with the captain had thrown her mind into overdrive, left her with so much to think through. Bottom of the list should be spending more time with Leo Kennedy-Edge. And yet here he was, and now he was within touching distance, the last thing she wanted to do was to walk away from him.

'How's your leg? The swimming wasn't enough exercise for one day?'

A tiny shake of his head was followed up with a more serious expression. 'It's still weak. I've given myself the rest of this trip for recuperation, but I need to be back to full speed once I'm home. It's non-negotiable, if I want to salvage any of the UK season. And I've plans to head to Argentina for a few weeks this autumn, so I haven't got time to burn.'

'Argentina?'

'They breed the most amazing polo ponies, so I'll be on the lookout for some more mares. Both to compete and to breed from. Long-term, the stud's where I want to concentrate my efforts.' He paused, as if weighing up what to say next. 'I can't play high goal forever. I need to have backup plans. Especially if . . .'

When he didn't finish his sentence, Bella was left wondering what he meant. If he didn't manage to get back to riding at the level he wanted – was that what he meant? Or was it something else?

'I hope I didn't get you into trouble earlier,' he said. 'With Captain Kirque.' He smirked. 'I'm sorry, I can't say his name out loud without wanting to laugh.'

'You and me both,' she said, happy to grab a moment of levity.

'Every time I see him, I want to make that Vulcan hand sign.' Leo lifted a hand and as he held it aloft, he forced the index and middle finger away from the other two, eyebrows raised in triumph.

Bella had seen the symbol before, her dad a diehard fan of the original series of *Star Trek*. Up until this moment, though, this particular hand gesture hadn't interested her in the slightest, and as she tried to make it too, frustration bubbled when her fingers wouldn't cooperate. Before she realised what was happening, Leo moved close enough to take hold of her hand, pressing her ring and little finger together within his fingers.

'Now try,' he said.

This close to him, she could see a bead of perspiration trapped in his hairline, feel the warmth of his fingers around hers, and as she drew in a breath the sweet scent of his body filling her senses. The last thing she could concentrate on was this strange hand gesture, her fingers continuing to lack the necessary coordination.

'Epic fail.' She extracted her hand from his grasp with a sigh.

'Did I get you into trouble, though? With the captain?'

'Who, Captain Kirque?' She was rewarded with an unfiltered laugh from Leo. 'No. It's all good.'

'I didn't want him to misinterpret. The fact that we were...' Leo swallowed, the muscles in his neck working hard as if he was supressing the rest of his sentence.

'What's to misinterpret?' Tilting her head, Bella held his gaze. 'Nothing to see here.'

'Well, quite.' Taking a step back, he held his hands out in mock defensiveness. 'Nothing to see here. I didn't want to overstep boundaries, that's all. I'm going to grab a shower; I'll catch you later.'

Nothing to see here. Exactly as it should be, Bella thought as Leo headed away from her. Nothing for Jean-Philippe to have an opinion on. No reason for him to be underwhelmed by the way she was performing in her job and no reason to view her in any other light than a professional member of his crew. Except that Bella couldn't shift the feeling that she hadn't wanted Leo to agree with her. That she wanted there to be something between her and Leo that *was* worth a second look.

With a sudden desire for military precision – or maybe it was the need for a moment to steady her thoughts – Bella headed into the gym and took some time straightening towels on a shelf before she remembered she was supposed to be fetching bottled water, and headed for the galley instead.

Chapter Ten

Felicia had no idea how long she'd slept for, but by the time she woke, the worst of her headache had lifted. Their bed on *Blue Sky* was incredibly comfortable, which helped, and the quiet on board the yacht was quite unlike anything on land. The closest she'd come to this lack of residual noise was a stay in fellow actor Anthony Harrington's ski chalet a few years previously, perched at the very top of a beautiful resort in the Alps, tucked away in its own private forest.

Nikolai was beside her, propped up by pillows and with his glasses on the tip of his nose, a hardback in his hand.

'What's the time, Nicki?'

'Never mind the time. How are you feeling? Better?'

'Much better. Thank you, darling.' A white lie. Amongst all the others, it would be well hidden.

'I have been thinking. Once we are home, I wonder if you should book an appointment with Dr Harding. These headaches, Felicia. They worry me.'

Now was the moment. Now was the exact time she should tell him. Tell him the truth. She should explain that she had already been to Dr Harding, that she went to him months previously with the persistent headaches. She had been expecting to be told she needed to cut back on her schedule, maybe take some stronger medication, or a proper break. She had been ready for the doctor to brush her concerns away. Expected to have the lecture about how she wasn't as young as she'd once been, and how working herself this hard wasn't something she would be able to do forever.

At the time she'd felt irritated before the consultation even began. Her defences had been well and truly in position, all the reasons why she couldn't cut back on her schedule on the tip of her tongue: she was as in demand on the screen as she'd ever been and if she didn't act, what was she? There wasn't anything else – apart from Nicki. Acting was what defined her. It always had.

Later she'd wished a lecture on overworking *had* been the doctor's verdict. How preferable that would have been to what she'd received. She hadn't been at all prepared for his decision to refer her to a specialist, or the trips to a private hospital she'd had to hide from Nicki, under the guise of lunch dates with her agent. For the tests and scans and biopsies she'd endured. She certainly hadn't been prepared for the diagnosis.

Maybe she should have told Nicki then. Thinking back, she wasn't entirely sure why she hadn't. No, that wasn't the truth. She knew exactly why. It was because Nicki would insist she receive every possible treatment, he wouldn't rest until every avenue had been explored. He would want to hang on to her for as long as possible. But which version of her would be left to hang on to?

The surgeon explained the likely outcomes, the paths she could choose to take. She'd asked for his complete candour on all the routes, all the scenarios and possibilities, and she'd got it. He'd explained what would likely happen if she took no action, the range of non-invasive treatments that might buy her a little time, all the way up to percentages on the likely results if she decided to endure the surgery required to try to get rid of this thing, this tumour growing and spreading its tendrils through her brain.

None of it sounded very appealing.

But Nicki would make it all sound possible, he would make it seem as if she could endure whatever it took, he would do his best to be the rock against which she would be able to lean, no matter what happened. He wouldn't listen to the negatives, to the likelihood that whatever actions she took there was limited possibility of emerging from this at all, let alone unscathed.

Felicia knew that, yet again, she was being selfish. To keep this to herself wasn't fair on her husband. But she wasn't a stranger to making life-altering decisions by herself, and there was no question that this was life-altering. And that it was ultimately *her* decision to make.

The trouble was, she didn't want to live a half-life. Her life had always been lived full throttle, all guns blazing. And it was frightening to think it might not last as long as she'd always assumed it would. That she wasn't still going to be attacking roles into her eighties, like Patrick Stewart. That she might not even see this Christmas. She'd needed time to process the information, to decide how best to move forwards. To decide which was better – to not see Christmas at all, or to stare at it through uncomprehending eyes.

She needed to tell Nicki, but the moment she did, everything in her life would change, regardless of her decision. She wasn't ready for that, not yet. Which was why she shuffled herself up until she was level with his eyeline, removed his glasses and folded them away, then she took his wonderful, beautiful, concerned face between her hands, told him she was absolutely fine, and kissed his worry away.

'All the guests are seated apart from J-P. I'm about to do water and wine service,' Bella relayed to Tobias in the galley, before pouring chilled water into tumblers. She moved unobtrusively from glass to glass as the guests chatted. The atmosphere was relaxed, an air of expectancy as they waited for the captain to join them for dinner.

'Darling girl – could I have some Svalbardi, rather than whatever it is you have in your carafe?'

A beaming smile accompanied Felicia's request, her lips perfectly coated in a vibrant red lipstick, its authenticity taking away some of the dismissiveness of the hand gesture that accompanied her words. That expression had graced millions of screens, both small and large. Almost hypnotic – Bella could see exactly how Felicia had charmed the world for so long.

'Of course.' Bella communicated the request via her earpiece;

hearing Tobias's snort over the radio, she covered her earpiece for fear Felicia might also hear it.

'I'll bring some with me.' Mel's voice, tinny through the earpiece, sounded enthusiastic, and she appeared a short while later – bottle of iceberg water in one hand, basket of Tobias's home-baked dinner rolls in the other.

As Mel served the rolls and Bella finished pouring water, Jean-Philippe finally arrived, formally attired in his whites, the rows of gold braid on each shoulder shimmering under the lights. There was another round of enthusiastic greetings as he took his seat, showered the ladies with compliments as he reached for his water and enquired as to how Nikolai was enjoying the charter, *Blue Sky* and all its amenities.

'As well as the jet skis we have an inflatable slide,' Jean-Philippe said. 'It attaches to the upper deck – I could have the deckhands set that up for you once we reach Elba. I understand it's a lot of fun.'

'I am keen to reach the islands,' Nikolai said. 'This coastline is fabulous, of course. But I am really looking forward to getting away from the hustle and bustle. Finding undisturbed coves and secret places.'

'Hustle and bustle?' Patti sounded mystified. 'I haven't had things this quiet in years.'

'Given the chance, I believe my husband would choose to live with a herd of goats on a deserted island,' Felicia said. The smile was back, radiant and beaming directly at Nikolai. 'Wouldn't you?'

'I would – you know me too well. But there would be a condition.'

'Oh, yes? A steady supply of your favourite cigars?'

'That would also be wonderful but was far from my mind in this instance.'

'So, what would the condition be?'

'That you would be there with me.' Nikolai covered Felicia's free hand with his. 'It is all I have ever wanted.'

Bella paused, the bottle of *Pouilly-Fumé* cold against her

fingers as she watched the interaction. Felicia's gaze intensified as she and Nikolai stared at one another. Bella wondered what it was like to have that level of investment in another person – to be so open about how much you loved them. After her experience with night manager – and general shagger of anything in a skirt – Paul, Bella had learned fast that not everybody was as honest and straightforward as they made out. That what people said, and what they actually meant, could be poles apart.

Between that time and now there had been other men in Bella's life – sometimes even boyfriends – but nobody had come remotely close enough to what she thought it must take to want to look at someone in the way Felicia was looking at her husband.

She sighed, wrapping a linen napkin around the neck of the bottle in preparation to pour the wine. The whole table had fallen silent, as if they too were captivated by the scene, and for a second Bella thought Felicia might cry – the whites of her eyes had lost some of their brightness and she blinked rapidly.

Patti broke the moment. Her loud American drawl sliced through the quiet. 'Oh, my Lord – will you two get a room already?' She glanced around. 'I mean, really? Can't we wait for the declarations of love until *after* we've eaten? I'm starved.'

Nikolai laughed, and Jean-Philippe joined in, but Bella couldn't help but notice that as the conversation continued around them, Patti glanced two or three times in Felicia's direction, her expression difficult to read.

With the French onion soup served and eaten, Bella and Mel cleared in preparation for the main course. Jean-Philippe was holding court, explaining the intricacies of negotiating the various marinas with such a large boat.

'Does the captain enjoy evenings like these?' Bella asked, as they headed for the galley.

Mel laughed. 'Nope. Especially when it's followed by a night sail. Guests don't appreciate how hard those are on the crew. But he never says "no" to an invitation to dine with charter guests. Whatever they want is exactly what they get.' She dumped a pile of plates next to the dishwasher. 'Although, he's an expert at charming them, then making an early escape – just wait and see.'

Back upstairs, with the large plates balanced precariously, Bella announced the next course.

'For your main course tonight, the chef has prepared pan-seared monkfish, on a bed of rocket and samphire, with a Sicilian lemon dressing. *Bon appétit.*' She felt a bit daft using the French phrase, but it was in keeping with the theme for the evening – the table decoration a flurry of the French *tricolore*, in recognition of Jean-Philippe's heritage – and the fish received a warm welcome.

'Tell me, Captain Kirque,' Patti said, lifting her fork in preparation. 'Do you ever feel like setting sail and, you know, boldly going where no man has gone before?'

Jean-Philippe pursed his lips; Bella could see Patti grinning as she glanced around the table. Like a naughty schoolkid baiting the teacher and waiting to find out whether her reference to *Star Trek* had been rumbled.

'It is not a particularly usual decision on board a yacht,' Jean-Philippe said, mild confusion settling on his face as Patti began to giggle. 'The ocean may look as though you may go wherever you please, but we have a manifest, shipping routes. So, we don't tend to be that dramatic. Not as a rule.'

'Right. That makes sense.' Patti hovered her fork over her plate. 'I suppose your guests always have plans, and they want you to "make it so".'

Bella did her best to muffle a laugh at another *Star Trek* reference, busying herself by checking the rest of the white wine was on ice.

'Patti, darling, do shut up,' Felicia said, digging her fork into her fish, flaking off a piece and popping it into her mouth. 'Oh, this is delicious. I've never been brave enough to prepare monkfish. It always looks so unappealing with all those teeth and the freaky spines.'

'Like you've ever filleted a fish for yourself, Felicia,' Patti said, spearing some of the rocket. 'Plus, you have a chef at home. What *are* you talking about?'

'And you're an expert, Patti, are you? A regular filleter of your own fish?'

'No, I never said I was. I'm pointing out facts, that's all.'

'Where you're concerned, Mom, that's also known as pouring on the gasoline and flicking a match.' Hannah lifted her wine glass, drained it, and glanced around for a top-up.

'At least there's heat when I'm around. I'd rather be a fire starter than a cold fish, baby girl.'

As Bella refilled her glass, Hannah laughed, but it wasn't from amusement. It was a hollow sound. 'Wow. So, I'm a cold fish now, too?'

'I didn't mean—'

'Yeah, you did.' Shoving the glass onto the table, Hannah rounded on her mother, the movement so quick Bella had to sidestep to avoid the wine bottle being caught in the motion. 'What do you want from me? You want me to jump him right here or something? For God's sake leave it alone, will you?' Twisting again towards Leo, her face clouded, and her tone softened. 'I'm sorry, I didn't mean to drag you into this, but she won't let it go.'

Bella couldn't keep up. She felt like she was watching a tennis match as her gaze swapped between Hannah, her mother and Leo. His expression remained guarded, and it occurred to Bella that he hadn't spoken a word since they'd sat down at the table. He ran tense fingers across his mouth, back and forth as though he had something to say but had determined not to allow himself to.

'Oh, my Lord, Hannah. You need to apologise to the table. And to Leo. What a thing to say.' Patti cast a worried glance around the table. 'I am so sorry for my daughter's behaviour. Truly I am.'

Hannah threw her napkin across her plate and stood. 'Well, no need to be sorry any longer, Mother. Apologies, everyone. Looks like Hannah still can't express her emotions in an adult fashion. Apparently, she's still confused about all sorts of things in her life. Probably best for everyone if I retire to my cabin and spend the rest of the evening in quiet contemplation about how I can improve myself.' She pulled the bottle of *Pouilly-Fumé* from Bella's hand. 'Or maybe I'll just get shit-faced and pass out.'

Shortly after Hannah stormed off, Leo excused himself from the table and headed after her. For a while it was quiet enough to hear the waves lapping at the hull of the yacht, the only other sound the occasional clink of cutlery against bone china, as the remaining guests struggled valiantly through the awkward atmosphere and the rest of their monkfish.

His plate empty and cutlery laid neatly together, Jean-Philippe pressed the napkin against his lips and cleared his throat.

'Well, I must get back to the bridge. I have checks to make before we head to Livorno province. Cruise ship traffic can be busy in and out of their modern harbour, so I must be alert as we navigate past that, *n'est-ce pas?*' He patted his stomach. 'Too much of this amazing food and I will be falling asleep at the helm. Not a good idea, I'm sure you'll agree.'

Felicia tinkled with a polite laugh. 'My goodness yes, Captain. That would be a terrible idea. Thank you so much for joining us. I'm sorry about . . .'

'About the terrible, spoiled American brat? Go on, say it.' Patti folded her napkin and slid it alongside her own plate. 'Well, I'm going to turn in, too. So you can talk all you like about us behind our backs.'

'We wouldn't dream of doing anything of the sort, Patti. You have a wonderful daughter, and we are all allowed to express our emotions. It's a healthy way to be. I hope you will be able to sleep well.' Nikolai stood, moving to hold her chair as Patti scraped it back.

'Thanks, Nicki. She's going through a tough time. I'm sure she'll be back on form tomorrow.'

Nikolai remained standing until Patti and Jean-Philippe were out of sight, then sank back into his chair. Lifting a glass, he held it until Felicia raised hers and chinked them together.

'Alone at last,' he said, his smile scrunching his eyes so much his wink was almost imperceptible.

'It would seem there's two of us for dessert, Bella,' Felicia said.

'Will Leo be rejoining you?' Although she appreciated his decision to go after Hannah, Bella found herself hoping he wasn't going to be spending too much time in her company. Silently, she told herself off – why did it matter how much time he spent with Hannah? *Nothing to see here . . . remember?*

'I don't know – he might.'

'Well, the chef can always prepare him something when he's ready, if he wishes.' Bella lifted their plates and, between them, she and Mel cleared the table again.

'Can you cope with the two of them?' Mel said. Now the captain had left, her enthusiasm from earlier seemed to have taken a sudden nosedive.

'Of course. Why?'

'No point all of us standing around, waiting for the next request. I'll go to bed now – if you like I can do early service tomorrow.'

It did seem overkill to have two of them on duty, and the thought of staying in bed past six o'clock the following morning was appealing. 'Sounds like a plan,' Bella said as they carried the plates into the galley. 'Maybe help Tobias with the clean-down before you knock off?'

'I can hear you,' Tobias said. 'Nobody ever tell you it's rude to talk about people behind their back?'

'There's only two for dessert,' Bella said, apologising when she saw Tobias's face drop.

'For shite's sake. Why?' He lifted a cloth on an entire tray of individual *panna cottas*.

Mel began to laugh, and Bella did her best to explain while Tobias turned out then garnished two of the *panna cottas* with delicate strands of fresh orange zest and a scraping of intensely dark chocolate.

'Don't forget the dessert wine to go with it.'

'Already taken it out.' Bella picked up the desserts and headed for the door. 'Thank you. These look amazing.'

'Of course they bloody do.' Tobias's words floated after her as she headed for the sun deck.

After dinner, Nikolai took Felicia and a bottle of Krug into the hot tub. Bella ensured there were plenty of their largest fluffy white towels and a couple of gowns within reach, and took the hint when Nikolai made assurances they wouldn't require any further assistance that evening. As she headed down the steps, she saw Felicia leaning back against her husband, the slowly rotating colours of the tub's internal lights sending out a vibrant glow, through which rising steam clouded the backdrop of the darkening sky.

She cleared the last of the decorations from the table, packing everything used to make the elaborate display back into their bags, and skipped down the stairs to shove them into the storage cupboard in the main salon.

As she walked in, Leo was occupying one end of a leather chesterfield, legs casually folded and his attention fully on the mobile in his hand. He looked as surprised as she felt when he glanced her way.

'Oh. Hi,' she said. 'Do you mind if I . . . ?' She gestured to one of the cupboards.

'No. Of course not. Carry on.'

After doing her best to shove the packets of beads and shells into the cupboard in some semblance of order, she straightened. 'Is there anything I can get you? Some food, perhaps? You missed most of dinner.'

She hoped it sounded as if she were simply concerned about him starving to death overnight, but she recognised there was a subtext to her questions. Who was she kidding? There was a massive subtext. *How long did you spend with Hannah, and why?* – that's what she really wanted to ask.

'No. Honestly, I'm fine.'

'Was everything all right? Hannah seemed very upset when she left the table.'

He sighed, laying the phone on the uneven studded roll of the chesterfield's arm, shuffling himself up to rest his elbows on his knees.

'It's nothing she hasn't been dealing with for a while,' he said. 'She'll be fine. She'll work it out.'

Not a particularly forthcoming answer, but there was no reason he should tell her anything about Hannah Prior, or their relationship – if that was what he was alluding to.

'Have you known her long?'

'I've known Hannah for years. She was about fourteen the first time we met, I think. I was maybe seventeen. At some gala evening for *Murder in Mayfair*, when Aunt Felicia wanted her extended family in tow. We see one another a few times a year.'

Bella felt her shoulders relax. They were casual acquaintances. Not that it mattered. But still . . .

'Actually, is there any chance I might raid the fridge for something to eat? Now I'm thinking about food, I could use a snack. Will the chef mind?'

Bella smiled. 'He won't mind at all. Let me fetch you something. What would you—'

Leo shook his head. 'I meant what I said earlier. I'll go and grab a sandwich, or something. I'm very happy to get it for myself.'

'A sandwich? Tobias will have a meltdown if all I let you have is a self-service sandwich.' She headed for the door. 'Come on. I've got a much better idea.'

Half expecting Tobias to still be in the galley, wiping down from the evening meal, or prepping for breakfast, Bella was surprised to find the space empty, the only sound coming from the churning dishwasher. Pulling open one of the huge fridge doors, she extracted the tray of *panna cotta* desserts.

'Have you ever had a back-to-front supper?' she asked.

'Never. What's a back-to-front supper?'

'Starting with pudding and working backwards. We did it at home, sometimes.'

Leo looked mystified. 'Why?'

'When my brother was small, he went through a difficult phase with his eating. I don't remember how it started; I was too young myself. Apparently, it had something to do with someone telling him where sausages came from. He loved them; they were his favourite food until that moment. He's still a vegetarian, but for ages he'd only eat pudding; he wouldn't touch anything he associated with meat. And he'd only eat sweet things once he'd established their ingredients. We had back-to-front suppers for ages to coax him into savoury food again, and even after normal service was resumed, the idea stuck and we did it for fun, every once in a while.'

She peeled the cover from the remaining dishes of dessert, watching as his eyes lit up.

'Is that *panna cotta*?'

Bella nodded. 'I didn't want you to miss out – especially as it's one of your favourite things, in one form or another.'

Leo took the spoon she offered. 'Yeah, well. I might be favouring this version right now. The other one has got some work to do if she wants to earn back her place in my heart.'

The mention of a place in his heart had Bella fumbling at the edge of the clingfilm, her fingers suddenly uncooperative, before she handed him one of the individual bowls. 'Do you mind eating it like this? I could try to turn one out for you, but I'm not sure I'd be able to match Tobias's presentation skills – it's more likely to end up all over the floor.'

'It's fine as it is, but only if you're going to join me. I hate to eat alone.'

They stood to eat, hips resting against the stainless steel island, their lack of conversation masked by the regular scraping from their spoons.

'God, that was good.' Leo lodged his empty bowl onto the counter, pushing it away with a sigh. 'Your chef really knows what he's doing.'

He was right. Even though Bella hadn't managed to eat much for the first day on board, she was slowly making up for it – and while Tobias's catering for the crew was excellent, this *panna cotta* was on a completely different level. It was sublime.

'Is it bad to say I want to lick the bowl clean?' she asked.

Chapter Eleven

Is it bad to say I want to watch you doing that? For a second or two, Leo wasn't entirely sure he'd kept that thought to himself. When Bella didn't react, he relaxed. He hadn't said it out loud, thank God.

Then she cleared her throat, perhaps embarrassed about what she'd said. 'Would you like another one?'

'No. Thanks.'

'Something savoury?'

'Do you know, I'm fine. I think that was exactly what I needed.'

Bella rinsed the bowls and spoons, lodging them in the sink. She smiled, then her face dropped, and she looked conflicted. Still she didn't speak. Eventually, he said, 'How much older is your brother?'

The smile reasserted itself. 'Three years.'

'Just the two of you?'

She laughed. 'Not exactly.' She explained that she and her brother were adopted at the same time but weren't biologically related, and in the intervening years how her parents had fostered other children. Digging out her phone, she swiped through until she came across some photos, pointing out Jay, and some of the rest of her extended family in group poses. In every picture she was the same – bright-eyed, seriously cute. And that smile. Like a bolt of lightning slamming him from the screen every time.

As she talked, Leo found himself relaxing. He rested his elbows on the cool of the stainless steel, watching her gesticulating wildly as she recounted tales of her childhood, of the disparity she perceived between her academic achievements and those of her brother, who was about to embark on the first year of his foundation programme as a junior doctor in the Royal London.

'Does he know what he wants to specialise in yet?' he asked.

'I'm not sure. I said he should choose anaesthesia, because he usually makes me fall asleep in no time. He didn't seem to find that as funny as I did. How about you? Any brothers or sisters?'

After all these years he should have been more prepared for this question. It wasn't as if he'd ever got to know his baby sister – she'd never even come home from the hospital, had died within hours of being born. Sometimes he wondered what life would have been like if she'd survived. Lily-Rose. *A pretty name for a pretty little girl,* his mother had said, *she would have made our family complete.* Amidst all the grief, Leo knew he'd had different emotions. He was four, hadn't wanted a brother or a sister to spoil his perfect world, hadn't been able to work out what all the fuss was about. It had taken him years to come to terms with that, to rationalise his guilt about his feelings at the time. Convince himself that his rejection couldn't possibly have had any bearing on why she'd died.

Of course, adult logic told him the wishes of his four-year-old self could have had no impact on the outcome – something had gone terribly wrong during the birth. His mother had been lucky to survive, and there was no chance of further siblings. But logic had never quite managed to erase the guilt. Or the lingering belief that without Lily-Rose their family wasn't complete. That he alone wasn't ever going to be enough. A belief regularly reinforced by his father's attitude towards everything Leo did.

Long ago Leo had realised that, in his father's eyes at least, however hard he tried, nothing was ever sufficient, or done to a high enough standard. Every match, win or lose, would be followed by an intricate explanation on how his father – if he'd still been riding competitively – would have taken certain shots, would have intercepted the ball more effectively, would have managed to score more goals than Leo had. As a young man, Leo had tried to work harder, to ride better, to impress – but lately he'd come to realise the futility of his actions. And he'd also begun to wonder how much of his father's angst was, and always had been, to do with the loss of Lily-Rose.

'No.' Pushing through the negative vibes of his thoughts, he focused his attention back onto Bella. 'No brothers or sisters. It's just me.'

'I think that's how Jay would have liked our home to have been. He found the constant upheavals of kids coming and going really difficult.'

'And you didn't?'

'Not really.' She shrugged, as if her willingness to share her life and home with whoever came into it was a normal attitude. 'Does Hannah have any siblings?'

Wondering why she had brought the conversation back to Hannah, he shook his head. 'No. She's an only child too. Why?'

'I wondered why she chose to come on this charter. If the two of you aren't . . .' She pulled in an awkward breath. 'If she finds spending time with her mother so difficult . . .' Shaking her head, she took a step away from him. 'Sorry. Ignore me. None of my business.'

'Contrary to whatever it is Patti thinks is going on, or what she'd like to have going on, Hannah and I will never be anything more than friends.'

He edged towards her, aware how much he enjoyed being near to her. It was as if Bella was a heat source in an otherwise ice-cold world.

'Why not? She's beautiful. I'd love to have her figure – it's perfection.'

A thought dawned, something that hadn't occurred to him before. Maybe he'd read the situation completely wrong. Perhaps Bella's interest was more than casual conversation – perhaps she'd read Hannah's signals more effectively than anyone else. Only one way to find out.

'Because Hannah would be far more interested in having a relationship with you than with me.'

The realisation dawned quickly on her face. 'Oh. I see.'

The flush of colour on her cheeks was momentary, the flash of embarrassment fleeting, but she didn't take her gaze away from his.

'She's having girlfriend troubles right now, which is weighing heavy – and her mother has always clung to the hope that her sexuality might be a "phase". However well it might sit with the media—' He mimed speech marks and adopted a newsreader's serious tone as he said, '"Felicia Kennedy's nephew in love tryst with Patti Prior's daughter, did the script writers see this one coming?"' He shook his head. 'Neither of us have ever been keen on explaining ourselves to the world, or being told what to want.'

'And what is it you *do* want?'

Bella's question was quiet, barely loud enough for him to hear, and it caught him totally off guard. *I want you.* The words came instantly into his mind, ricocheting inside his brain so loudly he had to suck in a breath to stop himself from saying them out loud. Covering his confusion with a laugh, he said, 'Not a shammed-up show-biz fake relationship; that's for sure. There are way too many of those already.'

'Something real and down to earth, then?'

'Yes. Exactly that. Something real. Someone real.'

Leo lost track of how long the words hung in the air, wasn't sure it mattered as he gazed at her. She held his eye, and he had to remind himself to breathe, his concentration on her was so all-consuming. Eventually, footsteps broke the moment, the whistling of a random tune loud and intrusive as Leo refocused. Bella turned away, her cheeks flaming red as another of the *Blue Sky*'s crew entered the galley.

'Can I help with something?' The chef was still in his whites, the pungent smell of cigarette smoke suddenly overpowering as he did his best to cover his obvious annoyance at finding a guest in his domain. The smile he pasted onto his face wasn't even slightly convincing.

'Leo wanted to try your *panna cotta*.' Bella stumbled over her words, and the chef arched his eyebrows.

'It was superb,' Leo said. 'I'm sorry dinner was so disrupted.'

'It's no problem. Can I get you anything else? Otherwise, I'm heading for my cabin.'

'No. Thank you.' Leo stood his ground, wanting to reclaim the quiet moment from before.

The chef's glance at Bella was measured, the smirk barely disguised. 'I'll leave you to it, then. Goodnight.'

But the moment had evaporated, because as Tobias headed off, Bella made it clear it was time for him to leave, too.

'Unless there's anything else?' she said. 'I should get my head down, as well. Another busy day tomorrow.'

'Of course. I'll let you get on. You're aware we're picking up Felicia's lawyer tomorrow before we head to Elba?'

She nodded. 'I'm sure the captain has everything in hand. I'll see you in the morning, Leo.'

Breakfast service was in full swing by the time Bella surfaced the next day. Sleep aboard *Blue Sky* was proving elusive. The noise from the engines hadn't been conducive to rest – she was pleased this was the only planned night sail. Or perhaps it was the churning of emotions – replacing the earlier churning of her stomach – which had made sleep so difficult. She woke sweating, and not only because the crew cabins were small and overheated; her shower was nothing like as refreshing as she'd have liked – although at least she had more space, with Mel already on early duty.

Once dressed, Bella headed for the galley, tucking her turquoise blouse into her khaki uniform skirt as she went. Tobias was stacking pancakes onto a dish, the jug of maple syrup ready on the countertop.

'Well, hello,' he said, his concentration remaining fixed on the final few pancakes. 'Good of you to put in an appearance.'

'Am I that late?' She checked her watch.

'Nope. I'm just intrigued. Apparently, Felicia Kennedy's nephew isn't up for breakfast yet, either. I was putting two and two together, that's all.' His eyebrows took on a life of their own, rising and falling like something out of a seventies comedy show skit. If he'd been wearing glasses, Bella wouldn't have been surprised to see him waggle them, too.

'What are you trying to say?'

'Did you shag him?'

'Of course not.' Her voice sounded overly loud, and she folded defensive arms.

'I wouldn't blame you – he's a good-looking bloke, and he's loaded. What's not to like? Plus, it was written all over his face.'

'What was?' Sweat was prickling at her armpits again, uncomfortable heat rising up her neck.

'I've started barbecues with smaller flames than he had smouldering in his eyes. I'm surprised you're not sunburnt this morning.'

'Don't be ridiculous.' The heat had made it fully up her throat now and was spreading across her cheeks.

'"Leo wanted to try your *panna cotta*."' He mimicked her voice, then said, 'That wasn't all he wanted to sample, sweetheart.'

'Stop it.'

Tobias laughed. 'Why? He's got a thing for you. Totally obvious to everyone but you, apparently.' He stacked the final pancake on the pile. 'These can go through whenever you're ready.'

Grabbing the platter and the jug, she swivelled and headed for the stairs, and some fresh air. Sidestepping Mel, who was coming from the opposite direction, a coffee pot in her hand, she made a hurried apology and kept moving. The last thing she needed was Mel's take on the whole situation. She didn't doubt for a moment Tobias and the other stewardesses would have discussed her and Leo in depth, and that Mel would be far less charitable in her opinions, even if Jessica, who was quiet and kind, might prefer to keep her thoughts to herself.

On the sun deck, conversation was subdued. Even though the table was positioned in the shade, Felicia had still opted for a pair of dark glasses – probably as a result of the bottle of Krug in the hot tub the previous evening – and Nikolai sat quietly, scrolling through something on an iPad. Patti and Hannah had chosen opposite ends of the table, each cradling a cup of black coffee and doing their best to ignore the world around them. Leo was nowhere to be seen. Bella couldn't decide whether that was better or worse than his being there.

Thankfully, breakfast aboard *Blue Sky* was a more relaxed meal, in terms of Bella's role. Rather than expecting everything to be served, dishes were either brought from the galley in individual portions, or on a large platter from which the guests could help themselves.

After explaining the variety of pancakes – some held a sprinkling of blueberries, others a trace of cinnamon, the rest were plain and perfect to have with some of the crispy bacon already on the table – Bella made her escape. She wanted to hide, to find a place to be quiet and alone. Almost impossible on a yacht.

She'd assumed, with her background of hectic work and equally hectic home life, the constant proximity of people on a boat wouldn't be a problem. After all, there was always somebody coming and going at home, always some kind of an interruption. It had played a large part in Jay's decision to stay in a London hospital for his foundation years, rather than coming home. Yes, his studio flat might be smaller than a Fairfax and Favor boot box, but it was somewhere he could shut the door on the rest of civilisation. All of a sudden, Bella wanted to be able to do the same.

Mel was on a high. A quiet word with Nikolai at the breakfast table had confirmed that a movie night was a good idea. When Patti joined them, they'd discussed which of Felicia's films should receive a screening. To be fair, the discussion had been largely between Nikolai and Patti – Mel didn't spend any more time watching films than she did television dramas. She would have struggled to even pull out the title of one of Felicia's films, let alone voice an opinion on it.

With a selection made, and Nikolai in charge of downloading *River of Dreams* while they remained in reach of decent internet connectivity, she was burning to tell J-P how well received her suggestion had been.

Add to which, the news that Tobias had caught Bella and Leo Kennedy-Edge behaving guiltily in the galley the previous evening had today shaping up well. Bella hadn't been on board for more than a few days, and already she was straying into dangerous territory with one of the charter guests. And it seemed Tobias hadn't taken kindly to Bella's interest in someone "above deck", either, however much the girl might deny it. Mel was well aware their chef had a history of flirting with every new female crew member, remembered entertaining the idea of a relationship with him when she first joined *Blue Sky*. Until she'd got to know J-P better, that was.

At this rate, there was no way Bella would make it through the season without stuffing up. Mel hoped for a magnificent fall from grace. Because while J-P liked to come across all liberal-minded and *laissez-faire* about casual relationships, his bottom line was undeniably selfish. To maintain his spotless reputation as a superyacht captain. And to that end, the crew needed to remember they were a direct reflection on him and were also, therefore, eminently disposable should something go awry.

At some point today, though, Mel should probably decide what to do with the diamond pendant necklace. Should she fish it out from the bowl of crystals on the guest suite deck and return it to Felicia's jewellery box? It was looking like Bella was going to drop her own yachting career overboard, without any outside assistance. Or, at least, without any help from Mel. If Tobias was correct, there would be plenty of help on tap from Leo. The more he confused Bella, the more likely it was she would make a critical error. Or perhaps Mel should leave the necklace where it was. Felicia Kennedy hadn't noticed it was missing – not surprising with all the other amazing jewellery she'd brought – and Mel might still need to plant it if the situation with Leo didn't yield results.

And there was the movie night to consider. If Mel planted the necklace now, and cried thief, the whole evening would be ruined. The evening she'd thought up. An evening which, if she played her cards right, would impress J-P.

Mel checked her watch. She was desperate to finish breakfast service, make her final list of provisions required for movie night, which with any luck Bella would assume as her responsibility to source, and then Mel could tell J-P how well her idea had been received. But J-P wouldn't appreciate being woken. The night sailing had gone smoothly, but most of the deck crew were still off duty. Yannis was the lone member up and about, taking on the endless task of cleaning down and hosing every inch of the yacht's outer shell and decking, the battle against saltwater a daily struggle.

No, she needed to wait a while longer before she offered to take fresh coffee and some breakfast to J-P's cabin.

With her mind racing with ideas, Mel grabbed a notepad and a pen, sliding into the banquette seating in the crew dining area to make her list.

This movie night was going to rival any evening ever seen on *Blue Sky*. She was going to ensure this charter season began with a bang, make it impossible for J-P to ignore her, force him to recognise her skills as a stewardess – to see the whole her. Not simply the bits he noticed to suit his libido. That aspect of the season could wait. By the time Mel was done with this group of charter guests, they would be singing her praises so highly J-P would be begging *her* to forgive *him*, not the other way around. And maybe, just maybe, she would.

Chapter Twelve

Thank goodness for their network of shore agents – that was all Bella could think as the morning ricocheted past way too quickly. When Mel had presented her with a list of items required for the movie night Jean-Philippe had sanctioned – and explained that the captain expected her to source them within the next few hours, Bella hadn't known what to say. But she was keen to build bridges, felt a slight thawing in the woman's attitude when she agreed to do her best to find everything. If Bella could pull this together, it could only be a good thing.

Over a coffee, she had been lamenting some of the items with Tobias.

'Where am I going to find all these different types of alcohol? Who knew there were so many versions of the movie-themed cocktail recipes Mel wants to try – and what even is Larceny bourbon?'

Tobias took the edge of the sheet of paper, pulling it from beneath Bella's palms.

'OK. Stop panicking.' He reached for the pen and ticked a few of the items listed. 'I know we have all of those in the storeroom. And I'm certain we have *crème de cacao blanc* – although I'll check. It might be the brown one.' He drew lines next to some of the list, including the Larceny bourbon. 'These I know we haven't got – that bourbon's infused with toffee, I believe. But in the yacht's "Bible" you'll find the number for the local shore agent. I think he's called Emmanuel and he's in charge of getting that final guest to us before we head to Elba, so he's already on standby. Once we know for sure what you need to source, phone him, and give him the list. You'd be amazed what these guys can magic up.'

As well as the half-dozen types of specialised alcohol, and various syrups listed, Mel had also made requests for more standard items – amongst them was popcorn, of course, which Tobias could provide without issue. At the very bottom of the list was an item that Bella took to be sarcasm.

'Is she joking with this?' Bella pointed to the request for a red carpet. 'It's a wind-up, surely?'

'What, more than the request for chocolate bitters and salted caramel Stolichnaya vodka?' Tobias laughed. 'She's having a go at pushing your buttons, no question. But we actually do have a red carpet on board.'

Bella frowned. 'Now *you're* taking the piss.'

'No. I'm not. Seriously, we have one. I've been the on-board chef for the owners a few times, and on occasion they've asked for it to be laid out – if they're welcoming a very special guest on board.' He doodled a stick figure in the margin of the list. 'It's underneath one of the chesterfields – there are storage compartments in the bottom of each of those sofas. It'll need a vacuum, but otherwise it should be good to go.'

'Wow.' Bella borrowed back the pen, and the sheet of paper, and ticked. Unbelievable – but one less thing to worry about.

Once she and Tobias had double-checked the store cupboard and drinks stash, Bella made a final note of what she still needed Emmanuel to source. The list wasn't anything like as daunting, now – and as she dialled the shore agent's number, on impulse she decided to add on her own request. Nothing like as weird and wonderful as the rest of the requirements, but something that would be appreciated – at least, she hoped so.

When the tender boat pulled alongside *Blue Sky* later in the afternoon, Bella was there to meet it. Yannis dealt with ropes while a lithe man transited from the small boat to the yacht. With the deep hair colour and tan of an archetypal native of the Med, the man was past his youth but not past his prime, significant crow's feet indicating a ready smile, which appeared as soon as he'd set foot on the yacht and caught his balance. Easier said than done, with the large box he cradled in both arms.

Emmanuel had arrived, with the provisions ordered from the mainland. 'Bella . . .'

For a moment, she wasn't sure if he was checking her name, or expressing happiness at making it onto *Blue Sky* with the contents of the box intact.

'Hi. Yes, I'm Bella.' She opted for the former. 'Let me help you with some of that.'

'Thank you.' He set the box on the deck. 'It is very heavy. Many bottles.'

'Did you manage to find everything from the list?' The anxiety had gnawed at her all day.

'It was very hard work, but I managed.'

She only realised he was deadpanning when he shook his head and said, 'My sense of humour is not for everyone. But this list was not a problem. I know a very good *vignaiolo*. He is not only interested in wine, he also stocks many interesting spirits. The rest was easy to find in the – how you say – the cash and carry?'

'That's fantastic, thank you.'

'But you will have noticed, I think, I come without the man. Signor Jeremy Giles.'

Her concentration had been so firmly on the provisions, the arrival of Mr Giles – or rather his non-arrival – had slipped Bella's mind. 'Oh no – what happened?'

'He missed his flight, was delayed and now cannot reach us today. This is the problem, not the bottles. I think I will speak to the captain. We must make a new plan.'

After Yannis had batted them both away from the box, hefting it up as if it were full of nothing more substantial than feathers and disappeared in the direction of the galley, Bella alerted Jean-Philippe that Emmanuel was on board, but that he had arrived solo. She led the way to the bridge, even though she felt sure Emmanuel knew his way around *Blue Sky*, then made an about-turn to leave them to it.

'Before you go—' Jean-Philippe said. 'Will you speak to the principal guests for me, sound out their preferred plan – to remain here and wait for Mr Giles' eventual arrival, or to head for Elba. I would prefer to stick to the manifest and sail to the islands. There are other ways of getting him on board, they just aren't so convenient for him. But it is their decision.'

Bella found Felicia and Nikolai in the main salon and was surprised by Nikolai's reaction to the news of Jeremy Giles' delayed arrival.

'The man is an idiot.' Visibly irritated, he scratched at a perceived imperfection in the leather of the sofa.

Felicia laughed. 'You know Jeremy has a fluid relationship with time. He's always been the same.'

'How you have tolerated him for so long is beyond me.'

'And we've all missed a flight at some point or another.' Felicia's tone was soothing, but there was no mistaking her amusement at Nikolai's reaction.

'No. We haven't.'

'Well OK – *you* haven't. But the rest of the civilised world has, darling.' A glance at Bella and she said, 'My husband can't stand tardiness. The one way to ensure you're on time for something? Make sure to go with Nicki.' Distracted by her mobile buzzing itself to life, Felicia cocked an eyebrow and answered the call. 'Are your ears burning, Jeremy? We're discussing you right now. Yes . . .' Felicia rose to her feet and headed for the deck as she chatted. 'What happened? Oh no, really . . . ?'

'Do you enjoy being punctual, Bella?' Nikolai settled his topaz-blue gaze on her.

'I do try my best to be on time, I suppose.'

He nodded, holding her with his gaze – it was hypnotic in its intensity. 'There are exceptions, of course, but I believe habitual lateness to be a sign of a lack of respect for others. To decide it is acceptable to have others wait for you – and then to make excuses we are supposed to accept without complaint?' He drew in a tight breath, his gaze briefly flitting to Felicia. 'It will be interesting to hear his excuse *this* time. Felicia is always too kind to him, too forgiving. I appreciate he has been her lawyer for many years, from the very beginning of her career, but still . . .'

'We can wait here for him, delay Elba for twenty-four hours, or . . .' Bella didn't get a chance to complete the options, Nikolai was already shaking his head.

'No. We will not change the itinerary for that imbecile. Is there another way to have him join the yacht?'

'Of course, I can have the shore agent liaise with Mr Giles – he could travel to Elba independently and join *Blue Sky* there.'

'Then that is what will happen. Thank you, Bella.'

'Should we wait until Ms Kennedy returns from her call?'

Nikolai stood, shaking his head again. 'No. The decision is made. Felicia will agree with me. Jeremy will join the cruise tomorrow.' His expression softened, and he slid another glance at his wife. 'Felicia knows nothing about our movie night later – I thought it would make a wonderful surprise. How long will you need to complete your preparations?'

After she relayed the rough timetable, he nodded. 'I will suggest we spend time in our suite. Perhaps Jeremy's late arrival might work in our favour – had he arrived on the tender as planned, Felicia would wish to entertain him. This way, we have no such distractions.'

As Bella sorted through bottles and leafed through cocktail recipes in the galley, Nikolai's reaction to Jeremy's arrival struck her as interesting. Not that she knew any of them well, and – judging by the photograph on the guest manifest – Jeremy was no direct threat to Nikolai in terms of his physical attractiveness, but there was more than a hint of jealousy in Nikolai's reaction. It felt defensive, as if he was threatened by the fact that Felicia and Jeremy had known one another for longer than he'd been a part of her life.

Pulling bags of multi-coloured cocktail-garnishing popcorn from the box – Tobias had drawn the line at making that, although he was happy to prepare fresh popcorn to be consumed during the screening – Bella peered into the bottom and couldn't help smiling as she went to lift out the final few bags, her impulse order. With her back to the galley, she paused.

Dropping them back into the box, she shoved the cardboard against the wall, prickles of heat firing up the sides of her neck. Perhaps she should leave them in the box, pretend she hadn't ordered them. Play it safe and get on with her job. The last thing she needed was drama in the first week of the season.

But although Bella had long ago chosen a career that involved pandering to people who ultimately meant nothing to her, something in that previously untroubled attitude had shifted this week. It was probably nothing more than the extremely close quarters of a yacht, the feeling of living inside everyone else's pockets, a state of being she simply needed to learn how to deal with. But what if it was more than that?

Pulling at the box again, she tightened her fingers around the packets and yanked them out. They were just a couple of bags of sweets. She was seriously overplaying the situation, exaggerating the intensity of her attraction to Leo. How ultimately pointless her emotions would undoubtedly turn out to be. In which case, what was she worrying about? It wouldn't matter how her actions were interpreted.

Still undecided, she shoved the bags into a cupboard, then returned to the task at hand and continued to memorise the ingredients for Mel's chosen movie night cocktail recipes.

Felicia knew something was going on. However mysterious Nicki liked to think he was being, however subtle, she had become aware there was more to this evening than a standard dinner when he'd pulled out his formal black trousers and favourite Tod's loafers, then spent a full ten minutes deciding on a shirt.

Not that she minded, because watching him in his painstaking decision-making process, while wearing nothing but a towel wrapped tightly around his waist, couldn't be described as a hardship.

The sight of him still had the capacity to make the breath catch in her throat.

'What's going on, Nicki?' She set down the magazine she'd been pretending to read and folded her glasses.

'What do you mean?'

Waving a hand at his careful assemblage of clothing, she said, 'This. We're simply having dinner. Why all the drama?'

The frown was almost imperceptible; he covered it quickly. 'I wanted to make the most of it. After all, it's not every day we get to dine on a superyacht.'

'No. You're right.' She stood. 'I'll get dressed too. I thought maybe the Alexander McQueen?'

Nicki's excitement was palpable by the time they were both dressed and ready to leave the cabin. Slipping his hand into hers, he was lighter on his feet than ever. His enthusiasm was infectious, and even though the reason for the fervour remained a mystery to her, by the time they threaded their way to the main salon Felicia was buzzing like a teenager. Nicki squeezed her fingers hard at the doorway.

'I hope you love it,' he said, before letting her go and pushing open the doors.

The room was transformed. At one end stood a large screen; the chesterfields had been rearranged to resemble rows of seating, and down the centre of the room, from the doorway to the screen, ran a red carpet.

'What on earth is going on?'

Standing to one side, Bella held a large silver tray loaded with cocktail glasses. Felicia had to give the girl credit; with her long dark hair swept back from her face and a smile to rival any Hollywood starlet brightening the room, she seemed utterly unaware of her appeal. The black evening uniform only accentuated the cream of her skin, the subdued lighting making the fire in her eyes shine all the fiercer.

'Welcome to *Blue Sky*'s movie night,' Bella said. 'Would you care for a cocktail?'

With the cocktails explained, Felicia settled for a corn

margarita and Nicki chose one called the Big Media. The salt of the margarita was sharp on her taste buds, but the tequila and orange balanced out the sour. There was something else, too – something that was difficult to identify.

'Is there some kind of popcorn taste in this?' she asked.

Bella nodded. 'We sourced some popcorn syrup to make the cocktails extra authentic.'

'I don't think I've ever had it before – I like it. Thank you.'

With the arrival of Patti and Hannah, then Leo, the red carpet walked, and cocktails refreshed, everyone was encouraged to take their seats. Nicki insisted they sit at the front, with Patti and Hannah in the next "row", their chesterfield offset to allow a clear view of the screen, and Leo took his seat in the sofa situated furthest back.

'What are we watching?' Felicia glanced around, taking in the ambiance – an evening at the movies. It had been a while – and this was like a private screening. The screen fluttered into life, the numbered countdown to the start of the film bringing a wonderfully old-school vibe to the proceedings. It was hard to beat the excitement of the prospect of watching a good film.

Nicki threaded his fingers through hers as the screen went dark, then burst into a cacophony of colour and sound. The music was the first thing she recognised, her surprised squeal bringing a laugh from Nicki.

'*River of Dreams?*'

'Arguably your best film, don't you agree?'

'You know I can't bear to watch myself.' She squeezed his hand, aware that her words were pure affectation. That watching the film that gave her an Oscar nomination was possibly the kindest way for Nicki to explain that nobody had forgotten she'd been a sought-after film actress. A reminder from the most important person in her life that he valued her for more than her never-ending role in a television drama. And even though he couldn't realise the importance of this evening, she wouldn't ever forget the wonderful warmth she felt in this moment.

Turning once more before the opening credits had concluded, she noticed Bella lodge her tray onto a table, swapping it for a bowl. The girl paused, as if making a decision, then she headed for Leo and handed him the dish. Unaware she was being watched by anyone else, Bella exchanged a few words with him, her face a hotbed of expression only a fool wouldn't recognise as he gazed back at her. Felicia smiled, then focused on the film. Her nephew was becoming the centre of that young woman's attention. As Felicia's character appeared on screen, and Patti hollered in appreciation, she rested her head against Nicki's shoulder, wondering if Leo would prove himself to be worthy of Bella's interest.

Chapter Thirteen

During the screening, Bella made regular forays into the salon, gathering requests for snacks, and freshening up cocktails. *River of Dreams* was a great film – a bit too old for her to have an active memory of it, but everyone was enjoying it, and it was no surprise Felicia had been nominated for an Oscar following the performance. The room had an extremely relaxed, buoyant feel to it and Bella had to admit, Mel's idea had been very much on point.

Having made a fresh round of a cocktail called a Caramel Popcorn and with everyone comfortable and settled, she decided to take a moment, heading along the exterior to the stern of the boat. As she padded along the wooden decking and took the steps to the swimming platform, Bella wiped the sticky remnants of popcorn syrup from her fingers with a damp cloth, then leaned her elbows against the railing, breathing in the cool sea breeze.

Leo must have slipped from the salon as silently as she had; she certainly didn't hear him until he cleared his throat, shoving his hands into the pockets of his chinos as he approached.

'Hi. Sorry – am I disturbing you?'

'No. Not at all. Can I get you something?'

'You didn't need to do that.'

'Do what?'

'The sweets. I was messing with you when I mentioned sour cherries.'

Bella shrugged, stung by his seeming indifference. The last thing she needed was someone messing with her – she'd tried to be thoughtful, and maybe there had been more to it, a desire to see his reaction. He'd seemed surprised when she'd handed him the bowl, surprised and pleased. Had she interpreted it so wrongly? Was he simply being polite? Either way, she didn't need it thrown back in her face.

'And I was doing my job. Going above and beyond to keep our guests happy – that's the baseline for *Blue Sky*. No need to feel special.' She wasn't sure why she said it, the words unnecessarily harsh if the shift in his expression was anything to go by.

'I didn't mean it like that.' He turned to rest his elbows on the handrail as he stared out into the gathering dusk, the sea and sky both merging grey as the sun paled and sank from view. 'But really, a whole bowl of sour cherries? Above and beyond doesn't cover that kind of attention to detail, does it?'

'And I could only get the mixed packets. So, I used my white gloves and a pair of tongs to pick the cherries out. In case you were wondering.' Although she tried to keep her face neutral, she couldn't suppress the rise in her eyebrows, had to bite the inside of her cheek as she watched his expression morph again. 'Silver service sweets, you might say.'

'Now you have to be joking. Tell me you're joking.' His grin evaporated and Bella had to admit she enjoyed the shape his face made when his emotions shifted.

'You'd prefer me to have handled each one with my bare fingers?'

Leo gave a sharp inhalation, his brow creasing. Staring out to sea, he said, 'There are a few things I'd prefer right now, but I'm not sure any of them are achievable.'

'Like what? Maybe *Blue Sky* can source them for you.' She watched him carefully, wondering where the conversation was about to head.

A beat passed. 'No, that's not what I mean, Bella. I don't want anything purely because I'm a guest on this yacht. Most people would jump at the chance to experience this level of hospitality, because it is excellent. No question. My aunt is absolutely loving this evening – it was a fantastic surprise. But I want more than that.'

'More?' He'd said the service on *Blue Sky* was excellent – it didn't get any better. So, what did he mean? 'In what way more?'

'OK – I'll stick with the analogy and hope I don't sound too weird. I want someone to pick out all the sour cherries for me purely because they want to. Because they like *me* enough to choose to do that. Not because they're expected to do it, or because it's going to gain anybody anything. Not because it's part of the game we're all playing, whether we want to or not.'

'I don't understand what you mean. What game?' She was fishing, because she had a fair idea she knew what he meant.

He laughed, an under-the-breath huff. 'You know what I'm talking about. The one where some people swan around and act special and have everything handed to them on platters – or in my case, a bowl . . .' The moment of levity was fleeting, then he became serious again. 'And others keep their true thoughts to themselves while doing their best to keep those people happy. That game.'

'Do you think that's what's happening, then? This is all a game?'

'I don't know. And that's my problem. I've lost the ability to tell what's real, and more importantly, *who* is genuine.'

'What do you mean?'

'Most people I meet like me. Or at least, they say they do. But which projection of me do they like? Is it the Felicia Kennedy's nephew persona, or the high-goal polo player with all the accompanying adrenalin and excitement, or is it the persona who can provide a route into having lunch with members of the royal family? If I stripped all that away, would they still be so keen? *That's* what I mean. Because lately it's struck me that I'm not sure I can work out which bits of my life are real, and which bits are fake. Like I said before, most people are better at acting than any of us realise.'

'I'm not sure I understand what you're trying to say.'

He shook his head. 'Nor am I. I've got myself confused, now, too. I suppose the bottom line is that I want to share my bowl of sour cherries with someone who doesn't care about any of that. Someone who just likes the sweets, same as me. End of story.'

Bella wasn't sure how to respond, so she didn't. She focused on the horizon, on the way the colours of the sky and sea had begun to morph together as the last of the sun's light leached away, her hands resting lightly on the railing.

Eventually, Leo sighed. 'I've overstepped. I didn't mean to offload all that stuff on you. It's . . .' He shook his head. 'I'd better get back to the film. I wanted to say thanks for the sweets, that's all. It was a really lovely thought.'

'You are very welcome. It's all—'

'Please don't say it's all part of the service.'

'I wasn't going to. I was going to say it's all good, because now I get to go and eat all the cola bottles, and the crocodiles. Although for the record, I like the sour cherries, too.' She paused. 'I think I understand what you were trying to say.'

'Do you?'

'Mhmm. Not that it's ever been a problem for me.' She slipped a palm around the handrail as she turned to face him. 'I haven't got any personas, nothing anyone's going to be overly impressed by, anyway. I'm just me.'

'I'm not sure that's accurate,' he said. 'There's no "just" about you, Bella. Not as far as I'm concerned.'

A beat of time passed – a moment in which he seemed to weigh up what to say next. In the end he didn't say anything; instead he ran his fingers across her knuckles as she gripped the stainless steel of the handrail, his touch lingering as he held her gaze.

In those seconds, with his fingers grazing hers, Bella could have made any number of decisions. She could have pulled her hand from his, taken a step back or turned away. She could have reminded him of the differences between them or could even have played the "how dare you" card. She could have kept her focus resolutely on her job, on her determination to remain professional. And although logic suggested any of these options would be the sensible choices, none of them came close to what Bella actually wanted to do. Only one action made any real sense.

Once Leo had recovered from the surprise of her stepping up onto her tiptoes and pressing her lips gently against his, it didn't take him long to wrap his arms around her and pull her close.

If her action was the last thing he'd been expecting, it clearly wasn't the last thing he wanted, if his response was anything to go by. And his eagerness to return her kiss was good – very good. She spiralled, losing track of her surroundings, of time, of everything but the way his lips felt against hers, the abrasive rub of his beard super-sensitising her skin, the way the heat from his body spread through hers as she wrapped her arms around his neck, and he pressed her against the railings hard enough to force the radio pack in her waistband into the small of her back. Eventually the pain from the corner of the battery pack digging into the underside of a rib was too much.

'Wait . . . Stop. I can't . . .' She drew back far enough to eke the words out, only intending to have him release the pressure a little, but he sidestepped away from her, as though she'd slapped him.

She shifted the pack, holding it up for him to see. 'I'm sorry – it was digging into my back, that's all.'

Later, she wondered if pulling at the front of his shirt until they were kissing again had been a conscious decision, or whether it fell into the "losing grip on reality" category. Either way, she didn't much care. She had no idea whether she'd be able to control what she'd unleashed. They finally pulled apart and neither of them could breathe calmly as they stared at one other.

'I should probably . . .'

'I'd better go and . . .'

The subtext was obvious. It was the time and the place and the circumstances that were all wrong.

Leo headed for the salon. Bella pressed her fingers to her lips and made for the galley, on the pretext of collecting some fresh popcorn.

'How much longer on the film?' Tobias asked as she scuttled through the door.

'Film?' It took her a moment to readjust, to work out what he was talking about. 'Oh, um, about half an hour, I think. I came to grab some more popcorn.'

'Are you OK? You seem flustered.'

'Do I? No. I'm fine. How's dinner looking?' She ran a hand across her cheeks, unable to work out if they burnt hot with residual heat from the kissing, or the abrasion from Leo's beard. The last thing she needed was to be left with stubble-rash – how obvious would that be? Leo and Jean-Philippe were the only men on board with beards, and there was absolutely no chance of her ever getting that close to their captain.

'All the food is under control. Do you think they'll move straight from the screening to the table?'

As conversation about the rest of the evening continued, and Bella assured Tobias that Mel and Jessica would be through with turning down the guest cabins in time for service, she couldn't fight the urge to check her reflection in the only mirror-like surface in the room – one of the window panels.

'You look fabulous, *daaaling*,' Tobias said, attempting an aristocratic accent. It was bad enough to make her grin. 'What's with you tonight? You're like a cat on hot tiles.'

'I just . . .' Shaking her head, she struggled for words. There was no way she could confide in Tobias, because within moments, she felt sure, Mel would also know. 'I'll take them a final bowl of snacks and double-check timings for you.'

'Don't let them fill up on popcorn – there's a six-course tasting menu to get through. They'd better bloody appreciate it.'

With the bowl in one hand, she intended to head straight back to the salon. Halfway there she paused, realised she was shaking, and set the bowl down. Her head was scrambled, her emotions all over the place. Against all logic, she'd grabbed a guest and kissed him, and only hours after Jean-Philippe had told her that messing with charter guests was akin to playing with fire. And yet, she didn't regret doing it. More than that, she desperately wanted it to happen again.

There was nobody aboard *Blue Sky* she could describe as being anywhere close to a friend, but she needed to talk to somebody. Someone who would set her straight, tell her what she needed to hear, but also be there for her. Only one person fitted those criteria.

'*I kissed a guy.*' She fired the text off to her brother and chewed her lip as she waited for his reply.

'*That was fast work, baby sis.*' The reply was instant, the words followed by a line of kissing emojis. A line of dots denoted he hadn't finished, was typing something else, and she waited for it to appear. '*By the way, so did I.*' Emojis followed, including a full line of hearts.

'*OMG. Who?*' She hoped it wasn't his ex. Her brother's on-off relationship with a fellow medical student had finally been put to rest a few months previously – at least, she hoped that was the case. Ewen hadn't been good for Jay.

'*He's called Henry. Sending pic.*' More dotted lines pulsed until a selfie appeared on her screen. Jay with his arm round a clean-shaven blond with bright blue eyes, a square chin and an unfiltered expression for the camera. '*Found myself a Viking.*'

'*Nice.*'

'*Very. WBU? Details.*'

'*Guest. Polo player IRL.*'

'*Ooh. Fancy. And . . . ?*'

'*Dark hair/eyes like me, beard . . .*'

'*Like you . . .*'

'*Cheeky.*'

'*Jack Sparrow or Jon Snow?*' Jay pretended to balance out his *Game of Thrones* fetish by referencing other forms of entertainment, but Bella was way past believing he spent his spare time watching anything else.

'*Jon Snow, but cuter. I'm working tho. Not sure I should be doing this tbh . . .*'

'Against maritime law or something?'
'Not exactly.'
'Is he hot?'
'Extremely.'
'Too hot to handle?'
'Maybe.'
'Worth it?'
She laughed. *'Maybe.'*
'That good? Dang . . .'
'IKR . . .'
'Well, don't fuck up your summer tanning plans. You want advice?'
'Maybe.'

There was a pause, then a string of laughing emojis was followed by a serious one, a monocle in one eye. *'Always use protection. Seawater isn't a contraceptive. Medical fact.'*

'Jay!!!'

'You're a big girl. You know what you want. If it's him, what's the problem?'

'But . . .'

'We've both kissed some proper frogs, but they aren't all green and slimy. And there's only one way to find out. Gotta go, Belly. Keep me updated xx'

She wondered if his advice might have been different if there hadn't been a Henry on the scene, if he'd still retained some of the sting Ewen had left him with. Would he have been more cautious with his messages? Probably not, knowing Jay. And that's what she'd wanted. Unfiltered brotherly support with a healthy dollop of "go for it", and the safety net of someone willing to tell her she was being a prize idiot if he thought so.

Picking up the bowl of popcorn, Bella headed for the salon.

Mel didn't much enjoy serving at table, but at least with a tasting menu everything was already plated; it simply needed to be delivered to the guests. As Bella oversaw the arrival of each course, explaining the dishes, Mel wondered if she was aware how intently Leo was watching her every move. If it had been anyone else on crew, Mel might even have felt a twinge of excitement for them, could imagine herself covering for a fellow stewardess and aiding a budding romance. But not where Bella was concerned. Not when she'd taken what should have been Mel's position on the yacht.

Conversation revolved around the film and Felicia Kennedy's movie career. They discussed her successes, the tribulations of a life lived at Hollywood's behest, the roles she would love to have played. Blah blah blah.

When the obvious topics began to dry up, Patti changed the subject to Felicia's dress, how stunning it was on her, how beautifully it was cut.

'It's an Alexander McQueen, so the design is only ever going to be sublime,' Felicia said.

'And such a perfect choice for tonight – it looks as though it's made up of film stills torn top and bottom and layered back together,' Patti said.

'Very elegant, the monochrome roses on it are particularly clever,' Hannah added. 'But to be honest, Felicia, you could wear a sack and make it work.'

Mel had to physically prevent herself from rolling her eyes. If there'd been a bucket handy, she'd have happily thrown up into it. Not that sucking up to the principal by the rest of the guests was something reserved solely for this charter. It was a regular feature – especially if the guests wanted a repeat invitation.

'Thank you, darling girl. I think it would look wonderful on someone like Bella, too. Don't you?' Felicia glanced at the chief stewardess. 'Someone young and gorgeous, not an old woman like me.'

If Mel felt the bite of being ignored, then so did Hannah if her expression was any gauge. And by extension, so did Patti, on her daughter's behalf. Bella had the good grace to appear embarrassed, to stumble out some awkward words of thanks.

Her cheeks flushed fuchsia and she seemed not to notice Leo's gaze settling on her time and again.

'Bella has the right colouring – all that amazing dark hair. Like mine used to be – before I started seeking professional help at the salon to keep things tip-top.' Felicia beamed at Bella, who returned the smile.

Mel wasn't especially insecure about her appearance, but there was something about the exchange that riled her, reminding her she wasn't likely to be mistaken for a Hollywood actress any time soon. She shook her head and picked up a bottle of the Rock Angel rosé they were serving with the lamb course. Bella was very pretty – no doubt – but she wasn't film-star beautiful, either. Not in the same league as someone like Felicia Kennedy.

By the time Mel had made it around the table, topping up glasses, a comment had been made about Nikolai's surname. On top of the earlier cocktails, enough wine had been consumed to make the idea of attempting to spell it correctly into a drinking game seem appealing. For his part, Nikolai appeared to be taking it all in good humour. And it was amusing to listen to.

'B-j-e-r-e—' Hannah's attempt was cut short by Nikolai giving her the thumbs down. 'God damn it.' After a theatrical eye-roll, she took a large mouthful of wine.

Patti made it a little further in her attempt. 'B-j-e-e-r-r . . . No, wait – that's too many e's. Oh Lord, I lose. Leo – you're up.'

Leo flexed his hands as if he was warming up to play a musical instrument as he cast his gaze around the table. 'I'll give it my best shot – but be warned, I am three cocktails in and dyslexic, so don't judge me.'

A glance at Bella had Mel frowning again. Bella's concentration on the man was total. She looked worried for him as he stumbled his way through a few more letters than Patti and gave up, lifting his glass in defeat.

'Good job this is a safe space,' Leo said before he downed his glassful, his cheeks flushing with colour.

'And people wonder why I kept Kennedy as my stage name,' Felicia said, closing a hand over Leo's and squeezing. 'My turn. I'll try it at speed. B-j-e-r-r-e-g-a-a-r-d. How did I do?' She glanced around as Nikolai raised two thumbs and the rest of the table burst into a round of applause, ever the consummate performer as she effortlessly absorbed the praise.

By the end of the meal, Mel's calves were aching from all the toing and froing from the galley, but the evening had been a triumph. Bella made it clear to the guests the whole thing had been Mel's idea, and much to her surprise everyone stood and gave her a round of applause as vibrant as the one they'd given Felicia. As the guests wished one another goodnight and headed for their cabins, she couldn't help the grin that wouldn't leave her face. And it was possible her attitude towards Bella might have shifted slightly, too. If the roles had been reversed, Mel wasn't sure she would have been so generous with the allocation of praise.

She tended to operate as more of a lone wolf, rather than a team player – always felt she had to fight her own corner and was fully aware how much it took for her to drop her guard and allow anyone else in. The utter lack of foundation she'd felt when she was growing up had taken its toll, and now Mel had installed order in her life and created her boundaries, she wouldn't allow anything to crowd in and threaten her status quo. Not even if she might have started to recognise, even appreciate, Bella's attempts at comradeship. With everything cleared and prepped for the morning, Mel was still buzzing. She padded to the aft, checking the bridge and then knocking gently on J-P's cabin door.

More spacious than the rest of the crew quarters and placed directly behind the bridge in case of emergencies, the captain's cabin was equipped with a double bed and still had space for a wardrobe and a tub chair.

There he sat, with his laptop lodged in front of him, a film playing quietly on the screen.

'Hi, J-P. I don't mean to disturb you, I just wanted to let you know how this evening went.'

Closing the laptop and sliding it to the floor, he swivelled the chair to give her his full attention. 'Well, I hope?'

'It was fantastic.' Her grin was back. 'They absolutely loved it. The film played without a hitch, the cocktails were awesome, and Tobias knocked dinner out of the park.'

'I should hope so.' He might sound as though her news wasn't news, as if a successful evening was nothing special – that it should be the norm – but she could tell she had his interest. He leaned forward in the chair. 'Your idea, it was a good one then? You are pleased with yourself.'

She needed to tread carefully. J-P was a hawk, and he had a way of making her the rabbit. The adrenalin began to pump, because she knew one false move and it could all turn. 'It was a lot of hard work for everyone, but the team was amazing.'

'Well, this is good to hear. Well done, Melanie.'

She decided against telling him about her round of applause. Instead, she said, 'Crazy amount of walking, though, with six courses for dinner. My calf muscles are killing me.'

The hitch in an eyebrow was as subtle as the dip in his gaze, but they were both there. Mel knew J-P well enough to spot them both. She'd planned to play this as a longer game – they had the whole season ahead of them – but she didn't want to waste the buzz she felt from a successful evening, nor the adrenalin surge she was currently experiencing. Hitching a leg up far enough to be able to rub at her calf, she pretended to ignore him.

This could go one of two ways, she knew. He could brush off her obvious play, and she would leave the cabin with praise for a well-executed evening still ringing in her ears and more groundwork to do, or . . .

'Would a massage help?'

Or she could accelerate her plans, starting right now. 'Thank you, J-P, but I've intruded for long enough. You were in the middle of watching something. I'll let you get back to it.'

'It was nothing. Of no consequence.'

They'd played this game before, and he stood, gesturing to the chair he had vacated. They held one another's gaze for a moment too long before she slid into it and he held out a hand, cupped ready for her heel.

His thumbs pressed hard into the tight knots in her calf muscles, the pain balanced by the pleasure of his hands on her skin. It had been a while. She sank back into the chair, her eyes closing as she surrendered herself to the sensations. It wasn't long before his fingers strayed further, past her knee and working their magic on her thighs, one then the other. Inching the fabric of her skirt further up. She shifted, feigning discomfort.

'You are uncomfortable?'

'A little.'

'You want me to stop?'

'No. It's not that. J-P, I wonder . . .' She inched her gaze past him, and he released her leg, gesturing for her hand instead and pulling her to her feet. 'I've missed you,' she whispered, her lips inches from his.

'And despite everything, I have missed you too, Melanie.'

He released her hand. The next move was hers to make – except it wasn't. Not really. She wanted to be stronger, to remember the final time they'd spoken the previous season, but it had paled. She supposed people would label what they had as dysfunctional, not even a real relationship, but she couldn't have cared less. The lure of being able to control a powerful man – even if it was only fleetingly – fired intense emotions for Mel. It was as good as any drug.

And maybe this time it would be different. Maybe this summer would be the one when he realised she meant more to him than he had ever been willing to admit before. Maybe right at this moment in time she didn't care about any of that, as she slid onto the bed and he joined her. His fingers continued their journey, circling and pressing and inching their way until they reached the softness of her inner thighs while she unbuttoned his shirt and finally – finally – was able to touch his skin to hers, to taste him again, to lose herself in the way he smelt and moved and sounded, to block out all the negatives and do nothing but feel with every inch of her being, with an intensity she'd never managed to achieve with anyone else.

Chapter Fourteen

Bella wondered how many hours' sleep she'd scraped together the previous night – however many it had been, she needed more. They were only three days into this charter and there was no way she would be able to survive much longer on the ragged, patchy rest she'd managed so far.

It hadn't helped that Mel had crept into the cabin at some ungodly hour and headed straight for their shower. When Mel finally slid into her bunk, Bella asked if she was OK, but the abrasive, off-hand answer had her wishing she hadn't bothered. It seemed they were back to square one.

She poked at the skin under her eyes, willing it to lose its sleep-deprived puffiness, then gave up and dressed. The guests, despite their late night, had asked for a relatively early breakfast in order to set sail for Elba in good time. Well, to be more accurate, Nikolai had requested an early breakfast. It was as if he was keen to remain away from Jeremy Giles for as long as he could, that he was trying to outpace the latecomer, stay one step ahead of him.

Raking a brush through her hair, she opted for a French plait – a style she had perfected over the years and could complete with speed and little need for a mirror. Her head might be spinning like a sycamore seed, her thoughts and emotions blowing this way and that, but she could still look the part. She could pretend she was in control and able to remain professional. She could pull off that role.

As she fastened the tie around her hair, Leo's words from the previous evening floated to the forefront of Bella's mind. The involuntary smile creeping across her lips at the mere thought of him was tamped down by the frown clouding her eyes. What had she been thinking? In the cold light of morning, kissing Leo felt like a colossal mistake.

Trouble was, it was a mistake she'd been unable to stop thinking about all night. A mistake she couldn't wait to do again, somehow.

Nikolai hadn't lost any of his determination to make breakfast brief. Bella brought him coffee and a small omelette on the sun deck. The others opted for cabin service, and before long Jean-Philippe was calling for the anchors to be raised and the boat began to move.

'This is where my holiday truly begins, Bella,' Nikolai said as she cleared his plate. 'Quiet bays to be explored, scenery undisturbed by too many people, plenty of nature and beauty. Walking the Mount Capanne. I cannot wait.'

He stood at the guard rail, the breeze rippling through his loose linen shirt and tugging at his hair as *Blue Sky* picked up speed. He was still there when the island of Elba grew larger in the azure sea as they approached, the biscuit-dry rocky coastline and scrubby green of the vegetation becoming clearer as they neared their anchor point. The plan was to spend the next few days circumnavigating the island, starting with today's beach picnic in a secluded bay.

By the time the deck crew were lowering anchors and sorting out the water toys, all the guests were topside. Bella was ferrying backwards and forwards to the galley with orders for drinks while Tobias stood at the stainless steel counter, relentless in his chopping.

'What are you making?' she asked.

'It's like living in Groundhog Day,' he said, glancing at her as she fiddled with the coffee machine. He looked irritated. Her question must have annoyed him. 'Did you ever see that film? Grouchy Bill Murray chasing after a gorgeous Andie MacDowell? Never have understood how that type of man always ends up getting the girl, but that's not my point. He repeated the same day over and over until he changed his ways and got to wake up the next day, with the girl. It's like our lives on *Blue Sky*. I get up, chop stuff, cook until I'm exhausted, then go to bed and do it all again the next day. It's the same day, repeated over and over and over.'

Tobias had a point. Loads of tasks had to be completed every day, sometimes multiple times – Bella could imagine it would become quite easy to lose track of the days, especially for the chef, who spent the bulk of his time in this space.

'And I never even manage to get the girl,' Tobias muttered, more to himself than to her. Bella wondered who he meant, but he didn't give her the chance to ask, as he said, 'Keep your head down and think of the tips. It's not like it's forever.'

'Do you want to go ashore for the beach picnic?' she asked. 'Have a change of scene?'

'God, no.' He adjusted his bandanna, wiping his forehead with the back of his arm as he took a breath. 'No. I'm good. To be honest it will be helpful to have the guests out of the way for a few hours. I can concentrate on dinner – I want to make a layered terrine, amongst other things. It'll take a while to get all the layers to set. And it'll be nice to have the place to myself.'

'Are you fed up with us already?'

He reached for another onion. 'You know what chefs are like – you've worked with enough of us. Ignore me. I'm tired, that's all.'

'I'm not surprised. Dinner last night was a tour de force.'

'Ooh, very Mediterranean.'

'*Mais oui*. I'm almost fluent.' With the coffee ready, she shoved the cup onto the waiting tray and headed for the door. '*Ciao, bello.*'

She could still hear him laughing as she climbed the stairs – yet again – to the sun deck.

Preparing for a beach picnic was like readying troops for an invasion, thought Bella, as she packed yet another cooler box. Not that she had any experience of life in the military, but she imagined the attention to detail, the forethought and preparation of everything required once they left *Blue Sky* had paralleled the precision of a military manoeuvre.

She'd found herself relying heavily on Mel's experience and was relieved when her second stew proved helpful and supportive – a pleasant surprise after the shortness of their communication the previous night. Mel didn't want to come to the beach – another surprise; Bella couldn't wait to have dry land under her feet. Instead, she would take Jessica, give the third stewardess a chance to get out of the laundry room and feel the sand between her toes, as well as a couple of deck crew to help with the set-up. Mel seemed more than happy to stay on board, even when Bella suggested the laundry could do with being turned over, and the crew area needed a tidy-up.

It took a couple of trips to get everything to the shore, the smallest of the beach's grainy pebbles rough and sticking to her toes as Bella made the second trip, nannying a tray of delicate filled pastries on her lap, balancing it against the bump of the waves.

They had the beach to themselves – Jean-Philippe had promised as much; there didn't seem to be any obvious way to access the tiny cove from on shore. Large terracotta-brown rocks speared their way skywards from the shallows, giving the whole place a secretive, hidden vibe.

When the tender reappeared with the guests, Bella felt momentary confusion as Yannis lifted Felicia, and then a squealing Patti, clear of the breakers and set them down on the beach. Where was everyone else? Her emotions churned. Where was Leo?

'The others are coming on the jet skis,' Patti called, one hand on her enormous straw sunhat as she picked her way across the shingle to the picnic area.

'I hope they are careful,' Yannis said once he was in earshot. 'There are submerged rocks. But they insisted.'

They watched as the two jet skis appeared from behind *Blue Sky*, snaking their way across the brilliant blue, plumes of spray shooting from behind each machine. The sun glittered from the surface of the water, blinding the watchers every now and again.

'It's like something from a James Bond film,' Patti said to Felicia, as Bella pressed a Mimosa into her hand and tried to stop her fingers from trembling. She was desperate to see Leo, but didn't have the first idea what she was going to say to him.

'Oh, darling. Stop. For one thing, Nicki's far too old to be cast in a role like that and Leo's far too . . . well, far too beardy. No, neither of them will do at all.' Felicia shook her head at the drink. 'No, thank you, Bella. No orange juice for me – I don't want another headache. Just some of the pink champagne, please. Although, if we're having a genuine conversation about Bond – I think Hannah would make the perfect choice. Can you imagine? My name's Bond. Aimee Bond. I've always wondered how long it would take.'

'Or Jane Bond. Maybe Jamie? That would work, too.'

'And someone with her striking colouring would be perfect. It's a shame she doesn't act.'

'No. Well, we've been through this before. Because she's my daughter, doesn't mean she wants to follow in my footsteps. And she's such a fabulous designer.'

'How is her swimwear line doing?'

Bella didn't hear the rest of the conversation, her attention taken by the jet skis criss-crossing before they slowed and ran aground on the gentle incline of the beach. Yannis hauled the vehicles clear of the water while Nikolai, Hannah and Leo stripped off their life jackets and left them on the rocks to dry in the sun.

'Lunch is ready when you are,' Bella said, once all the guests had a drink. It was difficult not to notice the flecks of spray glinting on Leo's face, as well as those darkening the fabric of his loose swimming shorts and casual, washed-out T-shirt.

As everyone took their seats, Leo took a moment to stare out to sea, sipping at his Mimosa.

'How was the jet ski?' Bella didn't want to talk about the jet ski, but it seemed as good a way as any to strike up a legitimate conversation with him.

'Can we find a moment to talk privately today?'

'Um. Yes, certainly.' Bella ran hot and cold. Had she utterly misjudged the previous evening? Leo appeared starchy, awkward, choosing to keep his gaze on the panorama.

'Maybe after lunch?'

'Of course.'

Only after he'd drained his glass did he look at her properly, holding her gaze for a second before he headed for the table. Was the crinkle at the edges of his eyes because he smiled, albeit briefly – or was it simply a reaction to the strength of the sun, unfiltered as it glinted off the undulating water?

'Thank you.'

Bella fumbled her way through lunch, accidentally tipping a bottle of champagne over then watching its contents drain into the gritty sand rather than scooping it quickly upright, and making a mess of serving the lobster salad, shreds of salad leaf showering Hannah's plate as she nearly lost her grip on the tongs.

'Are you feeling all right?' Patti asked. 'You're all fingers and thumbs today.'

'I'm so sorry, I didn't sleep well last night,' she replied, her words heavy with caution.

'Nothing worse,' Patti lamented. 'I remember countless sleepless nights, back in the bad old days.'

Bella wasn't sure what she was referring to, but Felicia rushed to change the subject. 'Perhaps you should take a few moments for yourself, Bella. We're quite capable of helping ourselves to the rest of lunch, and Jessica is here to look after us.'

'I couldn't possibly.'

'Oh, go on. We won't tell the captain.' Felicia bestowed her brightest smile on Bella. 'Your secret is safe with us.'

To be honest it was a relief to walk away from the group. There was no way Felicia could know anything about the previous evening, but her choice of words – her *secret*? Bella hadn't ever been very proficient at subterfuge, and this was no exception. Not sure where she was going, Bella stumbled away along the beach, skirting a group of rocks and allowing the warm seawater to swill around her feet as she walked the waterline. The cove stretched further than had been initially visible, with a trail path scrabbling its way up a more moderate incline at the far end. Vegetation here reached as far down as the beach, salt-resistant shrubs with needle-like leaves and large succulents covered in spines on either side of the dusty path.

With her back to the shore, Bella stared at the watery vista, cupping her hands around the sides of her face to keep strands of hair out of her eyes. She willed herself not to sink into tired self-pity, or speculate on what Leo wanted to say to her. Instead, she was determined to give herself a good talking-to, to run through her private pep-talk of: *life could be so much worse – you're working on a superyacht in the Mediterranean, get a grip on your reality and concentrate on what's important,* when she heard footsteps, the splosh of someone wading through water.

'Sorry to disturb,' Leo said as he drew near. 'I thought now was as good a time as any.'

'Sure, why not.' Resting hands on her hips, she turned to face him. 'What did you want to say?'

'Can we walk?'

They walked in silence for a while, Bella concentrating on the silty sand squeezing up through her toes as she took each step along the very edge of the waterline. Leo chose to remain further out, up to his ankles in the eddying water.

'This is such a tranquil place,' he said.

Bella wished he would get to the point. 'Yes.'

'Lunch was fabulous.'

'That's good.'

'Bella – have I upset you somehow?'

'What?' Water splashed at her ankles as she stopped abruptly. She raised a hand to shield her eyes from the sun as she looked at him. 'No. I just thought . . . When you said you wanted a private word, I assumed you meant . . .'

'Meant what?'

Did he expect her to spell it out? She pulled in a breath. 'That you were going to tell me what happened last night was a mistake.'

'Is that how you feel about it?'

She flipped the question back on him. 'Is that how *you* feel about it?'

The firm contours of his face softened; the crinkles beside his eyes deepened. 'That's cheating. I asked first.' He ran a hand through his hair, the arch in his eyebrows undeniable. 'OK, then. No.'

That was as clear as mud.

'No to which bit? No, that's not how you feel about it, or no, that's not what you wanted to talk about?'

The crinkles spread as his whole face creased and he began to laugh. 'I'm not sure any longer. You've confused me.'

'I always thought I could have made a brilliant prosecution lawyer,' she said, the tension easing. 'Bamboozle the defendant into a confession. What do you think?'

Leo held up his hands. 'I did it. I confess.'

'Did what?'

'Oh, God. I have no idea. Lock me up anyway.' He held his wrists together, ready for handcuffs, then dropped them to his sides. 'But seriously, I did want to talk to you about last night.'

'Do you want me to apologise?'

'Apologise? Wait, what? No. Why would you think that?'

'Because it was me. I kind of . . .'

'I wanted so badly to kiss you . . .' Leo raked a hand through his hair again, and Bella swallowed the remainder of her sentence in favour of hearing the rest of his. 'Almost from the moment we got on board, if I'm being honest. Wanted to find out more about you. But I'm also painfully aware we're here for totally different reasons. I'm here at the whim of my aunt, and you're here to do a job. I have my life; you've got yours. And I'm not looking to just hook up with anybody right now.'

Ouch. Hook up? Was that what he thought she had in mind?

'I mean, like I was trying to say last night, I'm not interested in anything fake. Been there, done that. Got multiple T-shirts.' He paused. 'Did that sound as bad as I think it did?'

She nodded. 'Worse, probably. Although, to be fair I'm struggling to get past the idea that you think I want to hook up with you.'

'No. I didn't mean that I thought *you* wanted to . . .' He shook his head. 'This could be the most confusing beginning of a relationship I've ever managed.'

'Relationship?' Her brow creased at his use of such a definitive word. 'But we don't know anything about one another.'

'I know, but I'm drawn to you – it's intense. I can't explain why, or make any sense of it. I mean, obviously you're gorgeous. That goes without saying.'

'Does it?'

He seemed not to have heard. 'All I want to do is find out more about you, spend time with you. But this whole yacht charter thing. The guest–crew dynamic. I don't know how to navigate it.'

'Ha, ha. *Navigate*. Very good.' She tried to lighten the moment, but his expression remained serious.

'Unintentionally amusing, but I'll take it as a win.'

'Are you trying to say we live totally different lives? That we're different animals?'

'I can be any kind of animal you want, Bella.'

She rolled her eyes at the corniness of his comment, but his expression didn't match her interpretation of his words. The base of her belly contracted, the sensation intensifying as they stared at one another until the corners of his mouth hitched and he shrugged.

'Too cheesy?'

The intensity of the moment seeped away, and Bella smiled. 'Like Roquefort left out in the sun. For three days.'

His laughter was like a burst of gunfire, loud and uninhibited. Up until that moment, his gaze hadn't strayed from her at any point during their conversation, and as he glanced up and down the stretch of beach, she wanted him to look at her again. The longer she was the subject of his scrutiny, the happier she felt.

'If it's any consolation,' she said, 'I have no idea how to navigate this, either.'

'But you want to try?' His gaze bored into her, and for the first time she grasped what Tobias had been telling her about lighting a barbecue with less of a flame. She understood the expression in Leo's eyes, partly hunger, partly anxiety, and with an intensity that was totally transfixing.

'I think I do.' What was she saying? Her head was telling her this was madness, that juggling her job and an attraction of such ferocity wasn't going to be easy – not even for the limited time he would be on board *Blue Sky*. Meanwhile, the rest of Bella's body was telling her something quite different, insisting that she could pull this off. That she could have both.

One of Leo's eyebrows hitched. 'So, should we look at the charts together, then? I'll grab a compass and we can map out a route across the high seas . . .'

'Stop it.'

'I'll check with my parrot and then we'd better splice the mainbrace. Or do something to the rigging. Or is that the same thing?'

'I don't know, and if you say "me hearties", I'm walking away right now.'

His fingers encircled her wrist as he drew her closer, suddenly serious. 'No. Please don't do that.'

Walking away was the last action on Bella's mind, especially as he wrapped an arm around her waist and she burrowed against his chest, the thud from his heart loud in her ear as she gazed out to sea.

Chapter Fifteen

Even though Leo and Bella were out of sight, Felicia heard the pistol-crack of her nephew's laughter as it resonated across the beach. His unfiltered guffaw sometimes reminded Felicia of her brother-in-law, but despite that, she loved the idea Bella was making the boy laugh that loudly. It had been such a long time since she'd heard him laugh so freely. In fact, it had been far too long since she'd spent any quality time with Leo – she'd missed their aunt–nephew trips, but over the last ten years or so both their work schedules had taken precedence.

'What's going on with Leo and the stewardess?' Patti said.

Felicia paused. Patti understood some of the difficulties surrounding her relationship with her sister's family, but she wasn't privy to all of it. And in return, Felicia knew many of the challenges faced down by Patti. Working together for a decade and a half had a way of bringing two people together, however hard they might have fought it at the start. Although still a dysfunctional pair, they'd grown closer than Felicia had ever imagined they would on initial meeting. Rather like her fictional character in *Murder in Mayfair* – or *MIM*, the acronym Patti had coined early on. And it was possible Felicia had come to rely on Patti more than she'd care to admit. Felicia hadn't ever found it particularly easy to make friends with other women – men were no problem, but she'd always seemed to elicit suspicion from her fellow sex. Somehow, she and Patti had cut through that – and the proof of the pudding was in the eating. After all, you didn't invite just *anybody* as your guest aboard a superyacht.

But while Felicia knew Leo was someone she would always feel strongly protective of, she wasn't sure how to tell her friend exactly what she thought was going on. Wasn't sure she wanted to discuss Leo in this way. She was fully aware of the tricky dynamic – which had always surprised Felicia, if she was being totally honest – the difficulty Patti had in accepting that no matter how many times she dangled Leo under Hannah's nose, neither party was interested.

Leo's empty chair and half-eaten salad told Felicia plenty, a fairly obvious clue as to what was going on with him and Bella, in her opinion – and she was aware that Patti had probably reached the same conclusion. Perhaps Patti wanted to know if Leo had confided any pearls of gossip. Perhaps she'd noticed, as Felicia had, the way Leo had slipped from the movie screening the previous evening as soon as Bella left the room.

She supposed Patti's question wasn't far from her own musings. If her nephew and Bella did intend to start something on board *Blue Sky*, what was it? A fling, or something else? Something more . . .

Generally speaking, her nephew's love life wasn't of any immediate significance to Felicia. But the whole purpose of inviting him on their charter was specifically because of changes she intended to make for him – changes that would radically alter his life in the long term. Give him the opportunity to get away from his overbearing father once and for all.

It was the reason Jeremy Giles was joining them – should he ever manage to get his act together and reach *Blue Sky* – so perhaps now was the time for Felicia to pay her nephew's love life closer attention.

Whatever his obvious attraction to Bella became, and although Felicia felt she held a proprietorial viewpoint on the whole situation, whatever was "*going on with them*" was hardly any of Patti's business. But her friend had always been nosy. And determined.

'You know what this generation is like.' It was a catch-all generalisation, a throwaway comment holding nothing in the way of information or definite opinion, which Felicia hoped might be enough to satisfy. She coupled her remark with a shrug.

Patti laughed. 'I don't know why you say things like that. Nothing's changed. Young people are young people, never mind the decade. Honey, you of all people should be aware.'

'What's *that* supposed to mean?'

'We were both young women at the same time – and in Hollywood, of all places. I remember it, too. Come on, Felicia, are you trying to tell me we all wafted around in ankle-length dresses, waiting for Mr Right? We all wanted to get laid, plain and simple. Nothing's changed.'

'*Mom* . . . Jesus Christ.' Hannah pushed her plate and stood. 'I've heard enough. If you're going to continue your discussion on sex in the eighties, I might take one of the jet skis out. Nikolai, how about you?'

'Actually, I might head back to the yacht,' Felicia said, catching Jessica's attention. 'I would like to go back to *Blue Sky*. Can you arrange that for me?'

Sliding her dark glasses over eyes that suddenly smarted from the bright sunshine, a wave of tiredness swept over Felicia. If she could get to her cabin and rest, perhaps she could stave off another headache.

Before they skirted the mounds of rocks separating the rest of the cove from the picnic, Bella tried to slip her hand from Leo's. His fingers tightened against hers, tugging her to a stop.

'Just one minute more,' he said. 'Let's not go back yet.'

'I should go. I've already been away too long.'

'If you could choose one place to visit, where would you want to go?'

'On Elba?'

'No. Well, not necessarily – not unless it's your dream destination. I meant where in the world?'

'I have no idea. I've never really been anywhere.'

'But you're here. So, you must be interested in seeing new places.'

'I am. I'm interested in new places and new things. That's exactly why I took this job.'

It hadn't escaped her notice that while she talked, Leo slid his hands around her waist and pulled her close. 'And new people?'

'Yes, and new people.'

Although, as he kissed her and she wrapped her arms around his neck, somehow Leo didn't feel like someone new. It felt as though she'd always known him. And while Bella was rarely lost for words, chatting this effortlessly to someone she felt such a heightened sense of attraction to hadn't come this easily to her before, either.

'Where, then?'

'Anywhere in the world?' When he nodded, she said, 'I'm not sure I can narrow it down to one place.'

'Well, don't. Give me the full itinerary.'

'All right. I want to visit the Australian outback. And Japan. The Amazon rainforest. I've always wanted to see penguins in the wild. And hippos. I love hippos.'

'Random selection.'

'Rude. I want to visit mountains – proper mountains, in the winter. Like the Canadian Rockies, or the Alps, with all those terrifying twisty-turny hairpin roads.'

'And you say you've never really thought about it?'

'Well, maybe I have a bit. Basically, I'd be happy to visit anywhere that's not Cornwall. Not that there's anything wrong with Cornwall, I suppose. But those would be my highlights. Why?'

Before Leo had a chance to reply, their attention was taken by the sound of the jet skis firing up.

'I need to get back.' She'd been away from the picnic for far too long – the others must have become restless.

Leo nodded, leaning in for a final kiss, his lips soft and gentle against hers, the touch fleeting and gone too soon. She wanted to stay right here, right now – wanted it so badly it was almost pain, something lodged within her belly.

'Give me a minute?' Not that anyone on the other side of the rocks would be under much of an illusion. It would be obvious they'd spent the time together, but Bella needed a moment to adjust back to her role as chief stew. To work out how to compartmentalise what was going on and try to hang on to a sliver of professionalism. Which meant they could hardly wander back to the others hand in hand.

A wave of guilt washed over her, cooling the heat created by his brief kiss. This was crazy – she was acting like a stupid teenager hanging out behind the gym block at school. That thought and its accompanying confusion had her pulling away from him. Without saying anything further, she slipped between the rocks, heading for the others. Time to get back to work.

If he'd thought things through, Jeremy would never have worn a suit for this journey. Even with his jacket slung over one arm, his charcoal Savile Row suit – not off the peg, after all, he *was* heading for a superyacht chartered by Felicia Kennedy – was already creased to Hades and patches of uncomfortably warm sweat pooled in his armpits. The last couple of days had been a living hell. A driver with as much sense of direction as a blind flamingo had managed to get them so lost after taking a roadworks detour, that even *with* satnav they arrived at the airport so late that he'd missed his flight *and* all his connections to reach *Blue Sky* at its anchor point.

He could only hope Felicia wouldn't mind his having added the extra travel costs onto his expenses tally – if not . . . He shuddered to think how much this charter boat out to Elba was costing, on top of all the other expenses. The last thing he needed was more personal outlay.

What he really *could* do with, though, was a generous measure of Grey Goose. On ice. And the promise of a decent laundry service on board. The shirt he was wearing was probably wrecked – a shame, he liked the way the blush pink made him look younger, maybe even edgier – but at least he hadn't sacrificed the tie he'd almost added to the ensemble. A vibrant fuchsia silk Hermès with self-coloured pattern, which he wasn't prepared to risk being ruined by his sweat. If the shirt was toast, at least he could repurpose the tie. Perhaps he could even add the shirt to his expenses. After all, it had been ruined purely as a result of a work commitment.

Jeremy sighed, resting a hand against his briefcase. If he could pull this off, if he managed to get Felicia to sign the extra paperwork he'd brought alongside the requested updates to her will, he could stop worrying about the loss of a shirt. Or whether he could find a decent laundry service. In fact, he'd never need to have another shirt washed. He could go from owning nothing more than the literal shirt on his back, to joining the ranks of those for whom a shirt was a disposable item, like a face mask or a paper tissue.

The beauty of his plan was she'd never even know what he'd done. She'd never miss the money – and it wasn't as if she didn't owe him.

He and Felicia went way back. So far back that he'd all but forgotten how they'd even met. At a party, if memory served, in Soho. Trendy and bohemian. Back in the days when he had a full head of hair and Felicia had been absolutely radiant. There had never been any question she would go far – he could tell immediately. Some people shine, and Felicia had always been one of those.

Early on, he'd hoped she might be interested in him as more than just a friend. He would have been a fool not to hope, and hope had a funny way of never letting go, not even when Felicia began a string of ill-advised romantic liaisons. Although Jeremy had recognised that he had been firmly "friend-zoned" – wasn't that the expression nowadays? – and settled for his role of solicitor, her go-to man for all things financial and legal, he'd never entirely given up hope. The lovers came and went, and all the time he had kept Felicia Kennedy free from the grasp of countless unscrupulous agents, unfavourable exposure in the press, the inevitable hangers-on, requests for charitable donations – all that nonsense. Shielded her from intrusive attention. He'd been there for her, especially during her most challenging times, and in return he'd earned her trust.

And then she met Nikolai Bjerregaard. Met and married

him within a matter of months – a whirlwind romance. He might have been approaching ten years her senior and utterly enigmatic, but he was yet another person to find himself instantly under Felicia's spell. Jeremy had attended the wedding, but while everyone else danced into the small hours and celebrated, his hopes of making his friendship with Felicia into something more had shrivelled away.

Nevertheless, Jeremy had continued to protect Felicia and her assets.

He'd earned this.

Jeremy pulled a cotton handkerchief from a pocket and patted at the back of his neck.

'You are hot, Mr Giles?'

The shore agent hadn't eased up on his smile at any point during the journey. Being paid by the hour, Jeremy assumed. 'A little,' he said.

'Not far to go now. Elba is only ten kilometres from the mainland. It takes no time to get you to *Blue Sky*. And then you can relax, yes?'

Felicia had to laugh. Once she'd persuaded a very hot, bothered and tetchy Jeremy to take all the time he needed to make himself at home in his cabin, he had emerged in a bubble-gum pink polo shirt and a pair of khaki shorts that made it clear his legs hadn't seen the sun for at least a decade.

He did look fresher, however, his hair slicked back from the shower and a more relaxed expression on his face. Although that could have more to do with the tumbler of vodka in his hand, large chunks of ice clinking against the crystal.

Bella bounced onto the sun deck, beamed a smile around the assembled group and announced that dinner was ready, if they would like to take their seats. Tonight, they were eating in the formal dining room on *Blue Sky* – after spending much of the day outside and on the beach, it was a welcome change to sit inside. It was difficult to believe, but there was such a thing as too much fresh air.

The table was dressed beautifully. This evening, rather than flowing fabrics and nautical objects, the most had been made of the feature chandelier. Each pendant of crystal glittering against the hundreds of tiny lightbulbs, the waterfall of hues catching every possible version of blue as they altered depending on the viewpoint. The bottom-most tips of the chandelier hung marginally above the crystal ornaments adorning the table's surface. Candlesticks and condiments and a rolling sculpture of what could be the sea, or maybe the concept of the *Blue Sky* yacht itself, all fashioned from crystal, adorned the highly polished wooden surface. It was a feast for the eyes, as the glittering light played from the cutlery and glassware laid around the table.

With Nicki to her left, Jeremy to her right and Leo opposite, Felicia couldn't resist commenting.

'All my favourite men in one place.'

'What am I?' Patti said, as she took a seat beside Leo. 'Chopped liver?'

'Well, darling, you're hardly one of my favourite men, are you?'

Patti raised her eyebrows, challenging Felicia until she relented. 'Oh, if you insist. All my favourite people in one place. Is that better?'

'I guess.'

'You know I don't "do" the girly thing, Patti.'

Patti rolled her eyes, but her expression was one of gentle amusement. 'Yeah, Felicia. So you keep telling me.'

Bella wafted into the room, pouring water and lingering longer than was strictly necessary at Leo's chair. She announced the starter, poured the accompanying *Picpoul de Pinet* and refreshed Jeremy's vodka.

It was only as she left the room that Felicia noticed Jeremy's attention lingering on their chief stewardess, almost as intently as Leo's.

'Has our beautiful Bella earned herself another admirer?' she said, tone light and airy, even though she couldn't help the tug of irritation. Usually, Jeremy only had eyes for her. Over the years it was something she'd grown accustomed to.

'Hardly. I'm easily old enough to be her father.'

'That's not exactly a barrier,' Patti said.

'Maybe not, but there's something about that girl.' Jeremy shook his head, taking a sip of Grey Goose. 'It'll come to me. She reminds me of someone, that's all.'

'Tomorrow we are heading along the southern side of the island. More quiet beaches and a chance to enjoy the yacht. I will ask for the Seabobs, I think, in addition to the jet skis. And perhaps the waterslide?' Nikolai glanced around the table.

Felicia wasn't interested in any of the water toys, but it might be pleasant to swim from the back of the yacht. 'Whatever you choose will be fine with me, darling.'

'I'm going to have a go with a jet ski,' Patti said triumphantly. 'I've never ridden one before, but how hard can it be?'

'Not difficult at all,' Leo said. 'You'll love it.' He failed to keep his attention on Patti for long, as Bella was back to clear their plates.

'How was the terrine?' she asked, her brow furrowing slightly as she reached for Felicia's barely touched plate.

'Excellent. I'm just pacing myself.' Felicia's comment wasn't strictly true. She didn't have much in the way of an appetite this evening. It was possible she'd overdone the medication on her return to the yacht. She only seemed to have replaced her creeping headache with stomach pains.

'I've worked it out,' Jeremy said, as Bella exited with a couple of plates, and the blonde stewardess – Mel – took the next few. 'I've worked out who the brunette reminds me of.'

'Who?'

'The hair threw me, because of course yours had a natural wave before you cut it short, but the tone is an exact match to yours before you began to col—before it started to go . . .' Jeremy shifted uncomfortably at his error, then covered his blunder as best he could by finishing with a totally different sentence. 'She looks like you.' Glancing at the rest of the people around the table, he rolled his tumbler in his hand, his expression one of expectation as he waited for their agreement. 'Strikingly similar to Felicia as a young woman. Don't you think?'

Jeremy's comment provoked a mixed reaction, but Patti nodded. 'Sure. Now you come to mention it, there's something in the smile. And her eyes.'

'No there isn't. You're being ridiculous.' Felicia frowned, sipping at her wine. There was nothing quite as tactless as someone pointing out how a beautiful young woman was reminding them of how you *used* to look. A damning indictment of the ageing process.

'I always thought you and Nicki would have made the most beautiful children,' Patti said. Indelicate, as always – Patti was fully aware of Nicki's stance on children. For him it was a dealbreaker, always had been. Then Patti wrinkled her nose at a thought, always a sign it was going to be followed up with something outrageous. 'Maybe she's your long-lost daughter, Felicia. The daughter you never knew you had.'

Felicia's fingers tightened around the stem of her wine glass, the other hand knuckling white against the base of her chair. She threw a wild glance at Jeremy, his ears pinking as he met her gaze and then looked away.

'I think I would remember having a child.' Sometimes being an actress paid dividends in unexpected ways, she thought, as she kept her voice level and concentrated on her breathing. Fixing her gaze on Patti, she challenged her to continue the conversation at her peril.

'No, well – yes, of course you would. I was messing around. But do you remember that storyline on *MIM* a couple years ago – the two kids who'd been put up for adoption and didn't know anything about the other one? I think we had that guy from *Killing Eve* playing one of them, the one who got pushed off the roof. Anyway, I digress, because in *MIM* the two kids learn their birth mother died and left a ton of money, and each one tried their best to kill the other so they'd get all the cash. Don't you remember?'

Patti continued to explain the finer details of the plotline, but Felicia wasn't listening any longer. She remembered that episode very well. It had brought up a raft of dangerously uncomfortable memories. Because nobody around this table, apart from Jeremy, knew that Felicia *had* had a child – a daughter – way before she'd even met Nicki. A daughter she'd given up for adoption for the best and the worst of reasons. A daughter she'd done her best not to think about for the last twenty-four years.

Chapter Sixteen

Felicia couldn't shift the lump that had settled in her throat, couldn't seem to swallow past the golf ball of emotion lodged behind her tongue. This holiday was supposed to have been full of joy and special moments, precious time with Nicki, the provision of a change in her will to favour the nephew she had always loved in place of her own child. A way to make the best of the future she still had. Not a way to rake up the past.

The conversation continued around her, and she did her best to tune back in to it. Patti had moved onto another of *MIM*'s more improbable storylines – there were plenty to choose from – but Felicia simply couldn't get a grasp on any of it. Blood roared through her ears, and she worked at loosening her fingers from the frame of her chair.

Jeremy continued to look awkward, swigging at his glass with increased rapidity and punctuating the conversation with laughter she recognised as a sign of nerves. Trying to act normally always translated into over-exaggerated movements and sounds, and Felicia was amazed nobody else seemed to have noticed.

Even though there had been no way to keep the baby – not without ripping her entire life apart, and the lives of those around her – Felicia still carried the guilt of having given her daughter up for adoption as if it were a physical weight. No matter how many times Jeremy reassured her the adoptive family had been chosen with extreme care, the child would want for nothing, it was all for the best and that the truth would never be revealed, it didn't lessen the heavy, muffled feeling she experienced every time adoption was mentioned. While the world carried on around her, it was as if she was drowning, weighted down with arms and legs that felt as if they were encased in lead.

It was purely chance that Bella resembled her in certain respects – it had to be. There was no way Bella could actually be her daughter. She might be the same age as her child, and share passing similarities, but that didn't mean anything. How many people in the world shared their colouring? Millions. And hadn't Bella stated that she had a brother – that the pair of them were adopted at the same time? Felicia was sure a brother had been mentioned.

Felicia needed to relax, breathe, and take a moment to restore her equilibrium. Allow the intensity of the unexpected turn in the conversation to ebb away. Jeremy wouldn't say anything further – he had clearly realised the level of his error. One look at the pink tips to his ears, and the request for yet another top-up of vodka was enough to establish that he would be keeping his mouth firmly closed for the rest of the evening.

It came as a relief when Nicki took her hand and suggested they have an early night. She allowed him to lead her away from the table, vaguely remembered wishing the rest of them a good night and felt nothing but a sense of numbness when Nicki pressed home the door to their suite.

After what he considered to be a polite enough interval of time, Leo left Hannah, Patti and Jeremy in the main salon and went in search of Bella. There was no sign of her in the dining room, the space devoid of any hint that dinner had been eaten there shortly before. The chandelier dominated the space above the huge table, but the rest of the crystal had already been packed away. The storage facilities on this yacht must be formidable, and before he continued his search for Bella, Leo couldn't resist opening cupboards to search for where all the paraphernalia was stowed. It hadn't been an idle request, when he'd asked if he could see the engine room – he really did enjoy poking around behind the scenes.

Dinner had been interesting. Having Jeremy Giles on board

had already changed the dynamics. Never the chattiest of people, Nikolai had become even quieter, more watchful. He seemed increasingly protective of Felicia, not that Leo could see any reason – Jeremy and his aunt went so far back that the origin of their friendship was lost in the mists of time, and their working relationship had always seemed to stand Felicia in good stead. She might be headstrong in many ways, but his aunt always maintained she listened to advice on her career, and between the legal input from Jeremy and the professional input from her agent, she'd managed to avoid many of the pitfalls into which others in the public eye tripped and fell – in fact, Felicia Kennedy was so well regarded she was regularly described as a national treasure by most of the media.

But the dynamics on board were changing rapidly for Leo, too. And in ways that had nothing to do with Jeremy Giles' arrival. He closed the door on a cupboard full of soft drink cans and refocused. Nosing around the underbelly of the yacht was not a priority. Finding Bella was.

Abandoning his search in the guest area, Leo took a breath and pushed open the door to the galley. Muffled voices became clearer as he rapped his knuckles against the open door and announced his arrival.

The chef had his back to the door, slotting a tray into a large fridge. The blonde stewardess continued wiping at a wine glass with her tea towel as she broke off mid-sentence and they both turned.

Suddenly tongue-tied, Leo said, 'Fantastic dinner – I wanted to say thank you.'

'I'm so pleased.' The chef looked anything but as he fiddled with the bandanna tied around his head and wiped at his forehead with the back of an arm.

'I'm sorry to intrude – I was wondering if it was possible to have a word with Bella?'

If the chef made any attempt to keep his expression under control, it wasn't obvious. His eyebrows arched and his mouth quirked up on one side as he glanced at the stewardess. 'Do you know where she is, Mel?'

'She's off duty. Probably gone to bed. Why?' Mel's question sounded innocent enough, but her expression wasn't. 'Is it something I could assist you with?'

The chef coughed and spun away, but not before Leo clocked his smirk. He frowned.

'No. Thank you. It can wait. Sorry to disturb.' Beating a hasty retreat, barely concealed laughter followed him as he slipped through the dining room and headed for the steps leading to the swimming platform. Was he surprised that Bella had disappeared off duty without letting him know, or was he expecting too much from her? Since she'd seized the initiative the previous evening and kissed him, the internal workings of Leo's head had become messy, to say the least. A strong and unusually instant connection with somebody was one thing. Even better was to discover that the other person might be feeling a similar way, but in Leo's experience all that did was set into motion a whole onslaught of possibilities for messing up.

He'd only ever felt like this once before, and he'd come on way too hard, way too fast that time. Emily had run a mile, and with the beauty of hindsight and a great deal more in the way of life experience under his belt, Leo had long since reached the conclusion that he didn't blame her. The episode had stung his young self badly though, badly enough to make him wary of anything that wasn't obviously casual in the intervening years.

Maybe he'd come on too hard on the beach and Bella was feeling pressured by him. Or perhaps since they all arrived back on *Blue Sky*, she'd realised she was muddying the waters by messing around with him. After all, with a smile like hers, if she wanted to, she could have a boy in every port. And another on the crew. The way the chef had eyed him during their brief conversation had given enough away. Leo was well aware what jealousy looked like.

Maybe some fresh air before he went to bed would allow

him some clarity on the situation, at least in his own mind. Help him deal with the shifting sands of his thoughts.

He'd made it halfway down the steps to the swimming platform before he realised someone was already there, sitting at the very edge with their legs dangling into the water. In the darkness it was more of a sense of a presence, difficult to make out who it was until she spoke.

'Leo?'

'I've been looking for you,' he said.

'And now you've found me.' Pulling her feet up onto the platform, Bella wrapped an arm around her knees, shimmers of moonlight playing on the water running from her calves.

'Can I join you?'

A flash of her brilliant smile had him crouching, then sliding onto the wooden decking beside her.

'I've discovered this is one of the quietest places on *Blue Sky* at night,' she said, tilting her head to survey the star-studded sky.

'Until I come lumbering along and ruin it for you.'

'Well, quite.'

He'd been hoping she'd brush away his self-deprecation, not agree with him. She sighed. 'Look at that sky. There's not a single cloud.'

'I think that's the Big Dipper.' He pointed to a random cluster of stars.

'Is it?'

'Definitely. Unless it's Orion's Belt.'

Their shoulders bumped as she turned to him. 'You have no idea what you're talking about, do you?'

'Those are definitely names of groups of stars.'

She laughed softly. 'But do they bear any relation to the stars you're pointing at?'

Waving his hand in the general direction of the sky, he brazened it out. 'They're all up there, somewhere.'

'You're an idiot.'

In the reflected light, he could see the flash of brightness as she smiled. 'You're probably right,' he said.

Lodging her elbows on the decking behind her, she leaned against them and looked back to the sky. 'Well, I suppose the stars don't much care what names they've been given by random humans, so why should we?'

'Agreed.' He mirrored her actions until he, too, was staring at the sky.

'That's a bit like a giraffe, though, don't you think?' Extending one arm, she pointed skywards and circled with a finger.

'Definitely,' he agreed. 'And next to the giraffe is a motorbike.'

'If you look really closely, there's a frying pan to the right of the giraffe's foot.'

'You may have discovered a new star system. Pandromeda.'

She giggled. 'I'll have to tell Captain Kirque.'

It was his turn to laugh, holding his hand aloft with fingers spread in the Vulcan greeting. 'Does *Blue Sky* morph into an intergalactic spacecraft, by any chance? We could boldly go where no—'

'Woman has gone before . . .'

'Exactly. Would you?'

'Go into space?'

'If you had the chance to – would you?'

She shook her head. 'No. I'd settle for exploring the world we've already got.'

Leo drew a packet of sweets from his pocket. 'Do you fancy a sour cherry while we watch the stars from afar, then?'

'You haven't eaten them all?'

'Not yet.'

'Go on, then.' She dipped a hand into the packet. 'Thanks.'

They chewed in silence. Leo remained acutely aware of how close she was, shoulders almost touching, the hairs on his arm super-sensitive to the heat from her skin. He shuffled closer, pressing his body into hers and pausing as he felt her push back. Looping an arm behind her, he drew her closer and closer until he lost all pretence of being interested in the stars and filled his vision with her, instead.

He wasn't sure if it had something to do with the quiet darkness, or the fact that they'd kissed before, or the way Bella sank back against the wooden decking, but there was an intensity to this exchange he hadn't felt before. She slid her arms around his neck and tugged him closer, her fingers running under the collar of his polo shirt and momentarily flowing over the skin at the base of his neck. She shifted, her hand gone, and then he felt her pulling the hemline of his shirt, tugging it up. He stripped it off, tossing it into the darkness before his lips found hers again and he sank down on top of her. Her hands raked their way across his naked back, her fingertips on fire, and when she shifted again under his weight and wrapped her legs around his hips, Leo had to pause, suck in some oxygen and make himself slow down.

Now was not the moment to lose control. He didn't want to spook her with what was going on in his head; he wasn't sure how far she wanted to take this. He might know exactly what *he* wanted to happen next – and she must sense it, too, because she must be able to feel how hard he was, must be able to sense how turned on he was. But this wasn't a one-night stand – at least that wasn't what he wanted it to be – and he needed her to understand that.

Running his fingers up the inside of her thigh, he kept going past the fabric of her skirt, pushed until he felt the edge of her cotton underwear, pausing as she let out a soft moan but didn't push him away. He wanted to please her, wanted her to understand what he hoped this would become. Not a quick fuck in the dark, but something she would want to come back for, again and again.

Bella knew she should make him stop, but she didn't want to. If she'd wanted to put a limit on this evening, she wouldn't have wrapped her legs around him. But it had seemed so natural, it hadn't even been a conscious decision – her body was choreographing its own movements, without bothering to ask for any kind of permission. Certainly her brain wasn't getting much of a look-in, logical thought parked in a far corner and being ignored.

If she'd wanted limits, she should have pushed him away, stopped his fingers from travelling up her thigh, made him remove his hand before she felt him easing her underwear to one side, before he found the very centre of her being and pressed his thumb against her, before his thumb began to circle, gently at first and then with more pressure, before his tongue and his lips were searing a path down her neck, before she heard herself moaning and felt the hot air of his breath against her ear as he pushed his fingers inside her, before she felt him moving his hand, moving and moving and moving until she was moving too, pushing against him until every joint in her body liquified and all that existed was his touch and his tongue and she didn't even realise how loudly she was moaning until she was coming and he swallowed her noise with his mouth, kissing her and kissing her as she shuddered and the waves began to subside as he slowed but didn't remove his touch.

She wasn't sure for how long they lay there in the dark, both fighting to recover their breath, but with him making no further moves. Wasn't sure whether he expected her to reciprocate, or what should happen next.

Eventually, he adjusted her clothing back into place, gently shifting away until they lay side by side. Meshing one hand with hers, he pointed to the stars with the other. 'Definitely a wheelbarrow over there. Can you see it?'

'What are we doing, Leo?'

'I'm not sure. I just know I want to do it a lot.' He drew his knees up until his feet were flat to the decking, the loose fabric of his shorts barely disguising the hardness still held within.

'Are you expecting me to . . .'

He glanced across, frowning as her gaze dipped to his shorts. 'Expecting? No, of course not. I wanted to touch you. I couldn't stop.'

'*You* couldn't stop?' She couldn't stifle her grin, but it slid away when she saw the seriousness of his expression. 'I didn't want you to stop. It's never felt that good.'

He seemed not to hear her praise, his expression difficult to interpret. Neither of them spoke further; instead she allowed her vision to fill with the glittering of the star-studded sky, and her other senses to absorb the sensation of their fingers firmly entwined, and the sound of the sea lapping gently against the hull.

They couldn't have been lying there for more than a few minutes, although it might have been hours – Bella was so settled it was difficult to judge. Then the rest of the world began to creep its way back into the moment, the fleeting sense of peace disrupted by the worry of being seen and she shifted, loosening her hand from his.

'Leo, I'd better go.'

He leaned over to kiss her. This time it was tender and sweet, and even though it was nothing more than lips pressed against lips, Bella felt a massive tug in the base of her belly, wanted desperately to hang on to him as she stood and he reached for his discarded shirt. 'I'll see you in the morning,' he said.

Chapter Seventeen

At breakfast the following day, Felicia was struggling to keep control of the conversation. She'd made a simple observation about Bella having a brother – about their being adopted at the same time and being siblings. It was nothing more than a way to finally put her own demons to rest. But Leo had contradicted her. Told her that Bella and her brother were adopted together but weren't biologically related.

'What on earth do you mean?' she said, panic prickling at the back of her neck. 'How would you know that?'

Bella chose that moment to crest the steps onto the sun deck, bringing croissants to the table.

'Bella – settle an argument for us, would you?'

'It wasn't an argument, Patti. Leave the girl alone – she's got enough on her mind dealing with our breakfast orders,' Felicia said.

Perhaps she should have kept quiet – Patti worked best when she was pushing against a perceived resistance of some kind, the last thing she would do now was back down. Especially when she sensed the unearthing of a truth. Not a million miles away from her *Murder in Mayfair* character.

'When you told us you and your brother were adopted together, did you mean you were already siblings?' Patti asked.

Bella laughed. 'Me and Jay? No.'

'Told you,' Leo muttered.

'So, you and Jay aren't biologically related?' Patti said.

'This sounds like a script from *Murder in Mayfair*,' Hannah said. 'Apologies for my mother's nosiness.'

'It's no problem. It's not like it wouldn't be obvious if you'd met both of us – Jay's Chinese. We were adopted at the same time; that's what I meant. More coffee, anyone?'

'Not for me.' Felicia kept her tone light, flicking at some imaginary lint on a sleeve as she added, 'When's your birthday?'

'My birthday? It's the fifth of September. Why?'

The rushing was back in Felicia's ears, louder than ever. Over the internal noise, she heard Jeremy clearing his throat, asking Nicki about plans for the day, deflecting the conversation as best he could. She risked a glance in his direction, knew instantly the same thoughts were running through his mind. It was an impossible set of coincidences, too many to ignore, and it was all Felicia could do to suck in sufficient air to stave off a panic attack. It was difficult to comprehend, but not only did she look strikingly similar, had been adopted and was the same age as her own daughter – but Bella also shared the same birthday...

Mercifully, the others were fully occupied with the water toys after breakfast, allowing Felicia time to catch her breath, and speak to Jeremy on the sun deck.

'I had no idea my observation would upset you so much,' he said, fiddling with a button on his lemon-yellow cotton shirt. 'It was an idle comment, 'Licia, I didn't mean anything by it. Don't listen to an old fool like me.'

'But I do, Jeremy. You know me better than most – and if you noticed a likeness, I'm not able to ignore it. Add that to what the girl said this morning... Her birthday... She's the same age...' She sighed. 'I've worked so hard to get past what happened all those years ago, to forget her. But this has brought it bubbling back to the surface. What if it is her...?'

'I'm sure it's nothing more than coincidence.'

'Coincidence? Surely not. And don't you remember Poirot's attitude to coincidence? That there's no such thing?'

'Poirot is a made-up character in a fictional world, 'Licia. Manufactured and manipulated for the viewer. If anyone knows how that works, it's you. This is real life – coincidences happen literally all the time. Come on, old girl – chin up.'

Jeremy didn't subscribe to modern sensitivities surrounding mental health – his was a far more old-school, grin and bear it attitude. Usually, it was an attitude Felicia embraced – as a young girl she remembered being told by her own mother to stop crying, suck it up and get on with it. "*Laugh and the world laughs with you, cry and you cry alone*" had been one of her mother's go-to phrases. But this situation wasn't one to be brushed aside with an enforced positive mental attitude. Nor did Felicia believe in coincidences to this extent – regardless of what Jeremy said.

'And what makes it even worse is that Leo seems to have a thing for her.'

'A "thing"?' Jeremy shifted on his chair and plucked a soft case from the table, pulling out some tinted glasses.

'Yes, Jeremy. You know what I mean. He's clearly very attracted to her, and she seems to like him. Stupidly, I was beginning to think how lovely it would be if he did find someone special – if he started thinking about settling down, especially with the changes to my will I've asked you to prepare.' She broke off, fixing her gaze out across the water while she regrouped her thoughts.

Leo had always held a special place in her heart. As the only official child of either of the Kennedy sisters, and after the painful loss of his baby sister, everyone had done their best to patch up their ripped hearts by soaking up as much of his innocent *joie de vivre* as they could.

It had been a particularly difficult time for Felicia, because while her sister had been losing her baby, she had had to keep her own pregnancy a secret. Perhaps that went part-way to explaining the reason for the strength of her emotions towards Leo. She'd often wondered if she'd transferred the love she would have given her own child on to him. A mother's love, by proxy – as well as from arm's length. His father had made sure of that.

Lately, once she'd learned of her own failing health, leaving Leo the bulk of her estate had seemed the obvious next step.

But what Felicia had found out in the last twelve hours about Bella had sent her into a complete tailspin.

'I'm worried it's becoming physical – that Leo and Bella are becoming romantically involved.'

She watched Jeremy as he calculated – his eyebrows flexing as he worked out the possible permutations. Eventually, his eyebrows settled, and he said, 'Even if they do like one another, we're only here for a matter of days. Hardly enough time to get serious, is it? Chances are it'll be nothing more than an on-board fling – he'll walk away at the end of the week and they'll never see one another again.'

Felicia sucked in a breath. 'But, Jeremy, they could be *related*. It's not right.'

He reached across and patted her hand. 'If – and this is a massive if, don't forget – if she is who you think she is, then yes, she and Leo are related. But I think you're getting ahead of yourself. There's a massive difference between them sharing a few kisses and cuddles on board a boat for a week and something more serious. And even then, there's no legal impediment to prevent first cousins from marrying, should it come to that – and I'm joking, Felicia, of course it won't come to that . . .' He frowned, sensing his words weren't having the desired effect.

Felicia didn't want platitudes, she needed practical solutions, and she drew her hand away from his.

'How about this, then . . .' Jeremy never finished his thought, as Bella appeared to take a refreshments order and Felicia hushed him. The conversation was over, for now. Felicia would need to think of something, though. And quickly. Her meeting with Leo was imminent.

As Jeremy sat across from Felicia, he pondered over his recollections of that time in Felicia's life. Most of his memories from so many years ago were hazy at best, but those concerning Felicia were crystal. Back then, she'd been hot property in Hollywood and had managed to attract the attention of top directors, securing roles with which she could have catapulted herself into the stratosphere, if she hadn't fallen pregnant.

Not that Hollywood ever knew. In fact, with one desperate phone call from her, he had swept into action, spirited her away to see out the latter stages of the pregnancy in a secluded rented Scottish lodge – where she'd worn a blond wig every time she set foot outside – and he'd played the role of her doting husband, with no acting required for his part. It had been some of the happiest months of his life. Perhaps it was selfish to have felt that way, knowing all the time that the experience was ripping Felicia apart, not to mention seriously harming her career prospects. Despite his best efforts to quash any negativity, while they were holed up near Gleneagles the rumour mill had run through every scenario for why she could be enduring such seclusion.

During the entirety of their stay, never once did she allude to the father. Jeremy had racked his brains trying to work out who it could have been – by that stage Felicia was mixing with Hollywood royalty, had worked with names like Affleck and Wahlberg all the way through to Clooney, and he'd always presumed the father was someone who would have made her sign an NDA before they'd so much as bought her a drink.

He remembered her telling him the paternity wasn't anyone's business – and he supposed he could understand her reasons for seeing the pregnancy through. It would have been far more logical to have had a termination, but after her sister lost her baby when Felicia was no more than a few months pregnant, he supposed he could understand her reluctance to terminate. It was an aspect of her that only made Jeremy love her more, however hopeless it might be. Settling on a rapid adoption had seemed the best solution all around. The baby got a decent life – Jeremy made sure of that – and Felicia got her career back on track.

It was funny how things had turned out. As he sat on the sun deck of *Blue Sky*, in companionable silence with the only woman he'd ever loved – a woman who looked through him every time she glanced his way – the thought struck him with the same force he'd felt on that grey September morning, when Felicia's waters had broken and the private midwife they'd paid handsomely for help and her silence had swung into action. Felicia could have had it all. Those precious moments she'd spent with her baby, moments when Jeremy had never seen her more exhausted – or more beautiful – could have lasted forever. He would have taken the baby on as his in a heartbeat, if she'd only agreed to marry him. Instead, when the agency came and took the baby away, he'd endured listening to her gut-wrenching wails, he'd had to watch her crumple and lie on the flagstones of that lodge weeping until she had no more tears.

There had been no need for any of it. If only she'd accepted his offer they could be sitting here as a family, enjoying the gorgeous weather and this exceptional yacht, all three of them together.

He eyed Felicia carefully, wondering how deeply she'd managed to bury her emotions surrounding the tiny scrap of a human she'd given away. Wondering if her display of protectiveness towards Leo was genuine, or whether it was also her way of making up for the decisions she made all those years ago.

Chapter Eighteen

Leo checked his watch. Time to head back to the yacht. He'd messed around on a jet ski, then given that over for Patti to have some lessons from one of the deck crew, swapping it for a paddleboard. Not something he had a great deal of experience with, but the dead calm of the water today was giving him the perfect opportunity to have a go.

He figured it would be good exercise for his knee, the constant adjustments to his balance and the sheer physicality of it giving him a good workout. Plus, after the previous evening, he could do with something to exhaust his body, and hopefully his mind. It had been difficult enough to set foot on the swimming platform that morning without the aftershocks from the night before ricocheting through him. As he stared at the place where he'd been lying with Bella, he wouldn't have been surprised to see his thoughts branded into the wooden planking, announcing to the world how he'd managed to make love to the hottest girl he'd ever met, and how much he wanted to do it all over again.

He'd lost count of how many times he'd thought about it since he'd woken – actually, cut the crap, he'd been thinking about it all night, and remembering the softness of her skin now was enough to have him wobble uncontrollably on the paddleboard, fighting for equilibrium before he overbalanced and hit the water with an undignified splash. Laughter had him glancing up in time to see Bella waving at him over the railings.

Doing his best impression of a Navy Seal, he bench-pressed his way back onto the board and waved, before paddling to the back of the boat. Time to park his thoughts of how to achieve some more alone time with Bella, because right now he needed to shower and present himself to Felicia. Presumably this meeting would reveal the core reason for his invite onto *Blue Sky*, and it involved Jeremy, so it didn't take a rocket scientist to work out the reason was something financial. Past that, Leo didn't have much clue.

He padded his way along the corridor to his room, towel in one hand as he did his best to rub away some of the water from his hair.

'You're doing it again.'

Her voice had him turning, one arm still on his head. His instant response to seeing Bella had him sucking in his belly and flexing the muscles in his arm. The effect this woman had on him was getting ridiculous. 'Doing what?'

'That thing with the towel.' She drew closer, lowering her voice. 'It's incredibly sexy, did you realise?'

Her words could have been an electric charge; the effect would have been the same. He was instantly hot, nerve endings crackling. Once she was close enough, he tried to wrap the towel around her to tug her tight against him, but she squealed and wriggled away from him.

'I'm glad you noticed,' he said. 'I've done it often enough to try to gain your attention.'

'Oh, you've got my attention, Leo,' she said, remaining out of his reach. 'But right now I have work to do. And you're dripping all over the parquet. Enjoy your shower.'

'I'd enjoy it more if you joined me.'

The flush of colour on her neck and her conflicted expression was better than any spoken reply.

'I'll see you later,' he said, and she nodded, regaining her composure and heading around the curve in the corridor.

After the fastest – and most vigorous – shower ever, Leo headed out to the sun deck to meet with his aunt.

'I've asked for coffee,' Felicia said, patting the chair beside her.

'Actually, the sun *is* almost over the yardarm,' Jeremy said. 'Might change my mind and order something a touch stronger.'

'Coffee's good for me,' Leo said.

'I expect you're wondering what this is all about,' Felicia said, pausing long enough for him to nod. 'The thing is, I'm not getting any younger . . .'

'None of us are,' Jeremy said, laughing at his own quip.

'Oh, Jeremy, do shush. You're ruining my train of thought. Leo, there comes a time in everyone's life when thoughts turn to the bigger picture. To what will happen once they're gone, I suppose. To decide if the flippant bequests they might have put in the will someone persuaded them to make in their thirties are truly up to the job. And for me, that time is now.'

There was a theatrical pause, one which Leo felt obliged to fill. 'Aunt Felicia, surely there's no need for you to be thinking about your will – not yet.'

A flash of a smile, edged with something else, crossed her face. 'Would that you were correct. But the time is right, and the time is now. It's all very simple, in actual fact, and it barely even needs your attention – but I wanted you to be aware of my plans. As you know, I am and always have been enormously fond of you, as has Nicki. Plus, you are the only person who will take the Kennedy name forward into a new generation – in due course, I mean.'

Felicia paused as Mel delivered the coffee and Jeremy ordered himself a Grey Goose.

'To cut a long, rambling, self-indulgent speech short, I'm leaving you everything.' Without waiting for her words to sink in, she clarified by saying, 'As you know, Nicki has no need of my money, so I have decided that, apart from a few small legacies to acting charities and so on, you are to be the main benefactor.'

'What?' Leo spluttered into his cup, unable to absorb what she was saying. She wanted him to inherit her fortune, her place in Beverly Hills, the London mews house, her classic Bentley. 'All of it?'

Felicia nodded. 'That's what I said. Apart from some charitable donations, a legacy for Mrs Davies and some of the other staff, and so on. I want you to have the rest of it.'

Setting his cup back into its saucer, Leo scraped his chair back awkwardly and stood. 'Do you mind if I take a moment?'

'Of course. I appreciate it's a lot to take in. You don't have to do anything; the will is already drawn up and I simply need to sign it. Jeremy has it with him.'

Pressing himself against the guard rail running around the perimeter of the sun deck, Leo tightened his fingers around the chrome and stared out into the blue, fixed his gaze on the furthest point where he could distinguish the transition between sea and sky. A bequest like this would mean he could set up on his own, away from his father and his overbearing one-size-fits-all attitude to the horses. Not that any of this would come to fruition for decades, though. His aunt wasn't far into her fifties – there was no reason for her not to live another thirty or forty years. By the time he saw any of the money, his career in polo would most probably be far behind him anyway – and that was if Pannacotta didn't take offence at another farm implement and decide to tap-dance on his head the next time. If that happened, his aunt would most likely outlive him anyway.

But – wow . . . Even though his family had discussed Aunt Felicia's accrued wealth, the fact that Nikolai was also independently wealthy in his own right, had speculated on what she would do with it all, Leo hadn't ever seriously considered this as a scenario. He supposed he'd imagined she might leave him something, a lump sum or a painting or something to remember her by – nothing like this though.

With his back to the view, he said, 'I'm a bit overwhelmed.'

Felicia laughed. 'Come here, Leo. Come and finish your coffee. I didn't mean to overwhelm you – I wanted to surprise you, but in a good way.'

Sliding into his chair, Leo shook his head. 'Why now, though? You've got more important things to think about this week, with Nikolai's birthday.'

Her smile faded, became the ghost of an emotion as something else crowded onto his aunt's face, something she concealed almost as quickly.

'Who knows how long any of us will be granted, Leo? I'm getting my ducks in a row, that's all. Being organised, for once.'

Jeremy laughed. 'It's taken me thirty years to get your aunt to do anything in a timely fashion – don't knock it.' He flapped open a manila folder, pulling out a thick wodge of papers clipped to which was a beautiful tortoiseshell-inlaid silver rollerball. 'Right, let's get on with it, shall we?'

Felicia reached for the pen. 'Absolutely. There's one teeny-weeny proviso, one thing I ask from you, Leo.'

'OK – what's that?'

'I'm going to make you a very wealthy man. And as such, I want you to be able to enjoy the finest things in life, but more than that, to enjoy it with the right person.' She paused, as if measuring what she would say next, rolling the words around in her mind. 'It's about Bella.'

'Bella?'

'I need you to reassure me that there's nothing serious going on between you two – that it's just a bit of flirting. Because she's not right for you, certainly not in the long term.'

'What do you mean?'

'I want you to call things off with her, let her down gently, whatever you decide is best. End it now, and I'll sign. We can get Patti and Hannah to witness everything, and it'll be done.'

'What? No.' His reaction was instant, and visceral. A wave of aggression flooded his senses, knee-jerk in terms of speed and exploding from somewhere deep inside. The kind of reaction he'd been fighting to dominate for so long – the kind of reaction that reminded him far too much of his own father. He took a breath, but the surge of adrenalin remained. 'How has any of this got anything to do with Bella? You're going to be around for decades yet; none of this will impact me or my life for tens of years. How can it matter who I choose to be with right now?'

The look on Leo's face was unexpected in its ferocity, the aggression barely shrouded from their view. It pressed Felicia back against her chair as she tried to regroup her thoughts.

'I'm not going to be around for as long as you might think.' Leo remained unmoved. She scrabbled around for what she hoped was a more persuasive angle. 'Truth be told, I'm worried she's using you. Surely you can see how girls on these kinds of boats operate. Seduce one of the guests and ask him for favours. They're not here looking for anything long-term, Leo. It's all about the money. Next week she'll be fawning over the new set of charter guests.'

Watching his face crumple wasn't pleasant, but Felicia needed to loosen his misguided grip on whatever he thought this was. She installed her best indulgent expression, tilting her head for good measure as she said, 'This is a passing thing, my lovely boy. Nothing more. You've got a crush on a pretty girl. I can see that's all it is, even if you can't. She'll break your heart, if you let her.' Felicia patted the pile of papers. 'Whereas this is something concrete. Something you can rely on for the rest of your life. That most people would kill for. So, what's it to be? An infatuation for a girl you barely know, or my estate?'

The chair scraped back again, the sound going straight through her head as the damned headache made itself felt for the first time this morning. Leo turned and made for the guard rail, staring out to sea for interminable minutes. Jeremy's vodka arrived and Felicia did her best to ignore the jingling clink of the ice as he made short work of the drink, then set the glass on the table. A glance at Jeremy's expression showed a similar level of incomprehension written across his face as she felt must be lodged on her own. He raised his substantial eyebrows and pulled a face and she replied with a shrug. She could guess what was going through Jeremy's mind. She could well imagine the total confusion that Jeremy, a confirmed bachelor, would be feeling at Leo's actions, trying to work out how there could be anything more than a momentary pause prior to Leo's total agreement. Bella? Bella Who?

'I don't mean to press you, Leo, but—'

'No.' Leo swung around and fixed her with an expression that reminded Felicia of her brother-in-law. Pure single-minded determination. It flashed across his features like ball lightning electrifying the sky, before his face softened a fraction. With deliberately careful pronunciation he said, 'Thank you for your stunningly generous offer, Aunt Felicia. Please don't think that I'm not absolutely bowled over by it. And you're right – I don't know Bella well at all. Not yet. But I want to – there's no way to describe how I feel around her, but it's something I've never experienced before. You must do whatever you see fit with your estate, but I can't agree to your conditions.'

Jeremy snorted, apparently in outrage. 'This is a huge mistake – don't be so stupid, young man.'

'I would be honoured to be named in my aunt's will,' Leo said, the steel resurfacing as he fixed his attention on Jeremy. 'But I won't be bought. It's as simple as that. Maybe I'm making a huge mistake with Bella, but I don't believe so.'

He maintained his advantage of height, standing over the table with the same unflinching determination, the same utter brick wall of inflexibility Felicia had experienced so many times over the years from his father. She felt herself shrink back in her chair – it had taken all her courage to stand up to Roger Edge. She had been devastated when her sister, Marianna, married him. Leo's generally laid-back attitude hadn't allowed her much insight into this side of his character. She'd believed Marianna's influence, and the time Felicia herself had managed to spend with him away from his parents in his formative years, had been enough to show him a better way of behaving. But Leo's reaction was unexpectedly strong, and her hand reached unconsciously for her forehead. The headache was suddenly like a tidal wave of pressure, her ears buzzing with a thousand imaginary flies.

'Perhaps you need to take some time,' she said, the words tailing off as she absorbed his expression, the shake of his head.

'Unless she proves me wrong, I believe I might have found someone important. I'm sorry, but that's how I feel.'

Felicia managed to reinstate an expression of benign generosity. 'As you wish, Leo. Perhaps we can talk about it some more at another time.'

Once he'd gone, Felicia sat quietly, allowing Jeremy's bluff and bluster, his words of disbelief, his obvious irritation as he shuffled the papers back into their folder, wash over her. Then she watched as he, too, disappeared downstairs.

Although Jeremy seemed unduly flustered at the setback, at the lack of signatures on documents, as she slowly composed herself, it began to dawn on Felicia that there was more than one way to skin a cat – alternative solutions, perhaps, to the immediate problem. There must be a way to permanently separate Leo and Bella. Because Leo had said it himself. *Unless she proves me wrong . . .*

Abandoning her coffee, Felicia headed downstairs to the occasional table holding the bowl of crystal chips – and a diamond pendant necklace.

Chapter Nineteen

Jeremy had taken the stairs quickly, heading for his suite. Once inside, he attempted to drop-kick the folder onto his bed, but all he succeeded in achieving was papers fluttering in all directions.

God damn it. What was wrong with that boy? It was nothing short of insanity to refuse the kind of legacy Felicia Kennedy had to offer. If Leo had half a brain, he would have grabbed her offer with both hands, and Jeremy could have slipped the extra documents under Felicia's pen without her even noticing. In the euphoria of a family bonding moment, nobody would have been looking too closely.

Instead, the papers remained unsigned, and were now decorating the expensive cream carpet and golden silk of the eiderdown.

Jeremy didn't consider himself a violent man, nor was he much into physical exertion, but right now he could happily beat the holy crap out of a punchbag. And he still hadn't broached the subject of who was paying for the extra flights and transfers, never mind the boat he'd had to charter to get him across to Elba.

He should have liberated some of Felicia's money years before, when his gambling had first caused him cash-flow issues. But he'd always been so sure he would win the losses back, and over the years he'd won enough to keep his head above water – barely. A couple of bad decisions recently had been all it took to spiral the situation out of his control, all it took to lead him to this moment, to being here now, scrabbling around on the floor of somebody else's yacht while he stacked the illicit pages back amongst the others.

With any luck, the boy would give Felicia's offer more serious thought and recognise the error he'd made; come the evening, Leo would be grovelling at her feet, desperate to apologise and for her to sign. Logic would prevail, surely to heaven?

Although, even as he envisaged it, Jeremy couldn't shift the memory of the determination over Bella etched into Leo's expression.

Nothing much he could do about any of it for now, he supposed. Hoping Leo would come to his senses and reconsider seemed a very weak plan, but it was the only one in play. Unless Jeremy could come up with something better. Picking up the phone on his wall, he ordered a double Grey Goose, on the rocks. He always thought better with a bit of lubrication for the mental cogs. A late-morning snifter and a game or two of online poker to settle the nerves and he'd be back on track.

Leo was still steaming when he got back to the privacy of his cabin. After slamming the door, he stripped out of his clothes and grabbed for a pair of swimming shorts. He needed to give himself some distance from what had occurred, from the fact that he might have thrown away the possibility of a multi-million-pound inheritance because of a girl he'd known for five days. Needed to rechannel himself into something physical, exhaust himself sufficiently to stop the torrential downpour of confusing thoughts. Gain the upper hand on his emotions.

The disbelief when he turned Felicia down had been written all over their faces – his aunt was clearly shocked, and it seemed Jeremy Giles had succumbed to an apoplectic fit. They'd acted as if asking him to choose had been a completely reasonable request. As if emotions and money were interchangeable – one for the other in a seamless trade. No, it was worse than that – it was as if Bella didn't matter, as if she were nothing but an inconvenient obstacle standing in the way of someone else's view of how his life should look.

Their obvious incomprehension lingered in his mind's eye. It would have been amusing, if he wasn't so utterly pissed off by the whole situation.

Were they really such terrible snobs? Bella worked in a service industry – but so what? Did that place her so low down on his aunt's radar that she was of negligible importance? It could be argued that his aunt worked in an industry not all that different. Instead of providing people with food and drink, Felicia Kennedy provided people with entertainment. It might be paid a whole lot better, but that was to do with scales of return, rather than simply a reflection of how proficient she was. Aunt Felicia was superb at her job, no question – but so was Bella.

He would have expected this attitude from his father, but although Felicia might move in privileged circles, Leo had never seen her in the same light. He'd done his best to battle his father's negative attitude towards his aunt – Felicia had never shown Leo anything other than kindness and unwavering support, had always seemed to extend her benevolent attitude to those around her. And her wish to leave him everything would have only reinforced that belief, if it hadn't been for the strange caveat about Bella. It didn't make any sense. Had Felicia lost sight of what was important in life? Or had Leo?

Still debating the point when he swept across the swimming platform and dived into the sea, he was vaguely aware of one of the deckhands shouting something at him. Surfacing some way from the boat he struck off in a rapid front crawl, ignoring everything but the sting of the salt in his eyes and the cooling effect of the water.

The noise should have been his first warning, reverberating through the water as he continued to slice through the undulations of the waves, but it took him too long to notice, too long to focus on anything other than the sensation of the water and its resistance as he pushed himself harder and harder. By the time he drew in an extended breath and looked around it was too late.

It happened in slow motion for him, even though they were moving fast, coming straight at him. Because he'd forgotten about the jet skis, forgotten that Patti was having a lesson, while Nikolai and Hannah had decided to explore the coastline.

Both jet skis were headed for the yacht, and he was directly in their path. By the time Leo raised an arm in warning, the first one was already on him, and it was all he could do to throw himself backwards away from the hull as it barrelled over the top of him.

'Oh my God . . .'

He heard the words, or perhaps he spoke them – he couldn't be sure because at the same moment his shoulder and the back of his head impacted against the side of the jet ski, and the burst of pain was all-consuming as the force sent him spinning away. Sky became sea, sea became sky, and his mouth was full of water as he tried to take a breath, the bubbling of the water filling his ears and his throat as he went under and stayed there, tossed around in the suck and pulse of the ski's wake.

Bella saw him from the sun deck. She was clearing the remnants of the coffee service when she caught sight of Leo diving from the back of the yacht, heard Dimitri shout to him about the returning jet skis. But Leo carried on swimming like he had a shark chasing him – straight towards the path of the pair of jet skis as they rounded the rocks outlying the cove in which *Blue Sky* was moored and headed directly for the boat – he mustn't have heard the warning.

Through her two-way radio, Bella shouted a warning to Dimitri, but didn't wait for his reply. Dumping the tray, she ran, slipping down the first set of stairs, then paused long enough to take another scan across the water.

It was almost impossible to see Leo, he was so streamlined in the water, his arms barely breaking the surface as he swam. Prickles of hot adrenalin and the ice-cold clamp of fear flowed through her as she watched the lead jet ski head straight for him. She waved her arms frantically, but the riders didn't see her – or Leo – and she could do nothing but watch as Leo realised far too late what was about to happen. He raised an arm, but the ski was already on him, and in the confusion of the spray, Nikolai's panic as he jerked the jet ski to one side, and the shouting coming from the swimming deck, Bella lost sight of Leo. Scanning the sea as the churn of white settled, there was nothing. She couldn't see him anywhere.

A splash from below and she was vaguely aware of Dimitri, with an orange life buoy skipping behind him across the surface of the water as he carved his way in the direction of the accident. When she looked out further, there was nothing but an expanse of blue where Leo should be. Nikolai had flagged down Yannis and both jet skis were crawling back to the site of the impact, all four riders scanning the water to either side, necks craning as they searched.

It was all happening too slowly, and there was still no sign of Leo. Yannis disconnected himself from his jet ski controls, dumped his life preserver and dived into the water, followed shortly afterwards by Hannah, who launched herself from the other vehicle. Frozen to the spot, Bella wanted to move, wanted to will her limbs into action, wanted to do more than stand there, helpless, swearing repeatedly between sobs – the sound of her own voice become louder and more high-pitched as she eventually got her legs moving and sprinted down the final steps to the swimming platform.

Afterwards, she wasn't sure what kind of help she thought she would be, but in that split second she wasn't thinking logically; she ripped off her khaki pencil skirt and dived in after Dimitri, swimming far harder and faster than when she'd raced around the buoy with Leo only days before.

By the time she reached them, the jet skis had bobbed, blocking her view. Sliding a hand onto the closest one, she sucked in a breath, then worked her way around it. It took precious seconds to clear the water from her eyes and focus on the scene: there were people treading water, someone was still seated on each of the jet skis, none of them noticed her as she swam across. And still it took far too long to work out which, if any, of the swimmers – all of them dark-haired and slick from the water – was Leo.

A Summer on the Riviera

'Where is he?' Unsure whether she spoke or thought the words, she'd reached the first swimmer and grabbed a shoulder, pulling at it until she could see faces, dragging in more air as another head turned and she finally saw him.

Bella wasn't particularly religious. She'd always hoped there was something more, an overarching entity governing the proceedings and promising an afterwards, but she hadn't ever been an active believer – not until this moment, when she found herself thanking God repeatedly as she saw Dimitri holding Leo firmly with the swim buoy wrapped across his chest.

'Is he all right?' She paddled closer. 'Are you all right, Leo?'

If the deckhands were confused by her presence as she bobbed around in her peacock blue uniform polo shirt and not a great deal else, they didn't show it. Nor did the guests. Even if they had, correct protocol was the last thing on Bella's mind as she continued to ask for reassurance about Leo's condition. Finally, Dimitri swung him fully around and at last she could see that Leo was conscious – he looked confused but was smiling and Bella couldn't see any obvious injuries. He saw her, and his expression strengthened.

'What are you doing out here?' he asked.

'I fancied a swim, what else?'

'You should've told me; I'd have waited for you.'

Before either one of them could say anything more, Dimitri and Yannis boosted Leo onto the jet ski still under Nikolai's control, before helping Hannah onto the other one, with her mother. The jet skis headed for the yacht, their speed a fraction of what it had been, while Bella and the deckhands swam their way back. By the time she made it, both deckhands were already there, dealing with the guests and the jet skis. Getting Leo onto the boat and checking him was the priority, although by the time she'd returned he was already on the platform, railing against all the attention. Dimitri grabbed Bella by her upper arms and tugged her onto the swimming platform, handing her a towel before leaving her to drip onto the decking as all attention turned back to Leo.

'I'm fine, I promise,' he was saying, 'I only hit my head – nothing vital.'

The fact that he was joking had to be a good sign; Patti was doing her best to lighten the situation too – she had clearly noticed that Nikolai appeared more shocked than anyone, resting her hand protectively on the towel wrapped around the older man's shoulder.

Although the wait felt interminable, it couldn't have been more than a matter of seconds before Leo pushed through the group, with a final determined declaration that he wasn't injured, that the impact had been superficial, nothing more. His smile faded and he wrapped his arms around Bella, the towel around his shoulders falling as she slipped her hands around his ribcage and pulled him close.

'I was so worried.' With her eyes closed, the image of him disappearing under the water loomed back into Bella's mind. 'I thought—' The words caught in her throat, suddenly tight with emotion. 'Are you really OK?'

'I'm completely OK.' The words resonated through Leo's chest. 'It was just a stupid accident.'

'I didn't know what to do . . .'

'You swam out to me?'

She nodded against his chest.

'With the world's slowest front crawl, you decided to come and save me?'

She tilted her face to be able to see his. 'Rude. But yes, I did. Clearly no brain damage from the impact then.'

His eyebrows arched. 'Not a lot of brain to damage, to be fair, but no – no damage.' A serious expression crowded onto his face. 'Thank you.'

'Don't thank me – thank Dimitri, and Yannis, and Hannah. They found you, not me.'

As much as Bella wanted to ignore the rest of the world and focus entirely on him, the world was still there. Dimitri was tying off jet ski ropes, Yannis bumped her arm and handed her the skirt she'd abandoned on her flight towards the sea.

'Captain is coming,' he said, his words clipped and heavy with warning. 'Didn't you hear him?'

Hear him? Bella felt up to her ear – the earpiece was gone. In her haste to get to Leo she'd forgotten about her radio. Checking the waistband of the skirt and then casting around the platform there was no sign of either the earpiece or radio set. And before she could pull her skirt back on, Jean-Philippe was there, his tone overly gushing and conciliatory with the guests, his gaze hawk-like and darting between the members of the deck crew before settling on her, as she pulled away from Leo's embrace and stood half-naked and soaking wet with her skirt in her hand.

'Get yourself cleaned up, Miss Mason. I'll see you on the bridge in ten minutes.' Jean-Philippe turned to Yannis and Dimitri. 'And I want to see you two right now.'

Chapter Twenty

From her location at the bottom of the bridge staircase, Bella could hear the pasting the deck crew was enduring. Jean-Philippe's voice was loud, his words a torrent of anger, which denied Dimitri and Yannis any opportunity to reply. Not that it sounded as though they were being asked questions – more like they were enduring something that a few hundred years ago would have been administered with a cat-o'-nine-tails. A tongue lashing rather than a physical one. Placing a guest in danger – even completely unintentionally – was one of the worst things that could happen aboard a chartered yacht; that much she could hear all too clearly. Having swimmers in the water at the same time as the jet skis was akin to mass murder.

Eventually the shouting died away, replaced by lower tones – the deckhands offering what Bella assumed were apologies, assurances that nothing like this would happen again, before all went quiet. They must have left via the external walkway.

Should she knock and go up, or wait? What she wanted to do was run away – not that there was much chance of achieving that. When Bella had decided she wanted a career change, taken a rare day off and cadged a lift with a friend to Fowey for the afternoon, where she'd eaten ice-cream and watched the boats come and go from the harbour – the day when a casual remark had started a train of thought that had brought her to this exact moment – this had been far from what she'd been hoping for. About as far from it as she could imagine. Five days in, and about to face the second major bollocking of the week.

She heard the captain calling for her through his radio, heard his frustration as he remembered halfway through that she didn't have one. He gave up and instead swore under his breath.

Before he could get wound up any further, Bella pressed her lips together and knocked at the base of the stairwell. She knocked again before she reached the top.

'It's Bella, Captain Kirque.'

His name was no longer a source of amusement, her mouth already dry as he called her in, reaching new levels of desiccation as he left her standing while he checked some instruments and pulled a ring binder from a shelf, leafing through it with deliberate and excruciating slowness.

When he finally faced her, his expression was granite. 'I'm not even sure where to begin.'

'Are you going to fire me?' She might as well take this bull by the horns.

'Do you enjoy the threat of losing your job so much? You would be wise not to goad me, Bella. Perhaps I should allow you to attempt an explanation?' The arch in his eyebrows gave a fair indication the question was rhetorical. 'To explain why a member of the interior team saw fit to abandon her work and throw herself, half-dressed, into the sea? To explain why you complicated the deck crew's job for no good reason. To find logic for leaving items of clothing strewn across the deck and dropping a valuable radio set into the ocean? We are not on a – how do you call it – an eighteen to thirty all-expenses-paid holiday in Benidorm, Miss Mason. We are aboard *Blue Sky*. We are providing the highest level of hospitality, everything slick and seamless and wonderful. This is not the setting for a wet T-shirt competition.'

He was shouting now, and Bella bit at the corner of her lip. When he said it like that, it sounded even worse than she'd thought it would.

'No.' He shook his head at her. 'No. You will not do that thing, that thing women do with the lip. You will not pretend to be overcome with emotion; you will not wriggle away from this by crying.' Running a hand across his forehead, he turned away, talking under his breath. '*Merde*. Perhaps this was a mistake after all.' Swivelling back, he fixed her with his hawkish gaze. 'How do you think it looked, to the other guests, you in an embrace with Mr Kennedy-Edge – standing there in your underwear when the concern should have been with his well-being?'

'Not good. I accept that.'

'There were many applicants for your job, Bella. And even though you had no on-board experience, I still believed in you, in your skill set, in my decision that you were the right pick for this job.'

'I know I can do this job, Captain.'

He barely paused for breath; the tirade continued. 'I took a risk in taking someone who has never worked a superyacht of this calibre, but I didn't think my risk would be so magnified. The last time we spoke, I suggested that discreet liaisons are occasionally a part of our life. *Discreet* being the important word. I also pointed out my desire not to spend a season working with a chief stewardess who is unable to control her emotional responses.'

'I can control my responses.'

'Can you? It didn't appear that way. In fact, it looked very much as though the opposite is true.'

'Captain Kirque, all I can do is apologise. I completely understand your reaction, but I saw the accident as it happened. I thought I could potentially be of some help, so I swam out. I am happy to pay for the radio out of my wages – that was stupid of me. I'm pleased Leo is OK, and I apologise for my lack of discretion.'

'No.' Holding a hand up, palm towards her, the captain shook his head. 'I do not want to hear this. These empty words. How stupid do you think I am?' He paused, then with a heaviness that Bella instantly recognised as an ultimatum, he said, 'Choose.'

'Choose?'

'Don't feign ignorance. I know you are an intelligent young woman. Choose which is more important to you. This job – in fact your entire career aboard charter yachts – or a man you hardly know.'

'But—'

'It should not be a difficult decision, surely? You seem to think this is an opportunity for your own holiday romance, but you are here to work. To be professional. So, which is it to be? Mr Kennedy-Edge or your job?'

His words hung in the air; everything slowed and narrowed until Bella knew she had no option but to respond.

'My job . . .'

It had to be. The whole of her future rested on making a go of this season, of proving to herself – and her family – that she could be more than the sum of her parts, that she was serious about her desire to travel, to work her way around the world, to see penguins and hippos and Ayers Rock. But even as she said the words, they dried in her mouth. What was she going to say to Leo?

'I should give you an official warning for your actions today, I should note this on your service record – but I am prepared to wait. Perhaps if you prove yourself, if you manage to focus on what is important, I will choose to forget this conversation. I will erase your frivolous actions from my mind. But only if you are serious about this. Do you understand?'

She nodded. 'I understand.'

He drew in a long breath. 'This is good. You have made, I think, the correct decision. I have one final request.'

'Yes?'

'Never be seen in your underwear outside of the bedroom again.'

Mel had heard some of the drama unfolding through the radio headset, was aware of the shouted warnings from Dimitri to Leo Kennedy-Edge and also the deckhand's frantic attempts at communications via the radio to Yannis out on the jet ski – who must have been momentarily out of range of the signal, because he didn't reply. Coupled with Bella's screamy shouts and Dimitri launching himself into full rescue mode, Mel knew something had gone wrong. And when Bella threw herself in after the deckhand and was still hugging Leo as if her life depended on it when J-P arrived on scene, she hadn't been able to quash her grin.

After the loud dressing-down J-P had dealt out to everyone involved in the accident, it was obvious to Mel that Bella was skating on thin ice. Although her attitude towards Bella had thawed since movie night, Mel wasn't about to worry about it if the chief stew was self-sabotaging. She wondered if J-P had given her a warning – verbal or written – or if it was worse than that, and whether she could persuade him to tell her, later.

The smirk was still in situ when she came across Felicia in the main salon.

'Ah, just the person I wanted to see,' Felicia said.

'How can I help?'

Felicia stood, dusting imaginary lint from her immaculate three-quarter-length trousers and observing her with an expression Mel couldn't identify.

'Can I get you something to eat? Or drink?'

'No. It's nothing like that. I would like you to come with me, though.'

When Felicia led the way to the curved corridor outside the main suites and came to a stop beside the occasional table holding the chips of crystal, Mel's scalp tightened and her grin faded. The necklace. It was still in the bowl.

Feigning confusion, Mel's hands tightened into nervous fists as Felicia dug in the bowl. She extracted the pendant, chain first – dangling it by its clasp, swinging it from side to side, her focus unwavering.

Mel did her best to amplify her confusion. 'I'm sorry, I don't think I understand . . .'

'Oh, you do. You understand perfectly. I saw you.'

'Saw me?'

'Drop the act, darling. I've worked with the very best actors in the world, and my advice to you is to keep the day job. You're convincing nobody. I saw you take my necklace and hide it here. Were you hoping I wouldn't notice it was gone, that you could take it for yourself once I had left?'

'I-I . . . No.' She could hardly explain her real reason for having palmed the necklace. 'I didn't take it.'

'Who do you think your captain will believe? Let's take this to him, shall we? Allow him to be the judge.'

'No. You can't—'

'Of course I can. What would he think of having a common thief on his crew?'

'Theft leads to a summary dismissal. I'd be off the boat within the hour.' Running a hand through her hair, Mel couldn't believe this was happening. 'I never intended to keep it.' At least that much was true. Aware she had incriminated herself, there wasn't much else Mel could do except try to wiggle her way out of this, somehow. 'I was going to put it back.'

Felicia bumped the pendant into her hand, dropping the chain in on top and tightening her fingers around it. Mel couldn't work out why the woman was smiling, as she attempted another explanation.

'Off the boat within the hour, you say?'

'Yes, but please—'

Holding up a finger to her lips, the glittering diamond visible between the curve of her knuckles, Felicia shushed her. 'Stop talking. If you want to keep your job, you will do something to help me. Something neither of us will ever admit to having done. Do you agree?'

Without waiting to discover what would be involved, Mel grabbed at the lifeline. 'I agree. What do you want me to do?'

'It's about Bella,' Felicia said.

Chapter Twenty-One

'Hi Jay, how's it going?'

After her meeting with Jean-Philippe, Bella sought sanctuary in her cabin and the unconditional support of the one person she could totally trust. Curling into a ball on her bunk, she clutched at her mobile as she waited for the dots signifying his reply, hoping he wasn't on rota at the hospital, or otherwise occupied.

She allowed a breath out slowly as the dots appeared.
'All good. You?'
'Nope . . .'
'Spill'
'I've messed up. Big time'

The dots pulsed, then stopped. Bella waited, willing the dots to resume their track across the screen. Instead, the phone rang.

'Hey there, Belly-button. This phone call better not cost me my week's rent. I'm practically penniless as it is.'

'Hi, Jay.' Just the sound of his voice had her shoulders notching down a couple of inches.

'So, what's up? Is it the gorgeous horse-whispering guy?'

'Sort of. Yes.' She ran through an explanation of the accident, annoyed that by the end he was laughing. 'It's not bloody funny.'

'But I remember you in the Swallowcliffe Leisure Centre pool learning to swim, and it wasn't pretty. Less Michael Phelps, more cat dropped in a pond.'

'Thanks a lot.'

'Pleasure. The image of you going all *Baywatch* in your knickers is solid gold. I'm adding it to my mental folder of embarrassing information about my sister.'

His laughter died away as she told him the rest of it, her meeting with the captain. 'I need to get serious,' she said, in conclusion.

'And that means what? Ditching the horse whisperer?'

'His name's Leo.'

'Leo. Sorry.'

She sighed. 'The captain made me choose – what was I supposed to do? I don't want to, but I don't see another way to get through the rest of this charter with everything intact.'

'Apologies for the public service announcement, but there are aspects of you that haven't been intact for some years.'

'Fuck off. You know what I mean. This is serious – but Jay, I don't want to choose. When Leo was in the water, and I couldn't see him – when I thought he might be . . . I can't describe it. Like a black hole had opened up and I wasn't going to be able to stop myself from falling into it. More than that, I *wanted* to fall into it, if he wasn't OK. Does that make sense? Those minutes before I knew he was all right – I've never experienced anything like it.'

'Wow – you're falling faster than Henry did for me.'

The overconfidence about his new boyfriend was mostly bluster. She knew how devastated he had been by his break-up from his former partner Ewen, and how long it had taken Jay to get back on track. 'For what it's worth, I've never heard you talking like this about anyone before.'

'I've never felt like this before. But you know how much this opportunity means to me, too. I can't risk screwing this job up.'

'I know, I get it – believe me. But I also think I know what it's like to meet the right person. That's not something to throw away, either.'

'No. I know, but—'

'Listen, here's my clinical diagnosis on your situation, should you choose to accept it. If he's really that important to you then find a way to make it work . . . Him *and* the job. Surely you can keep your brain focused for another few days?'

Was Leo that important to her? She wanted to believe so,

wanted to believe that's exactly why she'd lost her mind and jumped into the sea in the first place. She wouldn't have done that for any of the other guests – or crew. Or, for that matter, for any of her exes. She would have jumped in for Jay, even though he was a snarky sod, but she'd never experienced such an intense level of affinity for anyone else. But standing in front of Jean-Philippe had also clarified something in her mind – her determination to succeed as chief stewardess aboard *Blue Sky*. To prove him wrong. She wanted it all.

'Otherwise, what are you going to do? Although I suppose you could always dump the new man and come home if the pressure's already too much to take.'

'OK, so your advice is either do one thing, or do completely the opposite.'

Jay could always be relied upon to provide a motivational aspect, of sorts, to problems. 'Basically, yes. I like to tackle problems with a balanced approach.'

Bella huffed. 'Balanced? You are ultimately pointless; anyone ever tell you?'

'That burns me,' he said. 'Never call me again with your non-problems. You're like a paper cut. You look inconsequential, but you hurt like hell, and take ages to get rid of.'

'Harsh. But I still love you.'

'Love you too, fish-girl.'

Unable to stifle a laugh, she had to admit Jay had raised her spirits, even if he hadn't given her a definitive solution. 'I'd better go – I'm due in the galley to help the chef. Speak again soon?'

'Sure thing. Bye.'

Mel supposed she should be glad Felicia had seen her hiding the diamond pendant. In a twisted way it had led to this moment, the moment when she was nearer than ever to getting Bella off the boat and herself lined up for the role of chief stewardess, the job she knew she deserved. It would be difficult for J-P to source somebody to replace Bella quickly, and impossible mid-charter. This could be her chance to step up, to show J-P that between them, she and Jessica could hold the fort and rise to the challenge. If she played her cards right, she could haul Jessica up one step in the pecking order with her – with the two of them filling the chief and second stewardess roles, J-P need only find a replacement third. A far easier proposition – third stew was basically nothing more than a glorified cleaner, the usual entry position. Unless, of course, you happened to be Bella Mason.

She'd hidden the jewellery in a pocket of Bella's empty luggage, stowed at the bottom of their tiny wardrobe. Something Bella should have no reason to look inside. As Mel had ascended the staircase to tell Felicia it was done, she wanted to feel relief. Nobody had seen her. The crew area had been remarkably empty – any of the deck crew currently off duty must have been sleeping and there had been no sign of Tobias. Probably busy in the galley, as usual. She wanted a sense of excitement, the surge of an adrenalin rush to get her through the next few hours, when she'd need to do her best to appear as confused and disgusted as everybody else would be when the jewellery was discovered.

How was it, then, that all she felt was a growing sense of unease? A creeping sense that this was all wrong. Why did she have to choose this moment for the prickles of guilt to work their way up her spine? What was the point in thinking that maybe she'd started to like Bella, to view her as something other than an obstacle, to wonder if they might actually work well together, even end up being friends?

Because it was too late to go back, even if she wanted to. Felicia had threatened to reveal her as the thief if she didn't pin this on Bella. An ultimatum Mel couldn't escape. It was Bella's career, or her own. So, now was not the time to have an attack of conscience. She needed to stand tall, wait for the fallout and Bella's removal from the yacht, get rid of Felicia Kennedy from her life at the end of the charter and move forward. She had to remember she was closer than ever to getting everything she wanted, all she had to do was hold her nerve.

*

Felicia didn't give herself time to think. Almost as soon as Mel told her she'd hidden the special pieces of jewellery in Bella's suitcase, Felicia spilt the contents of her jewellery box across the counterpane, then began pulling clothes from her drawers. With the room suitably dishevelled, she headed up to the sun deck to find Nicki.

'I can't find it.' When her initial declaration only garnered a lukewarm response, she raised her voice and tried again. 'Nicki, I can't find it anywhere.'

'Find what, Fi?'

Nicki rarely looked tired, but as he scrabbled himself up on the lounger, she noticed he was carrying extra lines, and smudges of dark beneath his eyes. A pang of guilt lodged somewhere in her chest – although Leo hadn't been damaged in the jet ski incident, it was clear Nicki was suffering the aftermath more keenly than she had expected. Too late to back down, she pushed taut fingers through her hair until they rested against her scalp.

'The Bjerregaard Teardrop.' Hoping she hadn't overdone the dramatic tone in her voice, she slid a glance at Patti, now sitting up but regarding her with focus, rather than the quizzical expression she occasionally used when Felicia tried too hard to steal a scene.

'What do you mean you cannot find it?' Nicki was standing now, moving towards her.

'Nicki, I think it's gone. The earrings, too. Last night all the pieces were in my jewellery box with everything else and now they're gone. I've searched everywhere, and I can't find them.' She racked a breath over a tight throat for added effect.

With his hands resting comfortingly against her shoulders, Nicki reassured her that he would help her search, that the jewellery was probably misplaced, rather than gone. He remained convinced by his own words until he had taken a careful, and fruitless, look around their rooms.

'I want to see the captain,' he said, his voice uncharacteristically loud and demanding. 'I want the captain to come here. Now.'

With the order barked at the little stewardess with the corkscrew hair, the one who they'd hardly seen all week, Felicia sank onto the counterpane and played absently with the other pieces of jewellery. She was still there when Captain Kirque and Mel appeared at the door, followed seconds later by the others.

With the suite resembling a paparazzi tip-off, the captain began to collect facts. When had Felicia last seen the jewellery, where was it usually kept, was it possible the jewellery was somewhere else in the room? Felicia kept her answers brief, pushing him gently towards the need for a formal search. All three of the stewardesses had regular access to the rooms, she reminded him, although she tempered her comments with suggestions that she felt sure there was no way any of them could be involved – because they were all such lovely young women.

With the conversation steered in the correct direction and a search of all crew cabins imminent, starting with Mel and Bella's, then Jessica's, Felicia began to relax. This was going to work. Patti sat to her side, while Hannah had offered to continue to search the room and was systematically checking their wardrobes. Nicki remained in command of the situation – and Felicia assumed Jeremy to be holed up in his suite, probably working. There was no sign of Leo, but he would appear in due course. Perhaps it would be better if he wasn't around to witness Bella's fall from grace.

'Jean-Philippe to Bella, Bella report.'

Felicia tilted to hear the captain's side of the conversation, establishing that Bella was in the galley, issuing curt instructions for her to meet him and the other stewardesses in the crew cabins immediately.

The captain's tone altered significantly as he swung around to face her. 'Please allow us time to complete our investigations and I will report back to you and Mr Bjerregaard as soon as possible. We will leave no stone unturned, have no doubt about that, Ms Kennedy.'

*

Bella had to ask repeatedly before anyone would tell her why the captain and one of the deckhands were systematically taking her cabin apart. Pulling out every drawer, shaking out every piece of clothing, checking through and under the bedding and searching through toiletries. When Jessica finally explained, Bella wasn't any less confused.

'You're saying Felicia thinks one of us has taken some of her jewellery? Why?'

'Because she can't find it. Some family heirloom, apparently.' Jessica's voice was even quieter than usual, as the three stewardesses stood in awkward proximity in the cramped corridor.

'The set is called the Bjerregaard Teardrops, or something like that. Rubies and diamonds. Worth loads.' Mel lounged against the wall. Out of the three of them, she seemed the most relaxed, her voice level and calm.

'I've never even seen them,' Bella said.

'Are you sure? You were fiddling around in Ms Kennedy's jewellery box earlier in the charter, weren't you?'

'No. I've never . . .' Too late Bella remembered her search for Felicia's headache medication. Before she could clarify, Jean-Philippe had paused from his search, his attention tuning in to the conversation.

'You were seen looking through a guest's personal property?'

'She wanted headache medication. I wasn't sure which box I needed to find it, that's all.' Bella felt the heat spiking up her neck as her words came out all high-pitched and the captain focused on her, his expression intense. After their earlier conversation, Bella wasn't sure she could take much more of the captain's scrutiny. 'That's the only time I've looked in any of the guests' private belongings.'

'You can search where you like in my stuff, as far as I'm concerned,' Mel said, crossing her arms. 'I've got nothing to hide.'

'Nor have I.' The heat had made it as far as Bella's face, her cheeks burning even though she knew she wasn't concealing anything. 'She wanted some pills, that was all. Mel, you were there. I found them and took them to her. I haven't touched any of her stuff since.'

Captain Kirque's attention returned to the contents of the cabin, his attention moving to the shoes and bags at the bottom of the wardrobe. Mel sucked in a breath and seemed more intent, her gaze tracking the captain's every move. Once Mel's bag had been pulled out and searched, he extracted Bella's carry-on, set it on the bottom bunk and opened it. Mel craned to look, pushing her out of the way in her keenness to watch the bag being searched.

'No, please leave my bag alone. There's nothing in it.'

If Bella hadn't been so confused by the thought of being branded a thief, she might have been more circumspect with her comment, because it only served to make everyone ten times keener to check inside. To pull at every internal pocket and check every ripple in the lining fabric, to tug apart the Velcro and get at the internal structure of the case.

And then the whole situation magnified, confusion tugging at Bella.

Because right at the very base, hidden in the folds of the lining, the captain's hand tightened around something, pulling it into view.

'What's this?' he said.

Chapter Twenty-Two

Only when the crew members had left the room to begin their search did Felicia notice Leo, leaning against the suite doors. He advanced properly into the space.

'Oh, Leo – I've misplaced some jewellery. The Teardrop set – Nicki's family rubies. I can't find them anywhere. I'm sorry to say, but it seems as though they might have been . . .' She allowed her sentence to tail off.

'Stolen?' The arch in his eyebrows didn't seem wholly sympathetic as she nodded. 'Are you sure?'

'I can't believe it, but it seems possible, yes . . .'

He sucked in a breath and glanced at the others. 'Could I please have a private word with my aunt?'

'What can you possibly need to discuss in private at this moment?'

Nicki lodged defiant hands onto hips as he spoke, but Leo ignored him, fixing his gaze on her. Then his eyeline dipped and she followed his action, noticed something he was pulling partially from his pocket. It looked velvety, and a rich red colour . . . He waited until her expression changed, then pushed it out of sight as she sucked in an abrupt breath, and a flush of heat and panic washed over her.

Standing abruptly, she hustled the others out of the room, making up some excuse of needing some peace and quiet, ignoring the hurt expression on Nicki's face and the surprised protestations from Patti.

With the doors closed on them all, she swung around to face Leo.

'How much do you know?' she said.

*

Leo had been searching for Felicia. Partly to apologise. It seemed like a million years ago now, but he'd been rude earlier, had been caught off guard by the talk of her will, and the inexplicable caveat she'd added about Bella. Although he was uninjured past a few bruises, the jet ski incident – the understanding of what could have happened – had been a shock to him, and also to Nikolai. Leo wanted to explain about that, too. And assure Felicia that all parties were completely fine. Mostly, though, he wanted to clarify Bella's importance to him. To make Felicia understand.

She must know what it was like to fall headfirst for somebody – she'd done exactly that with Nikolai. It had been a major source of gossip at the time, had been in all the newspapers – Hollywood's newest piece of hot property stepping out with the enigmatic older man, a member of the Danish aristocracy, to boot. Leo's mother had kept the press clippings in a scrapbook, back in a time when social media consisted of a broadcast on local radio about what was happening in the nearest WI branch.

Added to which, Felicia had been extremely complimentary towards Bella for the entire trip – right up until the point of Jeremy's arrival. He wanted to ask if it was something Jeremy had said that had set her against Bella, to talk to his aunt without him around. He needed to set things straight.

So when he was unable to locate his aunt in any of the general guest areas, he'd headed for her cabin, surprised to hear his aunt talking in hushed but insistent tones, balanced by another female, her voice full of concern. Closing in on the suite door he recognised the other voice as that of the blonde stewardess – Mel.

About to knock and announce his presence, he hesitated when he heard what he thought was a reference to Bella. Stopping in his tracks, he remained out of their line of sight while he listened.

'I'm not comfortable doing this,' he heard Mel say. 'There's always the possibility Captain Kirque will think it was my doing. After all, Bella and I do share a cabin.'

'I don't really care whether you're comfortable or not, and I'm not sure you're in any position to argue with me on this. Take it and do as I ask.'

'When are you going to tell him?'

'Soon enough, so you haven't got time to waste. Hide it well. Nowhere she can come across it by chance. And be sure to tell me where.'

Leo was confused. Take what to hide, and why? And what did the captain have to do with this? Before he could make his presence known, Mel shot from the room like a cat with its tail on fire, mercifully heading in the opposite direction and appearing not to notice him, a soft velvet pouch dangling from one hand. The door to Felicia's suite closed firmly, aiding Leo's split-second decision; he followed Mel.

It had been harder to remain undetected as Mel headed for the crew stairs, and Leo doubled back, taking the guest staircase before catching sight of her again as she disappeared through the door leading to the crew's quarters. How would he explain his presence if challenged? Deciding to pretend he was searching for someone who could show him around the engine room – a request he'd mentioned to Bella and so would sound relatively convincing – he threaded his way down and into what must be the crew's dining room, just catching sight of the back of Mel's figure as she headed on through to a narrow central corridor flanked by rows of doors. The crew cabins.

He waited to see which one she entered, then retraced his steps to the formal dining room and forced himself to sit down and scroll through rubbish on his phone, in case anyone happened to come across him. After waiting for what felt like an interminable amount of time, although his watch told him it was less than five minutes, he headed back down the stairs. The words 'engine room' were on the tip of his tongue, but mercifully there seemed to be no one about. Tapping gently on the door through which he'd seen Mel disappear, he waited until a lack of response assured him the room was vacant. Mel had been and gone.

With the door closed behind him, he took stock of the space. Not that there was much to see. Tight living conditions didn't nearly cover it. And there were two of them existing in here – bunk beds and tiny cupboards with an en suite to one side. He supposed the compactness of the environment would restrict possible locations for the plush plum-coloured velvet pouch he'd seen in Mel's hand, but even so he wasn't sure where to start. His palms were slick and his breathing shallow and rapid as he'd begun his search.

'Tell me what you know,' Felicia said.

'Not nearly enough, obviously.' Leo stared at his aunt, then pulled the pouch from his pocket and emptied the contents onto a space on the counterpane. 'Looks like the Bjerregaard jewels are all here, doesn't it?'

Biting the edge of her lip, Felicia sank down beside the jewellery. Running a finger over the glittering gems, she nodded.

'What the hell is going on, Aunt Felicia?'

Leo had found the pouch at the bottom of a piece of luggage in the wardrobe, tucked into an internal pocket. Not exactly worthy of a CSI search, and not a place any self-respecting thief would hide something if they genuinely wanted to get away with concealing it and remaining in the clear. He'd watched enough detective series to know that hiding things in the bottom of your own suitcase was one of the most obvious ways of getting yourself caught. But then, that must be the idea. To incriminate Bella in theft.

Frowning, Leo had loosened the drawstrings at the top of the bag and tipped the contents onto his palm, sucking in a breath as he turned the jumble of jewellery over and recognised the pieces. They were a wedding gift from Nikolai. Three massive rubies and clusters of smaller diamonds set together in platinum and hanging from a substantial chain, with matching ruby and diamond earrings. The Bjerregaard Teardrop set. Of huge sentimental value to his aunt, an heirloom from Nikolai's family – and weighing in with substantial monetary value, too. But also the kind of pieces that could be broken down and sold as separate gemstones without much difficulty. Perhaps he'd been watching too many cop shows, or maybe his aunt was the one taking art and mimicking it in real life.

Sliding the jewellery into its pouch, then pocketing it, Leo had shoved everything else back into place as best he could before leaving the room. Heading out onto one of the exterior walkways, he'd taken a moment to process what was going on.

Not that it took a genius to work it out. His aunt wanted someone – presumably Captain Kirque – to find her jewellery hidden in Bella's property and come to the obvious conclusion. She wanted Bella to be accused of theft – and not any common-or-garden theft, the theft of significant and special pieces of her jewellery.

Leo's eyes had narrowed as he'd scanned the waves. First Felicia asked him to stop seeing Bella – a request he was still trying to work out the reason for – on top of which it now appeared that she also wanted Bella to lose her job and be removed from the boat.

In the moments it had taken him to reach his aunt's cabin, one thing had crystallised in Leo's mind. Bella's reaction during the incident with the jet ski had already strengthened how he felt about her, his emotions unfiltered and intense, and now a whole different set of priorities was kicking in. Whatever the cause for Felicia having taken against her, Leo was going to protect Bella, regardless of the cost to his relationship with his aunt, or Nikolai. Something about this whole thing stank, and he was determined to find out why.

Leo repeated his demand. 'You need to tell me what's going on with Bella, right now.'

'She's not right for you.'

From Leo's reaction, Felicia could tell her words were falling on deaf ears. And up until Jeremy's arrival, she hadn't thought anything of the kind, either. But even now, even with the look of disgust on his face, mixing with his total lack of comprehension, there was no way she could explain properly.

'You decide she's not right for me – and I still can't work out why you should think that – so you take it upon yourself to have your jewellery planted in her belongings, then plan to manipulate everybody into having them discovered by her employer. You don't think she's right for me, so you decide to destroy her career?'

'I don't want to destroy her career. You're being overdramatic, Leo.' His words stung, but perhaps she could still make him understand.

'No, I'm fucking well not. How likely do you think it would be for her to ever get another job in this industry with a black mark like this against her name?'

'I wouldn't have pressed charges.' Her voice sounded weak against his barrage of unfiltered emotions. She'd blocked herself from acknowledging who Bella might be, the uncomfortable shapes in her head when she thought of Bella and Leo together had overridden every other thought. The need to separate them topped everything else, but she didn't wish the girl harm. Even as she thought it, though, Felicia knew it wouldn't even be her decision, that Nikolai would insist on involving the authorities – wondered why she had been in denial about the full implications of what she'd planned to do to Bella.

'You're missing the point. You know how these things work – there are plenty of very talented actors nobody wants to employ, aren't there? Just because the rest of the world isn't party to all the unpleasant details, it doesn't stop word spreading through the industry, does it? This isn't any different. Even if you managed to keep the authorities out of it, everyone who mattered would still find out.'

She hadn't thought past getting Bella off the yacht. Hadn't realised the extent of the trouble she would have landed the girl in. Legal ramifications had been the last thing she'd wanted. But as she watched Leo's expression flex through various stages of disbelief to open loathing, she shook her head. 'I didn't intend for that to happen. That's not what I wanted.'

'Why does what *you* want matter so much? What's it got to do with you anyway?' Leo began to pace. 'But it's always about you, isn't it? Maybe Dad's right. He's always maintained you're completely self-obsessed, that you only spent time with me to allow yourself extra photo opportunities, but I tried so hard to see past his prejudices.

'Are you really that much of a snob?' Leo didn't even try to control the revulsion dripping from every word. 'Was the thought of having someone who works hard for their living – someone who doesn't have the safety net of inherited money, or a large bank balance to keep them afloat – was the thought of having someone far less fucked up than the rest of us as a potential member of the family too much to contemplate?'

Family. He had no idea how his casual use of the word hit her right in the solar plexus. It was as if he'd punched her.

'Is it because she's adopted, is that it? Did Jeremy fill your head with some nonsense about her background?'

'No.' The word was strangled; she could barely get it out.

'I don't believe you. I don't understand any of this, but I'm telling you it has to stop. Right now. You need to "find" this jewellery, you need to tell the captain you made a mistake, that it was simply misplaced, and you need to understand that after this week is over, I don't want to have anything more to do with you.' His anger spilled over. 'I'm done with this, and with you. I'd take a million Bellas over you, or your money.'

The pain came suddenly and was blinding. An explosion in the centre of her head. Squeezing her eyes shut, Felicia buried her face in her hands. A wave of nausea threatened to overwhelm her. 'I don't feel well, Leo. I need to get to the bathroom.'

'You've got to be joking.' Never had he sounded so disconnected, or so lacking in concern for her well-being. 'Are you seriously pretending you're suddenly ill? I can't believe you'd be that manipulative.'

'I'm not . . . I—'

Staggering to her feet, she opened her eyes sufficiently to be able to make out the door to the en suite and headed for it. Something went wrong on the way there, though, and she stumbled, falling to her knees barely halfway across the parquet flooring. Perhaps she'd tripped on the edge of the rug, she couldn't be sure. All she could be sure about was the pain. She rested the side of her pounding skull against the softness of the woollen rug and closed her eyes.

'Get Nicki,' she said. 'Please . . . Please, Leo, I'm begging you. Fetch Nicki . . .'

Chapter Twenty-Three

The captain unwrapped the package he'd found at the bottom of Bella's suitcase.

'Please don't.' Her requests fell on deaf ears. She'd forgotten all about it, hidden away at the bottom of her case for every trip she'd ever taken. Which up until now had consisted of visits to relatives and summer holidays in the Peak District.

Bella couldn't bear to leave it behind.

'It's nothing.' She tried again, but Jean-Philippe had already unfurled the scrappy parcel.

'What is this?' He sounded completely mystified, the small mess of wool perched on the flat of his hand not at all what he was expecting.

'What the hell is that?' Mel peered over the captain's shoulder.

'It's nothing. I told you.' Bella reached for it, a small plastic googly eye winking at her in the cabin light before she could pocket the woolly being. It was Edgar. The homemade hamster she'd told Leo she'd managed to lose when she was a kid. She *had* lost the hamster, had cried and searched for weeks. Not very effectively, as it turned out. Long after she'd forgotten all about him, Edgar was unearthed when her mum made her spring-clean her room. One way or another he'd been with her ever since, even if now he was consigned to the bottom of her suitcase.

As she slid him away into a drawer, and the search moved on to Jessica's cabin, Bella noticed Mel reaching for her bag – as if she wanted to continue the search.

'What are you doing?' Bella said. 'He's already looked. There's nothing in it.'

'I don't understand . . .' The expression on Mel's face was

pure confusion; there was no other word for it. Then she shook her head and the expression evaporated. 'I don't understand any of this.'

'It's mad, isn't it?' Jessica said, watching as her own belongings were turned over. 'This job isn't at all what I thought it would be.'

Bella could identify with that sentiment. She gave the third stew as big a look of encouragement as she could muster and they linked arms.

The captain never did complete his search of Jessica's cabin, as a panicky-sounding Tobias called for Jean-Philippe via the radio, and through their earpieces they all heard his words.

'We need you upstairs, Captain. It's the principal guest. She's collapsed.'

Once he realised his aunt wasn't messing around, that she had genuinely suffered some kind of an attack and wasn't playing for sympathy, Leo froze. She looked desperately uncomfortable, sprawled awkwardly on the hand-woven Turkish rug between one of the cream chairs and the low table, but he didn't dare move her. What if she'd hurt her neck as she fell? The last thing he wanted was to make the situation worse by blundering in and doing something wrong – he knew how dangerous that could be. Should he shout for help and stay with her, or run and risk leaving her alone?

In this moment he recognised how slick the deckhand's reactions had been earlier in the day, how quickly Bella had assessed the situation with the jet skis and acted. In comparison, Leo's legs felt leaden, his mind bombarded with conflicting messages, his system flooded with adrenalin. His first-aid knowledge, a course completed a decade ago in case of accidents on the polo yard, chose this moment to utterly desert him.

When his aunt repeated her plea for him to fetch Nicki, Leo jolted into action.

'Stay still; I'll get him. I'll be quick.'

Sprinting through the yacht and shouting simultaneously,

it still seemed to take forever to locate his uncle. Took even longer to get back to their suite, with Nikolai asking far too many questions to which he had no answer.

At the doorway Nikolai took one look at Felicia and came to a dead halt, swinging to face Leo. 'What did you do?'

'God. No . . . Nothing. She felt unwell, then she fell.'

'Nicki?' Her voice was tiny, muffled in the pile of the carpeting. She extended an arm out behind herself, reaching for him. It reminded Leo of a piece of bleached driftwood. Dead, its motion created purely by the current of the waves.

'Holy shit.' Patti arrived seconds later. 'Felicia? Doll – are you OK?'

'Out of my way.' Jeremy piled in behind her, shoving Leo to one side as they all fell to their knees beside Felicia.

On the periphery of the action for the second time in a matter of minutes, Leo framed his face with his hands. Had he done this? Had he caused her to collapse – had he been too harsh?

He'd never seen Lily-Rose's body, or her coffin – the family had shielded him from most of that aspect of his baby sister's death, but they hadn't been able to shield him from his own thoughts, his creeping deep, dark imaginings about his role in her loss. Seeing Aunt Felicia like this rendered him incapable of logical thought, took him back, mixed that time with this and threw his head into a spin.

Now Nikolai was lifting Felicia, as Patti wrapped the jewellery in the counterpane and pulled it unceremoniously to the floor, then yanked back the bedclothes. Between them, and with Jeremy flapping from the opposite side of the bed, they got Felicia settled.

For the first time, Leo became aware of a hand on his shoulder, glancing to see Hannah, her concentration also on the commotion. 'What happened?' she said.

'I don't know.' Dropping his hands, he shook his head. 'We had a disagreement; that was all. She was complaining about not feeling well.' His mouth went dry, unable to articulate his callous assumption that she had been faking it, that she'd been attempting to wriggle away from his onslaught. 'Then she collapsed.'

'Leo's right.' Felicia's voice was painfully thin and quiet. 'It wasn't anybody's fault. I simply took a tumble. I'm so sorry to cause all this fuss, but I'm all right, really.'

'You aren't anything even approaching all right. Don't play the heroine for our benefit. For once in your life, tell us the goddam unfiltered truth, will you?' Patti slid the sheet across Felicia's legs, then perched on the very edge of the mattress.

'As always, darling Patti, you're more on point than you realise.' Felicia looked away, her attention taken by the arrival of crew members in the doorway. 'Keep them out, please,' she said.

Leo asked the captain to wait outside, his gaze finding and lingering on Bella, her face full of concern as he'd known it would be. The look that passed between them was muted, but he was grateful for the strength it gave him.

'I need to talk to my husband,' Felicia said, her voice regaining some of its characteristic strength. 'Alone.'

'What you need is a doctor,' Jeremy said.

'It's a bit late for that,' she replied.

With the room emptied of everyone but Nicki, and instructions issued that nobody was to enter their suite until further notice, Felicia leaned against the pillows someone had propped behind her.

'I am very uncomfortable with this, Felicia. You must see a doctor.'

'Will you sit down, Nicki. I need to tell you something.' She patted the patch of sheet beside her, waiting for some of his adrenalin to seep away, waiting for his actions to slow and calm as he came to rest at her side.

'This wasn't how I wanted to explain, and I don't want you to be angry with me . . .'

'Never, Fi. I can't imagine ever being angry with you.'

'Let me finish before you make such sweeping statements,

my darling. I don't want you to be angry with me, but I'll understand if you are.'

'What on earth are you talking about?'

'The last thing I wanted was to have this come out on *Blue Sky*. We're here to celebrate you and your birthday. And I wanted to preserve that, more than anything else.' Blinking rapidly, she did her best to cancel the tears that threatened. 'I need you to believe me. This is the last thing I wanted to have to talk about.'

'I don't understand. I don't care about my birthday – it is simply the day on which my age changes. Celebrating is fun, but it is of no consequence.' He pulled her hand roughly into his, squashing her fingers as he said, 'Felicia, I beg of you – tell me what's going on.'

'Nicki, I'm dying.'

'You're ... No.' He shook his head as his brows drew together. 'You are making a bad joke. Let me check the calendar – is it the beginning of April?'

'Nicki, this is no joke. Please don't make me say it again.'

The expression that settled on his face felt like a knife through her stomach – as she'd always known it would. He had heard her correctly; he just didn't want to have heard it.

'No. That can't be right. Because you said ...'

She sighed. 'I did. It's true.'

'I don't understand.'

'My headaches. You suggested I should go to my doctor when we return from this trip – do you remember?'

'Of course.'

'I've already been to Dr Harding. I went months ago.'

'And you didn't tell me?'

'I thought it was nothing. I imagined he would tell me I needed to slow down, to cut back on work. I imagined coming home and telling you how you were going to get your wish, that I'd be home and getting under your feet while I took an enforced rest. I remember being annoyed at the thought of having my plans disrupted.' She paused, drawing in a breath. 'If only that had been what happened. But it wasn't.'

'What did happen?' His grip on her hand had softened, but the intensity of his gaze hadn't. 'What did he tell you?'

'The headaches – they're not going to stop. They're going to get worse.'

'Why? What is causing them?'

'It's a tumour, Nicki. In my head.'

As she explained the details and the prognosis, it would have been easier not to watch the changing expression on his face, to have focused on anything else in the room, to have closed her eyes and tried – as she had done many times when she had been alone since the diagnosis – tried to block it all out. But she'd known this moment was coming, and Nicki deserved more from her than to expect him to deal with it alone, while she hid from the fallout of his emotions. 'I should have told you sooner, but I didn't want to upset you.'

'How long have you known?'

'A couple of months.'

'You have been pretending there is nothing wrong for months?'

She gave him a wry look. 'I *am* an actress, my darling.'

'But with me you do not act. That has always been our greatest strength, the fact that we are always truthful with one another. Why did you hide this from me?' The wobble in his voice was unmistakable, the leaching of some of his vigour clear in his sigh. 'Why did you *want* to hide it from me?'

'I suppose I didn't want anything to change the way you see me. I don't want you to think of me as being weak and ill. I didn't know how to explain it to you, so it became easier not to tell you at all. Ultimately, it wasn't that I wanted to hide it from you, Nicki – more the other way around.' She shrugged. 'I wanted to shield you from it. From this. From the moment when I did this to you.'

'Did what to me?'

'Changed everything.'

'A long time ago, I made you a promise. Our vows might have been old-fashioned, even then, but I meant them. I still mean them. We tell one another everything, Fi. We share everything, remember?'

'I remember. And perhaps I should have told you straightaway, but I needed time.'

'Time for what?'

'To process the information, to decide what I want, how I want this thing to go. It's the only way I have any sense of control over it.' Her brows crowded together, a sudden stab of anger coursing its way through her, a flash of self-pity.

'But I could have helped you, supported you, instead of carrying on blithely with my life, without any idea of the burden you have been carrying.'

'I know, and that's why I love you, but I also knew you would want to insist I try all the treatments.'

'Of course you must. I will phone the doctor right now and have you airlifted home. There must be things which can be done.'

She cut him off, mid-flow. 'No, Nicki. You won't. I don't want to be airlifted home. That isn't what I want. I want to be here, celebrating your birthday with you in this gorgeous location, enjoying this amazing yacht.'

'How can any of that matter? It is now the very last thing on my mind.'

'And this is exactly what I was desperate to avoid. I had hoped we could enjoy this week; I could sort out my financial wishes for Leo and – once we were home – I would be able to find the strength to tell you. Because I'm not seeking any treatment. I've already made the decision. Any interventions, even a successful surgery, would be massive, entail a long recovery period and will in turn buy me only a little more time. But the surgery could cost me my mobility, or my speech, or my memories far more quickly than the tumour will.' She smiled. 'And let's not pretend I will be able to cope with any of those losses easily.'

A glance at him had the rest of her words catching in her throat, as she watched his face crumple. In all their years together she'd never seen him cry – not even when his sister died in a terrible car accident – and to watch it now was even more difficult than she'd imagined. If she'd had to guess how he would react to the news, she would have expected him to become larger, more imposing, stronger, as he had done in the past. To rail harder against the information, demand to see charts, to research everything to do with her condition and consult with the doctors. Leave no stone unturned.

And perhaps he would still try to do all those things, but right now he seemed to have shrunk. It wasn't because he was crying – the tears fell silently and it was as if he had no idea they were forming. He made no attempt to wipe them from his cheeks – it was more though he had deflated, lost his colour, had become a two-dimensional, monochrome version of the real Nikolai Bjerregaard.

'Nicki, say something . . .'

But he didn't. Instead, he drew his hand from hers and hid his face behind his palms as they sat there, in silence. Felicia reached for the glass of water on the bedside cabinet, sipping before she sighed and rested her eyelids.

A knock on the door had Nicki stirring, his sudden movement jolting her from a strange half-sleep. He didn't wait for whoever was knocking to identify themselves.

'No,' he barked. 'Go away. We need privacy.'

'I'm sorry,' Felicia said, once the footsteps died away.

'So am I. I should have realised, should have noticed something.'

'How? I've done my best to hide it from you.' Raising an eyebrow, she said, 'Brilliant actress, what can I say?'

Her attempt to lighten the moment fell flat, his expression clouding further. 'How much time do we have?'

'I don't know.'

He took her hand again. 'Years?' His grip tightened when she didn't reply. 'Months?'

'Probably.'

'Oh, *min stakkels skat*.'

She didn't understand the words, hadn't ever managed to

master much of his native Danish beyond *tak* – another of the things she'd thought she had all the time in the world to get to – but she did understand the sentiment behind the words, his thumb rubbing across the back of her knuckles as he pulled her close. They balled up together, and as she folded her body within the curve of his, the weight of his arm resting warmly across her, she too began to cry.

Chapter Twenty-Four

Leo had done his best to field questions from the others, but concern was gnawing away at him. It didn't matter that his aunt had assured everybody she would be fine, and her fall hadn't been caused by their argument, he couldn't shift the sensation of blame. She'd complained of feeling unwell directly after he'd shouted at her. Once he'd reassured the captain there was no need to continue to search for the jewellery – the pieces had simply been misplaced – Leo realised he still hadn't gained any firm understanding of why his aunt had begun that subterfuge in the first place. How his growing emotions for Bella could possibly have warranted such a vicious reaction.

Even as he assured Captain Kirque there was no immediate need to ready the tender to collect medical help from Elba, he couldn't shift the impression that everything was linked, and the only link on board *Blue Sky* that made any sense was him.

'We will remain at our mooring for as long as is required,' the captain was saying, although Leo was struggling to give him any attention. 'Please be sure to alert me immediately if your aunt requires medical assistance, or there is anything further any of us can do to support her.'

'Where's Bella? I need to speak to her. Privately.'

If the directness of his request was a surprise, the captain hid it well. Either way, Leo no longer cared. Any pretence had evaporated during the events in his aunt's cabin. He needed to know Bella was OK, reassure her nothing that had transpired was in any way her responsibility, and her position on *Blue Sky* was not under threat. More than that, he needed to tell her that the events of the day had changed nothing for him. Nothing had altered the strength of his conviction, the gut-deep belief that his connection to her was one of the deepest reactions he'd ever felt to another person. But he also needed to keep the truth of the events under a veil – he didn't want the actions of his aunt to convince her to run a mile from him. Although, if the shoe had been on the other foot, he himself might well have done just that.

'I can have her meet with you in the main salon, Mr Kennedy-Edge, if you would like?'

'Yes. I would like.' The words snapped from his mouth. His desire to remain calm and to shy away from pulling rank had evaporated. Well aware he was being overbearing, he brushed away the thought that he sounded like his father. He didn't care. Not today.

'Also, Captain Kirque, I want your total assurance that none of this week's issues will be laid at Bella's door. She has been wholly professional, under extreme circumstances. You're probably unaware, but I also happen to think a great deal of her on a personal level, so I would appreciate it if you would bear this in mind, going forwards.'

'Of course, Mr Kennedy-Edge. Your happiness aboard *Blue Sky* is our only concern.'

The captain's tone held more than a pinch of starch; his gait was stiff as he stepped back to allow him past, not that Leo was worried about how he'd made the captain feel. He wanted to see Bella – more than that, he needed to see her, needed to soak up some of the strength she exuded; as he hurried to the salon he was already planning what to say. When Bella arrived he had a speech all worked out, but the expression on her face brought him up short. He smiled, confusion rushing like a riptide when she didn't return it.

'What exactly did you say to the captain?' she said.

Jean-Philippe's tone had dripped with sarcasm when he relayed instructions for Bella to meet with Leo in the salon. It was excruciating to have to listen in silence as he repeated – presumably word for word – what Leo had said to him. But the real emphasis lay in what the captain didn't say. That this was Bella's opportunity to make her position clear to Leo, to explain her priorities on board *Blue Sky*.

The only relief Bella felt was that the message was relayed in person, rather than via the radio for everyone to hear.

By the time she reached the salon, she was prickling with frustration. Her question immediately had Leo on the back foot. His surprise had her repeating the question.

'What did you say to Jean-Philippe?'

'I wanted to make sure he understood you had nothing to do with my aunt misplacing her jewellery.' He sounded perplexed.

'Why? Did you suppose he'd think I was a thief?'

'No – no, that's not why. Not at all.' Leo's face flexed through a series of emotions. His words were measured but also seemed rushed, and not altogether forthcoming.

'Did *you* think I'd taken it, then?'

'No. Absolutely not.'

'So, why speak to him about me as though I'm a child? As though you need to explain *for* me?' She crossed her arms. 'I've known you for five days, and you're already speaking on my behalf?' She nearly told him he was entering red flag territory, that it was a total dick move, but stopped short. More important was to try to explain her decision to concentrate on her job. 'Leo, I have to work here. I need to make a success of this job, and in order to do that I have to stand on my own two feet, and if needs be fight my own battles. And I'm not sure I can do that with the situation between us as it is.'

'What do you mean?'

Something about his expression had her pausing, regrouping. He looked as though she had completely wrong-footed him. She sucked in a breath and softened her tone. 'How's your aunt?'

His strong, defined edges seemed to crumble, he ran a hand across the back of his neck. 'I don't know. She said she's OK, but people don't collapse for no reason. I don't understand what happened, but I can't shift the feeling I caused it, somehow.'

'How come?'

'We were arguing. One minute I was shouting at her, the next she was on the floor.'

'Sounds like she should be in a hospital, Leo.'

'I know, but Nikolai's keeping everyone out. And he'd be the first to insist on medical intervention if it was needed.'

'Why do you think you caused her fall? What were you upset about?'

'The missing jewellery, where it actually was and why she'd jumped to conclusions.' He rubbed a hand across his forehead. 'It's all such a mess.'

'The captain had our cabins searched.'

He pinched at the bridge of his nose. 'I'm so sorry. There was no need for any of that.'

'It was humiliating.'

'Nobody thinks you had anything to do with it, Bella . . .' He tailed off, sighed, and shook his head as if there was something he wanted to say, but had decided against it.

'Why would they?' Now was her moment, the perfect opportunity to tell him he should prioritise his ailing aunt and she should concentrate on her job. 'It doesn't matter, anyway.'

'But it does. That's the whole point. It matters enormously. *You* matter enormously.'

Shaking her head, Bella edged away. She was losing control of the conversation again. 'I should get back to work.'

'Please allow me to explain. I need you to understand the situation better, because it's complicated. My aunt sprung a huge surprise on me this week – one I wasn't expecting. The thing is, Felicia's always behaved like a second mother to me. I've always supposed it's because she never had children of her own, but recently we haven't seen much of one another. I've been concentrating on the polo; she's been busy filming. Our lives had moved on, or that's how I interpreted it. I suppose that's why her invitation to join her on this charter was rather unexpected.'

Struggling to understand what any of this had to do with her, Bella couldn't work out how to get back to the subject in the forefront of her mind – to find a way to explain to him that her job needed to take precedence over any romance. Before she could vocalise any of that, Leo continued.

'I've really struggled with it. Aunt Felicia's dynamics with my parents have always been difficult. My father won't speak to her unless he has to, and Mum's spent years exhausting herself playing the mediator. The whole thing is stifling. Sometimes I want to walk away from all of them and never look back.'

'Isn't that a standard feeling to have about your family? After all, I'm here – and Jay headed for London as soon as he could. Sometimes family are much easier to love from afar.'

He sighed. 'You're probably right, but that's easier said than done.' Leo frowned as he gazed at her. 'And this week has only served to complicate things. My aunt wanted to change her will in my favour.' The words came out in a rush, a conflicted expression crowding out his frown as he continued to hold her gaze.

'Wow – and you had no idea?'

'None. An inheritance like that would utterly change my life.' He paused. 'But I turned it down.'

Bella shook her head. 'Leo, I genuinely don't understand why you're telling me this. In fact, I think you should stop. It's none of my business.'

'It's totally your business. That's why I'm trying to explain it to you. Because as part of the agreement, my aunt basically wanted control over my future and the person I should end up with. She thinks . . .' He paused, then pressed his lips together with a slight shake of his head.

'But why would she want . . . ?' It took a few seconds for the tortured expression on Leo's face, his words, and the inference from the spaces between his words to land clearly in Bella's mind. When the chips were down, Felicia Kennedy didn't think she was good enough for her nephew. And as a direct result Leo had turned down the inheritance . . . Did that mean he was prepared to jeopardise his relationship with an aunt who had clearly meant an enormous amount to him throughout his life? Was he prepared to forfeit it all for a girl he'd known for less than a week? Throw it all away for her?

As she stared at him, Bella knew the answer – she could see it in the way his eyebrows quirked up to meet the worry lines on his forehead, in the way his jaw was set tight. In the stretch of his fingers as he reached for her hand, then faltered and stopped before they touched.

This was insane. However strongly they might think they were feeling about one another right at this moment, there was no way Leo should be deciding something of this magnitude on the strength of a few days. And if Felicia Kennedy felt negatively enough about Bella to make him choose, it didn't bode well for the rest of Leo's family, did it? Bella's mouth dried, her half-baked plan to try to find a way to tone down her and Leo's interactions for the rest of the cruise and somehow keep the captain happy was evaporating. Keeping her job *and* the prospect of a relationship with Leo afloat had been exploded out of the water. She couldn't allow him to throw away his future any more than she wanted to forfeit her own.

'Oh, Leo. No.' Bella shook her head. 'You're not saying what I think you're saying, are you?'

'I've never felt this way about anyone before, Bella.' He shrugged, a shy grin banishing the worry lines.

Bella ran hot and cold as she stared at him, the curve sliding from his lips as her expression failed to match his. 'Leo – I can't do this. You can't throw all that away for me.'

'I can. I have. It's done.' Intensity reasserted itself in his expression and he took a step towards her.

'No. I mean it.' However much she'd been hoping to find a way around the situation with Captain Kirque, to make some sense out of the crazy ideas circling her brain – to perhaps ask Leo to pretend they were nothing but charter guest and chief stewardess for the remainder of the trip, there was no way she could be party to this. The worries about her job paled. However excruciatingly aware she might be of where he was in a room – like a moth knows the exact location of a flame – there was no way she could be responsible for completely altering Leo's future in this way.

He might be able to turn her on with a single glance, but a purely sexual attraction didn't necessarily make for a solid foundation for anything else. She wondered if she might believe that, if she repeated it enough times. Wondered what else she could tell herself, to make what she was about to do more bearable. Because Bella wasn't prepared to be responsible for the disintegration of Leo's relationships with his family, or his future.

She needed to set him free, and to do that, she needed to make him view her in a completely different light. Extinguish the flame once and for all and allow the moths to flutter away into the darkness.

Pressing fingernails into the palm of one hand, digging until the discomfort claimed at least a portion of her conscious thought, she pulled in a deep breath. 'No, Leo. You misunderstand me. You can't do that, because I don't feel the same way about you.'

'What are you saying?'

Her throat tightened as she forced the words out. 'I was just having a bit of fun with you. No big deal. I had a bet on – with Tobias, actually – whether we would get a bigger tip at the end of the week if one of us managed to seduce a charter guest.'

As she watched Leo's expression alter, his eyes narrow and darken with the settling of her words, she willed her rules back into the forefront of her mind. Tried her best to reinstate them. These people weren't her people; they never would be. She needed to remember her mantra.

'You don't mean that.'

'Yes. I do.' Her words were like sawdust.

Leo said something under his breath, little more than a puff of air wrapped around an oath, then he nodded. 'I apologise for misunderstanding. Thank you for being so honest with me.'

Bella's stomach lurched as he stalked from the salon. She had to clamp one hand within the other to stop herself from reaching out to him. She knew she'd done the right thing, for both of them. It was the only thing she could have done in the circumstances. That thought was cold comfort, though, as she remained rooted to the spot, eyes dry but with a thousand unshed tears held tight behind rapidly blinking lashes.

Chapter Twenty-Five

'They won't let me in.' Jeremy threw himself onto one of the sun loungers on the sun deck. 'That man is hell-bent on controlling Felicia – even now when she should be going to a hospital.' It was difficult to keep his dislike – no, it was a loathing; it was time to be honest – it was difficult to keep the depth of his loathing for Nikolai out of his voice as he addressed Patti and her daughter.

'You know what she's like,' Patti was saying, her colourful sarong billowing around her legs as the breeze swirled. 'Always overdramatic. Jerry, it's what we all love about her.'

The frown accompanying her words didn't go unnoticed, nor did her uninvited shortening of his name – although at this moment he chose to ignore the latter.

'Did you know she wasn't well?' he asked.

Doing her best to smooth away the lines on her forehead, Patti messed with the dark glasses shoved up into her hair, slotting them over her eyes. 'I expect she's fine.'

'Did you know she wasn't well?' Jeremy repeated the question. He could spot evasion – especially on a face as expressive as Patti Prior's.

'There have been a lot of headaches. To be honest, I put them down to the fact that we were nearing the end of filming – the schedule for *MIM* has always been brutal. Back-to-back filming for sixteen episodes is enough to take down a bull elephant. But Felicia's been, I don't know, it's hard to explain . . . Lately she's been more reserved than usual. Even more snippy with the production team. Temper tantrums over the most ridiculous things.' She shrugged. 'I thought she was finding the pace too much, that's all. I didn't seriously consider there was a health issue. Why, what's Nicki saying?'

'Nothing. That's the whole point. He's keeping her all to himself down there and meanwhile, we're here in limbo wondering what the hell's going on. It's unacceptable.'

Patti laughed. 'Jerry, honey, he *is* her husband. They are allowed some space. And if Nicki thought she needed medical intervention, it would already have happened. Calm down and let's see if we can get hold of a drink, shall we?'

She didn't understand – couldn't understand the swirling of emotions rising and falling within his chest. Nobody understood how his thoughts formed into globules of concern or worry, like one of those lava lamps Felicia had adored when he'd first known her, forming and growing and rising only to run out of space and sink back down again, replaced by another, then another and another. What if she was dying down there? What if he never saw her again? The thought was too terrible to consider, his fingers gripping against themselves as he willed a new thought to replace it. But his follow-up thought was almost as bad. Because if Felicia did die – or needed to be hospitalised – there would be absolutely no way he would be able to get her to sign any of the paperwork he'd brought. And then he would be royally screwed.

The thought turned his armpits slick – the creditors he'd resorted to after his last downward spiral at the poker tables weren't going to be satisfied with an IOU. They'd already insinuated what would happen if he didn't manage to repay a significant wedge of the loan he'd taken out with them – plus the interest. The eye-watering interest.

As a money man, he had been well aware the terms were terrible – but he hadn't thought he'd need the money for long. He'd been so convinced he was due a winning streak. It always happened – if you gambled for long enough the tables eventually turned in your favour. It was the law of averages. Nobody lost forever . . . Did they?

Nausea tickled at the back of his throat – was this really what he had become? Someone for whom concern about the most important person in their life was tempered by the very real and pressing need to defraud her before it was too late? For both of them?

'What if she's had a stroke?' He was aware his voice sounded whiny; it was hard to control how any of his words came out. 'Or a heart attack. What the hell was Leo saying to her when it happened? How badly did he upset her?'

'It's not going to be that awful, Jerry.' Patti turned to Hannah. 'Find someone to get us some drinks, will you?'

Hannah seemed only too glad of an excuse to escape, bobbing immediately to her feet. 'Sure.'

'Jerry, you'll have a vodka, won't you?' He nodded. 'And – actually, I'll join him. And get them to bring out some olives, too. Some snacks. Give us something to concentrate on while we wait.' Patti glanced around. 'I'm surprised there's nobody up here with us. Bella's always around.'

With Hannah on the hunt for a stewardess, Jeremy worked at his shoulders, circling one then the other in an attempt to loosen them as they sat in silence, pretending to focus on the view. Jeremy wondered how long it would take Hannah to find someone, was about to suggest he might pop down to Felicia's cabin when Patti broke the quiet.

'She's gonna be all right, you'll see. Felicia's made of British steel – that's why everyone who comes near her needs to wear a hard hat.' Patti bathed him in one of her brilliant smiles as he did his best to acknowledge her joke. 'Am I managing to talk you down yet?'

'A little. And I appreciate it. It's just I've known her for so long – she's such an important person in my life.'

'You and me both, buster.' The smile faded from her lips, and she gazed out to sea again. 'You and me both.'

'I have to ask, what was all that about her jewellery?' Jeremy said. 'Do you know?'

Mel crested the stairs to the sun deck as Jeremy Giles asked the sixty-four-thousand-dollar question. She lodged the tray onto the large, padded area beside the hot tub and distributed the drinks, then the bowls of olives and pretzels, lingering to see if Patti had an answer.

Because she wanted to know the answer, too. What *had* happened with the jewellery? How had it disappeared from Bella's luggage, from the exact place where Mel *knew* she'd hidden it. There seemed no logical explanation for how it had magically reappeared in Felicia Kennedy's cabin – no explanation for J-P being told it had simply been misplaced. That it had been in the main suite all along. Because she knew that wasn't true.

Not that she could ask anyone apart from Felicia Kennedy for details – and she was cloistered in her cabin with her husband.

When Patti's reply to Jeremy was simply a statement about how Felicia must have misplaced the jewellery, followed by a quip about how only someone like Felicia could manage to lose the Danish crown jewels, Mel withdrew with her tray and, for want of a better strategy, headed for the galley.

'What the hell's going on?' For once, Tobias wasn't wielding a kitchen implement. In fact, there was no sign of any form of culinary endeavours. He didn't look whole, somehow, with nothing but a cup of coffee in his hand as he lounged against the stainless steel counter. As if he was inseparable from his usual furious chopping, surrounded by clouds of steam.

'I genuinely have no idea.' Mel dumped the tray.

'I can honestly say I've never been on a charter as bizarre as this one.' He reached for an empty mug. 'Coffee?'

'Please.'

'I mean, I remember more than one trip where every single guest spent the entire time completely wasted. Makes you wonder if any of them remembered any of it afterwards. Complete waste of money. And that one a couple of seasons ago with the two shite poos.'

'You mean the shih tzus?'

'Nope. I mean the shite poos. Little bastards kept coming in here, crapping on the floor. Surely you haven't forgotten?'

'I remember. Their owners maintained they had a problem with the on-board water – that was the excuse.'

Tobias poured the coffee and handed her the mug. 'Nasty creatures. And you understand I'm referring to their owners.'

She laughed. 'Of course.'

'So – are we going to make it to the end of this week without a death on board, do you think?'

Shrugging, she sipped from the mug. 'What do you suppose is wrong with her?'

'Whatever it is, it's playing fucking havoc with my menu plans.'

'You need to learn how to rein in your overwhelming levels of sympathy, Tobias – you're going to exhaust yourself.'

'But you know how these scenarios go. She'll emerge from her cabin as though nothing's happened and within five minutes they'll be demanding food.'

'True. Where's Bella, anyway? I thought she was helping you earlier.'

'She was – until everything turned to sewage. Haven't seen her since.'

'No. Well, she's probably with the nephew, pressing herself against the strength of his—'

'*J-P for Melanie. Melanie, report please.*' The voice was tinny, feeding straight into their ears and distracting Mel from completing her sentence.

'Saved by the captain.' Tobias lodged his mug on the counter.

'I *was* going to say shoulder.' Mel swigged a final mouthful, dumping the rest of the drink into the sink.

''Course you were.' Tobias headed for the cold store. 'I'll get some tuna steaks out to warm through. I can sear them quickly enough, I suppose.'

When Mel padded up the steps to the bridge, she found J-P sitting on the beige leather of the banquette seating, his laptop open in front of him, mobile phone to one side. He took a long breath, his expression stony as he closed the laptop lid and gestured for her to join him.

As she slid along the squashy leather, a quiver of nervous energy lodged in her stomach. It hadn't occurred to her that

J-P might have found out what she'd done, somehow, not until this moment. There was surely no way he would have found out, no way he could know.

But somebody knew – because somebody had found and returned the jewellery in the space of time between when she'd hidden it and when the search had begun. A period that could be measured in no more than ten or so minutes.

She pressed her lips together and waited for J-P to speak. Squashed her hands between the soft leather and the backs of her thighs to keep herself still.

His expression was surprisingly stern when he finally looked at her.

'I want you off the yacht, Melanie,' he said.

Chapter Twenty-Six

'What?' Mel's voice was little more than a whisper, her mouth instantly dry. 'How did you find out?'

'Find out what?' J-P sounded genuinely confused, then said, 'How are we to find out anything when the principal guest and her husband are refusing to answer their door? But this is an intolerable situation. I want you and Dimitri to take the tender and fetch a doctor. If they will not talk to us, they will perhaps talk to a member of the medical profession.'

J-P continued to speak, but Mel struggled to hear the rest of it. Her arms were locked tight, shoulders rammed somewhere close to her ears, her hands flattened and numb beneath her ramrod legs. The rushing of panicked blood through her ears was fizzing and there seemed no way to make it slow.

She'd been so sure he was about to give her notice – that whoever had found, and returned, the jewellery had seen her and told J-P what she'd done. In a wild moment she even wondered if Felicia, despite what she'd said about neither of them ever speaking of it, had double-crossed her and dropped the blame fully at her door. She'd braced herself, expecting her life to disintegrate. Somehow, this conversation was harder for her brain to compute.

'You want me to fetch a doctor?' The words tumbled past dry lips.

'Yes. Isn't that what I said? I have made contact with a local surgery on the island and the doctor will meet you in the *Marina di Campo*.'

'The *Marina di Campo*?'

'Yes.' Shifting to be able to look at her more directly, his brows crowded together. 'Are you ill, now, also? Why do you keep repeating me?' He shook his head. '*Merde*, I am surrounded by a crowd of *imbéciles*.'

'I-I just... Today has been a lot, that's all.' Pulling a shaking hand back to life, she ran it into the front of her scalp, rubbing the base of her palm against her forehead, pressing it into her eyelids. 'I'm exhausted, J-P, not ill.'

'I see that, Melanie. I made a bad joke; I meant to make you laugh, not feel bad.'

J-P had different smiles. He had public ones, the version reserved for charming the charter guests, another used for bestowing praise on the yacht crew or handing out the tips at the end of a successful charter. He had a smile that wasn't truly one at all; instead it was more reminiscent of the shape a jackal's lips made shortly before it attacked – and was used to deliver bad news, usually to a member of the crew. But there was another smile, one most people had never seen, and one that Mel lived for. It was little more than a twitch of his lips, the centre of its intensity instead located in the crinkle at the edges of his eyes, the dancing light held in his gaze, rather than his facial muscles.

She lowered her hand, and he took hold of it, tucking it beneath the table, away from casual view as he twined his fingers around hers. As he squeezed, his lips hitched and the smile was there, only for her.

'There is only so much I can offer you, Melanie. I don't think you fully understand.'

'I do, J-P.'

Shaking his head, he withdrew his hand. 'You believe you are in love with me.'

It was not a question. She nodded. 'I don't just believe it, J-P. I *am* in love with you. I expected too much of you, last year. And you're right: I probably didn't understand back then. But I've had time to think. To decide what I want. What I'm prepared to accept.'

'And you believe that having a part of me is better than having all of another man? You are a beautiful woman. Any man would be proud to be seen with you, but I can only ever give you a small part of myself. My wife, my daughters – the rest of my life in Marseilles? Nothing will challenge that; everything I do is for my family. I'm not sure you have thought this through, not fully. I will never leave them. What happens between us aboard *Blue Sky* can never extend any further, can never invade any other part of my life. It will always be a secret.' The smile evaporated, replaced instead by grey clouds of concern. 'And I'm not sure that's all you deserve, *mon amour*.'

'I am. I'm sure.'

'I have done my best to push you away. I need you to understand that. To make you my chief stewardess would have given you the wrong message, made the light too green. I have given as many ways for you to escape as I can think of. And yet, you are still here.'

'I'm still here.'

He shook his head. 'You must want to find someone to spend the winters with. To grow old surrounded by people you love. To have children.'

'Not every woman wants children, J-P.'

'But do you want these other things?'

'I want you. For now, that's as far as it goes. I understand that, now, too.'

'And I understand what I am asking of you, also. I thought you wanted to take from me, but now I see all you are trying to do is give. I'm not sure I deserve you, Melanie.'

Mel had to blink repeatedly to get herself under control. She never cried, and she certainly wasn't about to start now, especially when J-P was handing her the affirmation she'd been so desperate for. Would it be enough? After his behaviour the previous season, after his blatant disregard for any standard workplace protocol when he refused to even accept her application for the post of chief stewardess on *Blue Sky*, she'd railed against her situation and told herself she'd be better off walking away. But she didn't want a partner who would demand things from her she wasn't willing to give – the last thing she wanted was to lose her autonomy. To end up living in a breeding hutch of a house and feel under pressure to conform, to have children, to "fit in" was Mel's idea of hell, was a million miles away from any frame of reference she understood.

And despite everything, despite the fact that she knew exactly what kind of a man he was, she did want J-P. His nature was what had attracted her in the first place, what turned her on. And regardless of whether it was "right" or "wrong", perhaps she'd finally got him. The most important part of him, anyway.

Shuffling her way out of the bench, Mel stood.

'I'd like to think we all get what we deserve, sooner or later,' she said. 'I'll find Dimitri, and we'll fetch the doctor. Get this charter back on track.'

Felicia had no idea how much time had elapsed, wasn't sure whether she had slept, or if it simply felt that way, wrapped as she was in a tangle of Nicki's limbs, with her back pressed tight and warm against his chest. The tears were all gone, but it felt good to have cried. Cathartic – wasn't that the word? As if a weight had been lifted from her, partly through allowing her raw emotions to take the upper hand, and partly from finally having told Nicki the truth.

The last time she'd cried like that had been over twenty years ago. When they took her baby away. And even though the reasons had been clear, the path she had chosen the only logical one, it hadn't turned out quite as she'd hoped. Because as well as losing her daughter, to all intents and purposes she'd lost the rest of her family one way and another, too. Starting with the brother-in-law who stopped speaking to her shortly after his baby girl died, and in increments through the intervening years – concluding with Leo, this week, when he'd pushed her away with such outrage, such disgust.

The trouble was, she couldn't blame any of them – their reasons were as valid and crucial as her own had been. If the truth had come out, right at the beginning, perhaps the entire landscape of all their lives could have been totally different – might even have been better than what had transpired. It would have been a more honest form of a life, for all of them.

Ringing loudly through her mind, louder than the headache that had receded to its usual dull thud, was Nicki's comment about truth. About how they had always been honest with one another, and how much he valued their transparency. Except she'd lied to him throughout their relationship. She'd never told him she'd had a daughter, or that she'd given the baby up for adoption within days of her birth. That she'd got herself and her body under control and headed back to the glittering lights of Hollywood as though nothing had happened. That she'd met him a few years later and had all but erased the child's existence from her memory.

How had she managed to do that? To deny that a child ever existed. She'd sworn Jeremy to secrecy – not that it had been hard to make him promise. She'd always known he would do anything for her, always known – if she was being completely candid – that he had hoped for more from her. Much more. Had seen how he crumpled when she married Nicki and tried to bolster him with friendship, with a business relationship, with what was nothing more, in actuality, than a few pats on the head for a loyal Labrador.

How many people had she taken for granted in her life?

The answer followed hotly on the heels of the question. Everybody.

Not once had she tried to find out whether her daughter had indeed found the life promised by Jeremy. Never had she considered explaining to her sister the kind of man she'd married, or justifying why she'd spent Leo's formative years desperately hoping he'd grow up to be the image of his mother, not his father.

No, Felicia had shied away from the hard truths, had spent her lifetime – her entire lifetime, as it seemed to have turned out – dressing everything up, smothering it in makeup and dousing it all in the very best lighting. Along the way she'd forgotten it was impossible to polish a turd, that all you can do is roll it in glitter and hope nobody notices.

'Nicki, are you awake?'

'Yes. Sleep would be impossible for me at the moment.' His arm tightened around her. It was far more than she deserved.

'I think it's time to tell the others. They must be worried. And the crew have no idea what's going on, either.'

Once she had broken the news to the others, once they'd had time to absorb the information, she hoped Jeremy would be willing to help her. One thing had become crystal clear as she'd wept herself dry of tears – that if there was any chance Bella was her daughter, she needed to know. She needed confirmation, one way or the other. And not only because of Leo's interest in Bella, although that would need to be carefully navigated. But as she lay there with Nicki, it had occurred to Felicia that this young woman – this vibrant, wonderful, excellent human being – might *actually be* her daughter. She could, in the last few days, have met the human being she created, but never got to know.

Chapter Twenty-Seven

Bella was in the corridor when Felicia emerged from her suite, hand in hand with Nikolai and looking immaculate. Not a hair out of place, Felicia was dressed simply in a blue shift dress which, even though it wasn't supposed to be tailored, had still been cut to emphasise the great figure beneath.

The only hints as to what had taken place within the room were the ashen paleness of Felicia's skin and the poorly supressed emotion on Nikolai's face. His eyes were rimmed red, his whole demeanour one of exhaustion.

Bella laid down the duster – the pretence at cleaning an already pristine mirrored section of corridor had been suggested by Jean-Philippe to ensure a member of the crew was at hand outside the suite. It wasn't the only thing Bella was having to pretend to do. She forced herself to remain polite, to keep her true thoughts to herself as she smiled at the woman who thought her unworthy of her nephew.

Bella grazed the edge of her lip with her teeth, wishing Jean-Philippe had also offered some advice about how to approach the guests, what to say if they did happen to emerge before the doctor arrived. Doing her utmost to bite back the words she really wanted to say in favour of remaining quiet.

'Where are the rest of the guests, Bella?' Felicia gave no hint at any emotion, her voice level and her smile, framed in a gentle pink lipstick, calm. 'I would like to speak with them.'

'I think Mrs Prior and Mr Giles are on the sun deck, Hannah too. I'm not sure where Mr Kennedy-Edge is.' At the mention of Leo, Bella's cheeks flashed with heat, and she hoped – in vain, if the arch of an eyebrow was anything to go by – that Felicia hadn't noticed. Didn't want to give her the satisfaction.

'Will you locate him and ask him to join us upstairs? And would you be kind enough to bring up some drinks, too. Some of my bottled water, I think. And some spirits. I'll have a whisky, and I'm sure Jeremy will have a Grey Goose, or two.' She turned to Nikolai. 'How about you, darling?'

It was hard to ignore the crack in his voice, the soft resignation of his tone and his barely concealed emotion chipped at Bella's resolve to remain impartial. 'I could do with a whisky also. Thank you, Bella.'

These people weren't her people. She was here to do a job, nothing more. She needed to remember that.

Bella located Leo in his cabin, held her breath as she knocked on the door and struggled to hold his eye when he answered. 'Your aunt and uncle are heading up to the sun deck. They want to speak to everyone together.'

'How does she seem?' The worry was clear in his voice. Then he frowned and looked away from her. 'Never mind. I'll go and find out for myself. Thank you for making me aware.'

His formality was horrible.

'Your aunt has requested drinks – would you like anything?' When he shook his head, Bella continued, 'I know your aunt didn't want to see anyone medical, but the captain has sent for a doctor anyway. Would you be able to ask if she might have changed her mind? Otherwise, we will radio the tender and send it back. The captain is obviously very concerned for Ms Kennedy's well-being.'

'Of course.'

A muscle ticked in Leo's jaw; Bella could see it through his beard. She ached to rub a thumb over it, to wrap her arms around his ribcage and feel him hug her tight. To be able to rest her head against his chest and tell him that despite everything, she hoped there was nothing seriously wrong with Felicia Kennedy.

'The whole crew are,' she added.

Leo laughed, but there was no humour held within the sound. Instead, he studied her for a moment, then sighed and the thin smile faded from his lips. 'You are all very kind.'

As she remained completely still, he took a deep breath, closed the cabin door behind him and walked away.

In the galley, Bella was unsure whether loading a tray with drinks to take to the sun deck immediately was preferable to waiting. With no idea whether what Felicia had to say would need drinks before, during, after – or possibly all three – Bella was awash with indecision as she filled an ice bucket and found some tongs.

'How's it looking for lunch?' Tobias said. 'Any word on timings?'

'I think food is the last thing on anyone's mind right now.'

'You say that, but you'd be surprised. On one charter the principal found out his mother had died two days in. Hardly batted an eyelid at the news – then went off on one because the *vichyssoise* wasn't creamy enough. Skewed priorities, these people.'

Her anger flared hot and fast. 'These people? You talk about them as though they were a different species, a completely different breed. They're just people, Tobias. Same as you and me.'

Momentarily taken aback, he flared too. 'Just because you've got the hots for luscious Leo, doesn't mean you're suddenly one of them. You've changed your fucking tune.'

'No, I haven't. On both counts. I'm more aware than ever that I'm never going to be "one of them" as you so eloquently put it, but that doesn't mean they don't have emotions, same as you and me.'

Whatever Felicia was about to tell her friends, Bella felt convinced it was an issue that their status, their money, their sheer privilege wasn't going to be able to make a dent in. Because even though the two of them had appeared poised and calm, there had been something in the way Felicia and Nikolai had left their suite, something raw and human. And just because Bella could feel the sting of Felicia's rejection as acutely as lemon in an open wound, it didn't make her oblivious to everyone else's emotions. It hadn't made it any easier to witness the way

Leo had done his best to hide from her all his emotions, when only a matter of minutes earlier he had been prepared to give up his entire world for her.

It was as if they could tell there was a tempest coming, as if the skies were filling with clouds and the birds had all taken to the wing to search for safety, before the storm could inflict the worst of its damage. Leaving the earthbound to face whatever was heading their way.

'They couldn't give a rat's arse about us – don't forget that.'

'I appreciate what you're saying, Tobias. But I think there's something really wrong with Felicia Kennedy, and I don't think it should matter less to the crew on *Blue Sky* because she's just a guest.'

'She probably broke a nail.' There was a surly gruffness to Tobias's words, as though he was determined to stick to his point of view, regardless.

'Well, let's hope that's all it is. Then nobody need crawl out from their entrenched position to extend any sympathy, need they?'

By the time Bella hit the top step on the sun deck it was clear Felicia hadn't waited for the drinks. Everybody looked completely stunned, the silence broken only by Patti weeping gently into Felicia's shoulder, and the muted calls from a few gulls circling above.

Jeremy stood with his back to everybody, gripping the railing as he stared out to sea. Hannah flanked Felicia's other side, one of the older woman's hands clasped gently between hers. Leo and Nikolai sat to one side, and it was difficult for Bella not to react to the expression on Leo's face. To the tear he made no attempt to brush away, instead allowing it to slide down his cheek unchecked.

The tray of bottles and glasses chinked noisily as she set it down, the tongs toppling from their perch on top of the ice bucket and clanking loudly as they came to rest on the stripped pine of the decking.

'I'm so sorry.' Her words were barely more than a whisper

as she crouched to retrieve the tongs and slid them back onto the tray.

Desperate to be as inconspicuous as possible, she stood awkwardly beside the tray, feeling as though she'd crashed somebody's funeral. Leo stood, keeping a hand firmly on Nikolai's shoulder. Bella could see how tightly he gripped the older man, who in turn was staring into the middle distance, apparently unaware of his surroundings.

'Would you like a drink, Uncle Nicki?' Leo said.

'Whisky.' The reply was monotone, vacant. 'Please.'

Leo crossed the space between them, collecting more drinks orders on his way to the tray.

'Bella, would you mind leaving us alone? We need more time to . . .' A frown lined his forehead, and he sniffed, wiping at the tear with the flat of his hand as if only just noticing its existence. 'Please could you advise the captain that my aunt has no need of a doctor, but that she would like to thank him for his kindness and forethought.'

Bella nodded. Even though he was doing his best to push her away, she was desperate to ask him what had happened, but how could she? 'Is there anything else you need?'

The shake of his head was brusque, a huff of sarcastic laughter so soft she almost didn't hear it at all. 'No. Everything's perfect.'

'Leo, I . . .'

The twist in his mouth had her taking a step back as he snarled at her. 'We have everything we need. Some privacy would be a bonus.'

Bella escaped from the sun deck, the tears she'd been holding at bay finally breaking through and flowing freely as she headed for the crew deck and locked herself in her bathroom.

For possibly the first time in her life, Felicia had done her best to downplay her news. In a way it wasn't news – it was old, at least to her. She'd had months to adjust to her new status quo. Which was what made watching their reactions strangely fascinating, as though she were watching the whole thing unfold on screen – as if she'd delivered her lines and could stand back and see the reaction they created.

When nobody shouted 'Cut, that's a wrap', it occurred to Felicia that – although their reactions were Oscar-worthy – this wasn't pretend. This was real. These were her nearest and dearest reacting to the news she'd spent so long trying to hide from them, had spent almost as long hiding from herself. The truth, finally laid bare. No more pretending. No more hiding.

In any other scenario, she would have had something spiky to say about Patti snivelling all over her linen-clad shoulder, would have told her to get a grip. Not today. Theirs had started as a dysfunctional relationship, nothing more than a couple of jobbing actors thrown together for work. A few episodes of some TV nonsense, which Felicia had fully expected to be cancelled after the first series. The years had come and gone and somewhere along the way the dynamic had shifted. It might have taken her an age to have realised, but Patti had become her closest friend, the only woman she was truly comfortable spending time with, despite – or perhaps because of – all their jabbing and jibing at each other. It was no coincidence that she had been invited to join this charter, no fluke of chance that it was Patti whom she wanted to have witness the will, which Felicia knew would be her final one.

By the time Bella appeared with the drinks, the situation had become calmer. Patti was still crushing the linen of her dress, probably also smearing mascara all over the fabric, but Felicia was glad of it. Glad of the damp sensation as the tears soaked through against her skin, grateful to be able to finally tell her friend that she loved her and hear her reply with a similarly raw response.

She hadn't heard what Leo said to Bella, it didn't really matter – the girl made a tactical withdrawal and Leo poured everyone healthy measures of spirits. And even though the interaction between Leo and Bella had appeared stilted, one thing was clear.

Leo was in love with Bella – Felicia knew her nephew well enough to see it in his eyes. And yet . . . If Bella genuinely was Felicia's daughter, *she* might also get the chance to fall in love with the child she'd never known, before it was too late.

'I know this is hard for you all to accept – and I truly didn't want to have to tell you here, on *Blue Sky* – but we need to find a way to move forward. To enjoy the last few days on this stunning yacht.' Her words were met with muted derision, but she pressed on. 'No, I insist. Nothing need change. We're here to celebrate Nicki's birthday – and I want to do that. Now more than ever before.'

'You ask too much of us.' Jeremy's knuckles turned white as he gripped the shiny handrail, his vision fixed on some far-distant point. 'You always have, Felicia.'

He was crying. Felicia swallowed, trying to rid her throat of the lump stuck behind her tonsils. 'And I'm going to continue to ask too much of you, Jeremy. Of all of you. I mean – why break the habit of a lifetime? I love every one of you, but if anyone intends to spend the next forty-eight hours moping around then I'm buggered if you're doing it on *Blue Sky*. Not with these daily charter rates.'

She was being unfair; she'd given them less than half an hour to assimilate information it had taken her months to get her head around. She would have found amusement in the pun if it wasn't in such poor taste. But now was not the time for any of them to fall apart. It certainly wasn't the time for her to sink into the warm bath of self-pity that waited for her – there would be time enough for that when she truly began to disintegrate.

'Leo – find out if we can have a late lunch, then I think we should take the tender to the Marina di Campo. See if there's anything in the way of some retail therapy while we have a wander around.' Lodging her empty glass onto the table, she slipped from her chair and smiled. 'Chop chop, everyone . . . Please?'

Jeremy hadn't been able to eat more than a bite or two at lunch, but now – a couple of hours later and with their feet on dry land – he was experiencing the pinch of hunger. How was it possible that the body could be so cavalier with his emotions? That even though every inch of his conscious mind was awash with sadness and fear and – to his shame – the pressing crucible of his financial worries and how to resolve them ... even though his mind had no space to process anything else, his stomach still felt as though his throat had been cut.

The paper cones filled with triangles of *farinata di ceci*, the tubs of fresh olives bathed in olive oil and chopped garlic being touted by the street vendor smelled devilishly attractive, making his mouth water obscenely. Not that he could do anything to purge his sudden and overwhelming hunger, not with Felicia's arm through his, and certainly not with the conversation they were having.

She'd drawn him away from the others not long after they'd reached the marina. He would have felt flattered, couldn't stop the flutter of anticipation – even now, hope remained like a bird in a tiny cage – but he should have known, did know, that the conversation would be centred around her finances. Now he properly understood her need to sort out her final wishes, her legacy, her family's future. But this conversation was about much more than simply the wording of the will.

'I need to know about her.' Her surreptitious glances had him following her gaze. Nikolai, Leo and the women were all far behind the two of them, doing their best to act like people whose worlds hadn't just imploded.

'Know about who?'

'My baby. I need to know if she's Bella. I have to know, Jeremy.' The urgency in Felicia's voice was visceral.

'The records are all sealed. There's no way for you to find out – it only works the other way around.'

'Bollocks it does. I know you can find out – don't try to tell me otherwise.' She tugged him to a halt, levering her enormous dark glasses up into the thick layers of her bobbed hair. 'You *have* to do this for me, Jeremy. I *have* to know.'

It was true that he could find out. He shouldn't be able to

do so; that part of what he'd told her was true. But at the time of the adoption, it had seemed prudent to add in a few extra measures. After all, this was Felicia Kennedy's daughter – there had always been the possibility that someone would eventually put two and two together, get the correct total and come for one or the other of them. There were members of the media who were frighteningly resourceful – and while that threat had undeniably long odds, there had been nothing stopping the child herself searching for her biological parents once she turned eighteen. And there was no telling what an individual would do, should they suddenly discover they had been dumped at birth by one of the most famous women in the world of entertainment.

Monetary demands could have been the least of Felicia's worries.

But it hadn't happened. The child must have moved forwards with her life, with no inclination to find her birth mother, and Jeremy had remained passive, ready to act only should the need arise.

Never in a million years had he imagined needing to locate Felicia's daughter in circumstances such as these. It was as though the heavens had conspired against him, bringing unexpected and unwelcome complications. He swallowed, well aware he had to tread carefully with this request – if he wanted to try to get the signing of the will back on the table, and his own pieces of paperwork in the process, then he must think this through – he needed to work out how the chips would fall if the girl *was* Felicia's daughter, and also if she wasn't.

'Have you changed your mind about your beneficiary?'

She huffed, slotting the glasses over her eyes and walking on again. 'It's not about the money, Jeremy. Why is it always about the money with you?'

It was impossible not to recoil from the sting in her comment. What the hell else was it supposed to be about? After all, a business relationship had been all she'd ever wanted from him. And now she was behaving as though there was something wrong with *his* perception of the situation. As if the money was the only reason he was here, the only reason he'd hung around her for thirty-odd years.

'You want to get to know her – is that what you mean? You want to find your child?'

The momentary pause was fleeting. The sucking in of a breath could have meant a thousand different things, but then she nodded. 'Before it's too late.' Pulling away, she headed across the esplanade, staring out to sea.

Jeremy presumed she was referring to her illness but then she said, 'If it is Bella, though – it's already too late.'

'What do you mean?' Now Jeremy was confused. If the stars did align, and Bella was Felicia's daughter, the fact that the girl was here would make Felicia's wish to meet her child easier, not more difficult. 'Are you still concerned because of Leo?' Her nod had Jeremy confused. 'But we've already had this conversation, 'Licia. There's nothing here we can't overcome, no massive problem.' He paused, Felicia's conflicted expression and restless fingers speaking volumes. There was more to this. Jeremy knew her well enough to recognise that much. 'Unless there's something else, something you're not telling me.'

'God damn it.' Her teeth gritted together, her words somewhere between a snarl and a yelp.

'What is it?' He rested a hand against the back of her shoulder, waiting for her to shake it off. She didn't react, her face a mask. She seemed lost in her own thoughts. 'What aren't you telling me?'

Eventually she lifted her glasses, her expression one of indescribable sadness. It was enough to make Jeremy take a step back, all thoughts of food forgotten.

'If Bella *is* my daughter, then there is a massive problem. Because she and Leo share the same father . . .'

Chapter Twenty-Eight

Jeremy pressed his lips together as he absorbed Felicia's words – he needed to think carefully before he said anything, make sure he'd heard her correctly. Had she really just told him that her nephew and the girl who could be her daughter shared the same father? That could only mean one thing. The father could only be one person – Roger Edge. Felicia's brother-in-law. The frown lines on his face might have been well utilised through the course of Jeremy's life, their creases well established, but never had they been pressed into deeper service than at this moment.

He took a sideways glance at Felicia, whose gaze was still fixed somewhere in the blue yonder. 'Are you being serious?'

'It's hardly something I'd make a fucking joke about, is it?'

Her words came as more of a bark, and he could understand why.

'But . . . how?' So much for thinking carefully before he spoke – but he couldn't believe what he'd heard. Of all the people in Felicia's life back then . . . Roger Edge?

'That explains why you never married, then, if you still don't understand the mechanics of reproduction.' Laced with bitterness, her words would have been coated in arsenic had they been delivered in solid form. A venomous creature, cornered, spitting at anyone foolish enough to come within range.

'That's not what I mean, and you know it.'

She sighed, her shoulders visibly sagging. 'No. I suppose not.'

'Do you want to talk about it?'

'No. Not really. But I do need you to understand how important it is to find out the truth.'

It certainly explained her reaction to his lack of concern about Leo and Bella's involvement with each other. Jeremy's cheeks fired with colour as the implications embedded themselves into his mind.

Before he could reply, Felicia checked there was nobody within earshot, then said, 'It was only once – that's what made it so unbelievable when I discovered I was pregnant. I never loved him. God Almighty, Jeremy, he's my sister's husband – by then already a father and with another baby on the way. I could tell you it was a moment of madness, I could pretend we were both drunk, or that he forced himself on me, or any number of scenarios to try to present myself in a better light. But the truth is I seduced him. I was angry with Marianna about something – I can't even remember what it was now – and it was my way of getting back at her.'

'Seducing her husband?'

'I'd always known he liked both of us. I treated him like dirt right from the off – he was just another man doing his best to get my attention, and I wasn't interested. Sounds terribly self-absorbed, doesn't it? But it's true. Back then my looks were my weapon and my shield. They got me everything I wanted – and in lots of ways they were all I had. And there was something about him, something I couldn't put my finger on. Something that made me wary. Anyway, eventually he gave up on me and settled for Marianna instead. Married her and set about procreating, his way of proving he was utterly over me.'

'But he wasn't?' A familiar tale, Jeremy thought with a shake of his head. He'd been a fool to believe himself the only one obsessed by her.

'Clearly not. Either that or he wasn't as honourable as he liked to think. Anyway, he was raging with himself as soon as it was over. His anger extended to encompass me, too. I still remember the names he called me – although at the time I enjoyed his wrath. It made me feel victorious.' A sharp exhalation of air. 'That didn't last long, though.'

Felicia pressed her hands against the rough stone of the harbour wall, keeping her line of sight busy with the bobbing fishing vessels and, further out, the yachts small enough to anchor close to shore. She'd already said more to Jeremy than she'd intended.

'You have to find my daughter, Jeremy. Today. Will you do that for me?'

'I can try.'

'If it's Bella, I need to know. And now you understand why.'

His nod was definite. 'I'll make some calls. Give me a couple of hours.'

'And it goes without saying – this conversation goes no further. Your discretion is paramount. I rely on you so much, Jeremy – and I value everything you have ever done for me. I want you to know that. I haven't forgotten your kindness all those years ago in Scotland. Your unwavering strength.' Reaching across, she squeezed his arm. 'I couldn't have done any of it without you.'

His expression was difficult to interpret but having assured her he would do all he could to find out the truth, he pulled his phone from a pocket and told her he'd set up camp in a local café bar until he had news.

Once he had walked away, she turned back towards the water and allowed her thoughts to wander. She'd always wondered who Jeremy had decided was the father – they never discussed it, but she'd long ago concluded he'd taken her silence on the matter as the result of some kind of gagging order from one of the Hollywood A-listers she'd dated.

What Jeremy didn't understand, had never understood, was that if one of those men had been the father she would have kept her baby. Because no superinjunction they could have slapped on her would have been as crippling as what had actually happened.

Telling Roger had been one of the hardest things Felicia had ever done. She'd known his reaction wasn't likely to be favourable – Marianna was eight months pregnant by the time her own pregnancy was confirmed, the whole family gearing up to welcome a brother or sister for Leo, another baby

Kennedy-Edge over whom Roger could crow. She remembered the shock on his face, followed rapidly by his mental calculations needed to verify the baby could be his, and work out where that left him. It had taken him a while to speak, but when he did his words left her cold. He assumed she would be getting rid of it – told her he expected no less. That he already had his family, and he didn't want any bastard child hanging around. There had been such venom in his words – no doubt he enjoyed the restoration of power in his favour – but also a touch of fear in the mix, too.

A fear that magnified when she'd told him that any decision was very firmly hers to make. At that point, if she was being candid in her remembering, she'd been undecided. Bearing and keeping a child at that stage of her career would have had a significant impact on her future; terminating a pregnancy would have impacted her far more deeply on a personal level – a no-win situation. An impossible decision.

A decision that could have been totally different, if Lily-Rose had survived. Instead, her sister had lost her new-born daughter to "complications". While Roger went home to care for a tiny Leo, Felicia had spent an uncomfortable night in a chair in Marianna's hospital room, listening to her sister mourn her baby into the small hours, waking up the following morning after precious little sleep and with the scent of all those damned flowers choking the room's warm, oppressive air.

In that moment, in those seconds when she knew she never wanted to smell fresh-cut flowers as she woke ever again, Felicia also knew there was no way she could destroy the tiny life growing inside her – no way she could not have this baby. No matter what the repercussions. Not after that night.

But as time moved forwards, she also came to understand there was no way she could keep the child, either. She'd always maintained to Jeremy it was because of the impact it would have on her career. But it ran far deeper than that, because however much she might have liked to punish Roger for expecting her to terminate, she could see the terrible impact losing Lily-Rose

A Summer on the Riviera

had on him. On his entire family. She began to understand there was no way she could parade her child in front of them, pretend it wasn't his, nor could she live alongside her sister and watch Marianna breaking into smaller and smaller pieces every time she held Felicia's baby.

So, the die was cast, and Felicia began to make plans. Or, rather more accurately, she asked Jeremy to make plans. And a part of that plan was to have the baby adopted. As soon as possible after the birth. It seemed the logical solution – the baby would get to have a wonderful life, with parents who were desperate to love and wouldn't spend the rest of their lives bitching about one another, while her life could get back to where it should have been. And Roger could pretend nothing had happened. Everyone could pretend nothing had happened.

That's how it had been, those times eventually becoming nothing more than a memory, all ancient history – interred in the previous millennium. It had taken more grit and determination than she knew she had, but eventually Felicia had moved on, met Nikolai, made a different life. And that's how everything would have remained, if this week on *Blue Sky* hadn't taken an archaeologist's pickaxe to her carefully buried past and unearthed the stark whiteness of its bones.

She wondered if she'd managed – truly managed – to pack away any of it, though. Or whether it was impossible to completely suppress the emotions involved with giving away a child. It had certainly been possible to appear to have dealt with the situation, to make an amazing life and spend large parts of it being extremely happy. But then Felicia had never got to find out how she would have felt to have raised a child herself. Maybe the joys and trials of that kind of a life would have been even better, the emotions even stronger, the highs and lows even more life-affirming. She would never know.

Perhaps it was simply the pressing nature of her condition that was dragging these thoughts to the forefront of her mind. Somehow, she didn't believe that to be the case. The yo-yo of adrenalin and fluttering of nerves in the base of her stomach were unlike anything she'd felt in such a long time. Bella could be her daughter.

Bella could be her daughter . . .

Despite everything, Felicia couldn't dampen the swelling hope, the desire for it to be so – for her to get to know Bella and for them to become friends, for Felicia to make her understand why. To be able to explain how it had been – how it had had to be, how sorry she was to have missed so many years of knowing her.

She picked at a loose piece of stone on the top of the wall, pressing it between her fingers to focus her thoughts as she swung round to see the others heading her way. They'd kept their distance while she'd been talking with Jeremy, even Nicki had hung back, but they were incoming now. Packing her tumble of thoughts away, Felicia pulled in a deep breath. She smiled and walked towards them.

Leo wondered if his mask was anything like as effective as his aunt's. Here she was, in the idyllic surroundings of the Marina di Campo, looking as though life couldn't be running more smoothly if it tried. He wanted to ask her how the hell she did it. Because even though he had attempted to plaster a casual expression on his face, was doing his best to chat as normally as possible to Nikolai while Felicia and Jeremy were deep in discussion, Leo had never felt more untethered than he did at this moment.

Bella had just been having fun. She'd been playing him. He wanted to explode, to shout and swear and kick out. How had he misjudged her so badly? How stupid he must have looked, asking her if she wanted to make their attraction for one another into something more – he'd even mentioned the relationship word, for the love of God. She was probably having a great laugh with the *Blue Sky* chef right now, holed up in the galley drinking coffee and discussing how best to screw with the next group of unsuspecting charter guests.

Pinching at the bridge of his nose, Leo supposed he could

allow the tears to flow – nobody would question his display of emotion, would assume it was about his aunt. And it would be, too, because alongside his tumble of emotions about Bella, underlying all that was a deep-seated hollowness. A sense of loss already making its presence felt. Despite her manipulative behaviour, Aunt Felicia was, and always had been, very important to Leo. She'd been a haven, a home away from home when it all got too intense with his father, a rock in his life otherwise dominated by the shifting sands of his father's expectations.

To think that she would be gone, and not in thirty or forty years' time as he'd always assumed, but instead in a matter of months.

No wonder she'd wanted to discuss her will; her determination to have the paperwork sorted made so much more sense. Leo's cheeks burned with embarrassment – she'd been right about Bella, after all. And he'd been so blind to it all. Had his aunt been correct right from the off, that his feelings for Bella had been nothing more than a purely physical attraction? Would he have been over her by now if they'd just slept together?

No. Even though he burned with the sting of her rejection, even though he should be erasing her from his mind, consigning her to the overflowing dustbin of fake people he'd come across over the years, he couldn't. She might be able to switch her emotions on and off at will, but he couldn't.

Instead, he'd have to crash his way through the next few days as best he could, do his best to concentrate on his aunt, and hope that with enough space and distance from *Blue Sky* he would be able to begin to forget Chief Stewardess Bella Mason.

A season on a charter yacht always started off hectic, and only got busier. Mel already felt like she'd dodged multiple bullets, but some were still airborne, and she had no idea whether they still might find their mark. The reappearance of the jewellery she'd hidden in Bella's luggage seemed to have been lost in the drama surrounding Felicia Kennedy's collapse. Was it possible that particular bullet might have landed harmlessly in the sea, that her role in the attempt to get Bella removed from *Blue Sky* could fade far enough into the background to go undetected?

There were two days left before they got rid of these charter guests, two days to endure before she could finally breathe a sigh of relief and put the episode behind her.

With the entire cast of guests having headed for the nondescript port shortly after she had returned with the tender, the crew had the yacht to themselves for a few hours. Usually, given an unexpected opportunity like this, the entire crew would rush through their jobs in the hope of having an hour or two to kick back before the guests returned. Mel knew exactly how she would have liked to spend the time, and with whom. But not today. Today J-P had summoned all three stewardesses to meet him in the principal's suite.

Untouched since Felicia and Nikolai had exited earlier, on the floor at the end of the bed lay the counterpane, twisted like a makeshift sack. Once they were all present, J-P unfolded the material, a tangle of jewellery nestling in its centre.

'Our guest has shown a level of unparalleled trust – she has asked for her rooms to be tidied, and for these to be sorted and replaced into their boxes.' He gestured at the discarded jewellery case and a slew of smaller boxes on the glossy wood of the parquet flooring. His eyebrows arched. 'Perhaps she feels a sense of guilt over her mistaken accusation. Whatever the reason, and in light of earlier events, I think it is in all our best interests that this is not undertaken alone by any one of you. I will not have my crew accused so blatantly and falsely again.'

Mel's cheeks flared with colour, and she looked away, hoping nobody noticed as J-P continued.

'Therefore, you will all sort out and put away Ms Kennedy's jewellery, and I will be here to supervise.'

It wasn't at all the way she would have preferred to spend the time with J-P, but as Mel reached for the first box, she supposed the afternoon could have been far worse.

'Do you think the black pearls go in this one?' Jessica was the first to break the uneasy quiet as they settled on the floor and tried to work out which pieces of jewellery belonged in which container. 'It says Paspaley – that's a pearl jeweller, isn't it?'

'Is it?' Bella said.

'She is correct.' J-P had taken up residence in one of the cream armchairs, his focus on the three of them intense.

As she watched J-P approve of Jessica's knowledge, and while the third stew slotted the bracelet into its correct home, Mel reached for the deep ruby-red vintage velvet pouch. Her fingers melted into the softness of the familiar fabric, and she pulled at the cords at the top of the pouch, waiting for J-P to be equally impressed as she announced, 'The Bjerregaard Teardrop set goes in here.'

She saw Bella frown, but was already reaching for the necklace, untangling it from the silk of the counterpane and picking out the earrings. Sliding the set into the pouch, she added it to the jewellery box, and only then did she notice how still Bella had become, how carefully she watched her movements.

'How did you know those belonged in that bag?' Bella asked. 'There aren't any markings on it.'

Mel's cheeks flushed with heat again as she realised what she'd done. There was only one way she could have known that those items of jewellery belonged in that pouch, only one way she could have been that definite – if she'd seen it before, handled the contents. Shit. Had Bella made the connection?

'Someone must have told me.' The words sounded desperate, her gaze raking Bella for clues as to what she would do next.

Heat prickled up Bella's neck. Mel was lying. She was sure of it. Why would there have been the need for anyone to have told her those particular gems belonged in that pouch? It made no sense. And if Felicia had been mistaken, as she claimed, and the jewellery had remained in this very cabin all along, how would anyone except members of Felicia's family have a clue as to how she chose to store such important jewellery?

If the pieces were worth so much money, held an immense amount of personal sentiment for both Felicia and her husband, it would have made far more sense for them to have been kept in one of the boxes scattering the floor. That would have been her guess. Perhaps the burr walnut one, inlaid with mother of pearl – that one was beautiful, and far more befitting of such treasured heirlooms than an old velvet bag, surely?

Another thought pricked at the back of Bella's mind. When their cabin had been searched, Mel had seemed totally relaxed. On the other hand, Bella had felt a jumble of nerves, even though she knew she had nothing to hide – and Jessica had behaved similarly, her anxious laugh and worried comments testament to her underlying emotions. So, why hadn't Mel been worried?

The flash of warning in Mel's expression as she tried to bluff her way out of the situation was clear, though. Here, in front of the captain, wasn't the right place to accuse Mel of something. And accuse her of what? Nothing had actually happened with the Bjerregaard Teardrop. Plus, after her devastating conversation with Leo, after his coldness on the sun deck when she'd taken out the drinks, Bella couldn't cope with more confrontation. She felt as though she was drowning in emotion already; she couldn't cope with anything else falling apart.

Instead, she returned Mel's glance with one of equal forcefulness – one that intimated this wasn't finished with, even though her words conveyed the opposite sentiment.

'That must have been it.' The relief on Mel's face when Bella said nothing more was palpable, although her focus did remain closely on her as they sorted the remainder of the jewellery and tidied the suite. Jean-Philippe stayed present throughout the process and by the time the four of them exited the suite, Bella was relieved to escape the claustrophobic surroundings.

Mel was keen to escape, too, saying something about heading to the galley to see if Tobias needed any help.

'Could I have a word first?' Bella said.

'What, now? There's so much to get on with.' Mel was flustered, her sudden enthusiasm for the mundane tasks still to be completed at odds with her usual attitude.

'Yes. Please.'

A final cast around for help, which wasn't forthcoming as Jessica and Jean-Philippe had already disappeared, gave way to resignation. 'Well, what is it?'

Bella paused. How was she going to handle this? Not one to back away from an argument, she didn't hugely enjoy confrontation either – nor did she want to create a situation that would ruin the uneasy truce she thought she'd forged with Mel. On the other hand, had Mel intended to plant stolen jewellery in her belongings, only for it to be discovered by Jean-Philippe? She could have ended up in jail for something as serious as a theft like that.

She decided to access the conversation from a different angle.

'Mel, I know you don't like me much. And I assume you think the chief stew's job should be yours?'

The slight incline in Mel's head was answer enough.

'I get that – I understand it must seem as though I've parachuted in over your head. It certainly wasn't my intention to pull a job from someone else's hands. Jean-Philippe was very clear that it was a chief stew he was looking for, so I assumed everyone else on board was comfortable with that.'

'It is what it is.' Mel frowned. 'What's that got to do with anything?'

Bella had to hand it to her, Mel was pricklier than a porcupine. 'I don't fully understand what happened with that jewellery, but I can't shift the feeling there was far more going on than I'm aware of.' She decided against stating that Mel's reactions in their cabin had been off, especially when it came to the searching of her luggage. None of it proved anything. Instead, she said, 'Listen – you and I don't ever need to be friends. But if you think for a minute I'm not serious about making this job a success, then all that shows is how little you know about me. We can either work as a team, or the next few months can be hell – and that ball is currently in your court. I'm prepared to move forwards. Are you?'

Mel recognised a lifeline when one was thrown, and that's exactly what Bella had given her. She supposed it might all be irrelevant if Felicia demanded a repeat performance of the staging of a jewellery theft, although that seemed unlikely now J-P had instructed all three stewardesses that none of them were to enter any of these charter guests' cabins alone. There would be no opportunity for accusations of theft to be made about anybody.

Bella held her gaze, waiting for her to reply.

'OK.' Mel nodded. 'Let's draw a line and move forwards.'

'Good.'

Neither of them seemed prepared to go so far as an apology, and Mel was happy about that. The last thing she needed was for the situation to get mushy.

It was still unclear exactly why Felicia Kennedy had been so keen to get rid of Bella – obviously it was to do with Leo Kennedy-Edge, but it seemed likely whatever had been going on between Bella and Leo would end with the conclusion of the charter anyway, if not sooner. For the first time since they'd all boarded *Blue Sky*, Bella looked unhappy, and not simply about the jewellery. There was a heaviness to her movements that hadn't been there only a short time before, a resignation in her eyes Mel recognised. She hadn't been being purely bitchy that first night in the taverna – part of her had genuinely wanted to warn the newbie. Bella wouldn't be the first stewardess to fall for the charms of a guest, only to find themselves used and tossed away like a paper napkin at the end of a meal. Mel didn't necessarily go all in on "girl code" – she'd never been totally clear on what that even was – but warnings borne out of experience were for free.

In a way, this whole episode had offered her a clearer insight into Bella than she'd expected – the girl was tougher than she'd thought. Kudos for that. And now Mel was making definite inroads into her situation with J-P, maybe the other irritations could fade into the background. After all, you didn't have to like people to be able to work with them.

Chapter Twenty-Nine

With a surge of pride, Bella decided *Blue Sky* was looking immaculate by the time everyone was back on board. Which was more than could be said for the guests. Without exception they appeared exhausted. Tired and dusty from the shore visit, certainly – but it ran deeper than that. Still none the wiser about exactly how ill Felicia was, and fidgety about the itinerary of the remainder of the charter, Jean-Philippe had asked Bella to find out what was really going on. It was absolutely the last task she felt capable of achieving.

They might have settled on a truce, but the expression on Mel's face was crystal. She couldn't have made her reaction any clearer if she'd actually told Bella that being chief stewardess ran alongside being handed the most difficult jobs.

Despite everything, Leo seemed the best person to ask. She needed to consult a family member, but couldn't speak directly to Felicia, and by extension she didn't want to put Nikolai under any greater pressure. She caught up with Leo on the swimming platform. He'd swapped dusty clothes for a pair of swimming shorts, diving into the azure of the sea as soon as he returned. She took him a towel, and when he emerged from the water, he used it to rub at the back of his head as she asked about his aunt's health. His action with the towel was brusque, utterly different to his provocative behaviour of the preceding days. He wrapped the towel around his shoulders, holding it firmly against his chest. He hardly looked her in the eye, and she couldn't blame him. He must think her a complete bitch.

Bella hadn't been sure what she'd expected to be wrong with Felicia. There hadn't been any doubt in her mind that it was serious, but she'd expected a level of detachment from it – after all, she hardly knew the woman. Not personally, anyway. And Felicia had cast judgement on Bella without any clear provocation. Bella tried not to care, tried to remain distant from the information.

But the details were harder to absorb than she'd expected. On one level, Leo was talking about someone Bella had watched in films and on the TV ever since she'd been a little girl – someone for whom, it became clear, there would be no further series of *Murder in Mayfair*. No more film roles, maybe no more TV appearances of any kind. That hit Bella harder than she had been expecting. It was like having a premonition about one of those announcements played at the end of the nightly news – the latest celebrity death, with a quick rundown of a star's major roles, achievements, awards and a reminder of their legacy while a montage of their most beautiful images filled the screen.

But that wasn't the worst of it. Far worse was watching Leo's expression as he told her. The way he was visibly fighting back tears, all over again, and how much she wanted to wrap him up in a hug and have him cry openly and unashamedly, if that would make it any easier for him.

Instead, she stood at an awkward distance, and asked awkward questions, cursing herself at her lack of finesse when she said, 'How long does she have?'

'Months.' The word was strangled.

'Oh, God. Leo, I'm so sorry. We all are.' Fighting the image of Tobias and his off-hand remark about Felicia having broken a nail, she regrouped her thoughts. Maybe a practical question would help Leo regain his composure. 'And it goes without saying the captain is more than happy to accommodate whatever your aunt requires from the rest of this charter. We can stay here, and sail directly back to Monaco on Saturday, or we can stick to the rest of the plan – whatever she would like. Would you be able to find out?'

'Yes. Thank you.' Leo sighed, moving to push past her. Then he paused. 'She wants us to behave as if nothing's changed. But how is that even possible?'

'I don't know. Maybe she wants to pretend it isn't happening?'

A shake of his head. 'No, it's not that. I don't know. It's hard to explain, but she's expecting us to bounce back and have a wonderful day tomorrow to celebrate Nikolai's birthday. How can we – how am I supposed to do that? I don't understand how people seem to be able to pack away emotions at will, to suit a plan.'

Bella sucked in a breath as his gaze came to rest heavily on her. Her mouth ran dry as the arch in his brows suggested he wasn't purely referring to Felicia Kennedy.

'I'm sorry, Leo.'

'Yeah. So am I.' He rested his forearms on the guard rail and fixed his gaze out to sea.

'You'll get through this,' she said. 'And maybe she needs you to be stronger than she can be, right now. She needs you more than you realise.'

'I'm not as strong as people think.' His words were muted, his expression torture as he glanced a final time in her direction, eyes narrowed in what felt like pure accusation. She'd really hurt him; that much was patently clear. But there was no going back, no way she could undo any of it. She chose to ignore his expression.

'Yes, Leo. You are.'

Never before had Leo found so much confusion in one place. He'd been comprehensively rejected by this woman, rendered utterly insecure by the revelation of her true motives, and yet she continued to draw him to her. He supposed he was a moth to her flame – and had ended up in a similar way to the analogy. Severely injured moth.

What Bella didn't understand, and he would never be able to tell her, was how much of the strength she seemed to think he possessed had actually come from knowing her.

After he'd dressed, he headed for the sun deck, stopping off to collect some of his aunt's bottled water on the way. Felicia and Nikolai lay side by side on sun loungers, her hand resting gently on a sleeping Nikolai's shoulder. Leo wasn't surprised, his uncle must be completely exhausted.

At his arrival, Leo saw his aunt stiffen, her hand slipping from Nikolai's shoulder as she pushed herself up until she was seated. His aunt wanted him to be strong. Everyone thought he was strong. So be it.

And after all, he supposed he owed his aunt all the support he could muster. She'd always been the one who had his best interests at heart, unlike so many of the other people Leo had wasted his emotions on.

'Would you like some water?' He settled the bottle onto the padded area surrounding the hot tub and lined up a couple of glass tumblers.

'Thank you, that would be lovely.'

After he'd poured, and distributed, Leo said, 'I've been reading up on this water. I had no idea there was such a difference between spring water and water taken from melting icebergs. Fascinating.'

'Did you see the photos on the website?' Felicia said, her interest piqued by his. 'The chunks of iceberg that naturally calve from the main ice mass – I love that word, that image of a piece of ice calving. Then they collect them on a ship and allow them to melt before they bottle the water.'

'Amazing to think it froze way before any of the modern world existed, that it has no nitrates or pollutants in it at all.' He took a sip, then slid onto a lounger.

Leo wondered whether people actually lived their entire lives playing a role, just minus the cameras and adoring audience. Maybe his desire to find something meaningful – a deep connection with another human – maybe that was naïve. Perhaps that was the stuff of movies. Maybe real life was all about settling for something half-decent and not investing too heavily. That anything else was achieved through luck.

'It's ultra-low in minerals, too.'

The hitch in Felicia's voice caught Leo's attention; he watched as her animated expression crumpled, and tears welled.

'It's very healthy. It's supposed to be really good for the body,' Felicia continued, a few stray tears slipping from the corners of her eyes before she got herself under control. She laughed, but not from amusement. 'Ironic, don't you think? A bit wasted on me, now.'

'Never wasted,' Leo said. 'If you enjoy it, how can that ever be a waste?'

She nodded, gaining some of the strength back into her expression. 'You are so dear to me, Leo.' A frown flickered, and Leo waited, expecting her to say something further. But before Felicia had a chance to comment further, Jeremy crested the top step, taking everyone's attention with the volume of his puffing, the redness of his cheeks, the vibrancy of his flamingo-pink shirt. He flailed an arm in Felicia's direction, mobile clutched in his hand.

'Felicia. A word?' Jeremy glanced at the rest of them. 'In private?'

Felicia walked him to the far end of the deck, where they had a clear view out across the Tyrrhenian Sea. She allowed her eyes to adjust to which blue was the sea, which was the sky, allowing herself a momentary acknowledgement about how stunning the weather had been all week while she waited for Jeremy to speak. Her fingers tightened around the shiny chrome of the handrail, aware of its smoothness beneath her touch as she waited to find out if she'd finally gained a daughter.

Until this moment she hadn't realised how badly she wanted Jeremy to tell her Bella was her child. After the next few words, she would either have to wreck Leo's life – and potentially gain a daughter – or accept she would never know her child.

Jeremy was puffing so hard she missed his words when he finally did speak.

'For God's sake, Jeremy, take a breath – I didn't hear any of that.'

'It's not her, 'Licia. Bella isn't your daughter.' He waved his mobile at her, as if the slim piece of brushed steel and glass somehow constituted proof.

'What?' She'd heard him that time, but the words hadn't landed and her fingers slipped from the railing as she stumbled away from him.

Jeremy grabbed at her shoulder. 'Dear Lord. Don't fall again. Maybe you should sit down.'

Unable to understand how Bella couldn't be her daughter, Felicia batted his hand away. 'I'm perfectly fine, stop fussing. I don't understand how she isn't. She's the spitting image of me, you said so yourself. And her family circumstances – her birthday – how can that all be pure coincidence?'

'Because we're not living in an Agatha Christie Poirot novel. I told you, in real life coincidences happen all the time.' Jeremy beamed, clearly thrilled by the news. Then his expression clouded. 'Why are you frowning? I thought that's what you wanted – I thought, with Leo and her getting to be . . .' Swallowing, he failed to complete the sentence.

He was right: she should be happy – this was what she'd been praying for. At least, to start with. And for Leo's sake, she was pleased – of course she was. The thought of having to explain to her nephew that he'd fallen in love with someone so closely related to him – not to mention the fallout for the entire family from revealing *why* they were so closely related – had filled her with horror, and yet . . . At the same time, if Bella *had* been her child . . .

Felicia hadn't realised how large a part of her had wanted it to be Bella. How much of her was desperate to meet the child she'd never got to spend time with. How much she'd actually given up when she agreed to give her baby away. All gone. And now it seemed she'd never get any of it back, either.

Even if in the process she would have had to rip apart Leo's world, she would have found her child. Even if the revelation would have caused the decimation of plenty of other people's worlds . . . even with that thought, Felicia would have endured it all to have been able to call Bella hers.

Perhaps it was to do with her circumstances – perhaps it came with the knowledge that her time was limited. Maybe it was because Bella would have been the perfect daughter. A young woman any mother would be proud to stand beside.

And perhaps it was because Felicia finally understood herself to be inherently selfish – it had taken her long enough to work it out, but there was no way to glide around an iceberg of this magnitude. She was, and always had been, utterly egocentric.

But none of it mattered, anyway, because Bella wasn't hers.

Felicia gripped the handrail harder, steadying herself before she replied. 'You're absolutely right, Jeremy. This is wonderful news. Thank goodness for that.' It was possible she'd overplayed her reply, been too upbeat, made her smile too broad. 'Did you happen to find out my daughter's actual identity, then?'

His expression clouded further. 'You want to know who she is?'

'I think I do.' She'd come this far – if she couldn't have Bella, perhaps there was still time to find out where her real daughter was.

'Are you sure?'

'I think I need to know, Jeremy.'

God damn it, Jeremy thought. He'd assumed the reassurance that Bella was no relation would do the trick, would get the status back to quo and he could nudge the conversation towards reinstating the signing of the will, et cetera. With the emphasis on the et cetera portion of that statement. It might be wicked of him to still be concerned with his personal finances, but he would have to deal with the seven levels of hell at a later date. More pressing were the seven shades of shit that would likely get beaten out of him if he didn't get himself out from under his current debts. The thought of physical violence brought bile to the base of Jeremy's throat, but the threat had been unmistakable.

And now Felicia was going way off-piste with talk of finding her daughter. That knowledge was only a phone call away – his contact already had the information. If he relayed it to Felicia, though, would that prompt her to want to alter her will completely – away from Leo and in favour of this sudden, and incredibly fortunate, addition to the family? How quickly could he get the office to draft the new paperwork so he could print out a fresh set of documentation? It wasn't outside the realms of possibility to do it by close of business the following day, he supposed.

There was no way he wanted to fly back into Gatwick without the documents signed. Without something concrete to show to his creditors, to convince them he was only a whisker away from repaying them. They were the kind of people who might think it a good idea to meet him at arrivals. Who might decide there was no reason for him to go back to his flat, that he could find a dumpster in one of London's more squalid alleyways behind a fast-food joint or a Mandarin restaurant a more restful destination, if he came home empty-handed.

They were people who were at home in the shadows, but whose bosses were probably rich enough to own a fucking superyacht themselves.

This needed careful handling.

'It's just – I don't want you to rush into anything.' He sounded desperate. Not what he'd wanted to achieve.

'It's been twenty-four years, Jeremy.'

'No. I know. I didn't mean it like that. It's more that I think you need to consider how this will impact on the rest of your family, especially with your health—' He was making it worse; the expression on her face told him as much.

'I want to know who she is. I know it's too little, too late – but is wanting this so very bad?'

Shoulders sagging, he shook his head. 'No, it's not bad at all. I'll make the call.'

'Thank you, my dear friend.'

Her fingers rested gently against his forearm, her touch featherlight but too much for him to bear, as he pulled his arm away and fiddled with his phone. 'I do have a question, though.' She nodded for him to continue. 'Does this mean you might want to alter your will again?'

For a moment, Felicia looked completely wrong-footed. 'Do you know, I'd completely forgotten about that.'

Wasn't she the fortunate one – the documents in that stack continued to burn holes in his conscious thought. He could barely function without thinking about the repercussions of not getting them signed. 'It's just that, now everything is squared away with Leo, well – it makes sense to get things signed and sealed – don't you think?'

'Leo doesn't want my money, he said as much.'

'Yes, but that was when you were trying to warn him away from Bella. Nothing more than the words of a hot-headed young man with his blood up. All that can be forgotten now, can't it?' The desperate edge was back in his voice, nervous sweat pricking at his temples. Forcing himself to laugh, he added, 'After all, I'm the money man – the one who fixes all that stuff. That was the reason I was invited to join this charter, wasn't it?'

'Not the only reason, Jeremy.'

He barrelled straight over her words. 'And any further changes in favour of an extra heir would be easy enough to make at some point in the future, of course.'

'Do you think that was the only reason I wanted you here? Is that really what you think of me?'

'Well, I . . . er . . . I always assumed . . .'

'Have I really been that terrible at letting you know how much of a rock you have been in my life? No, not a rock – that's far too boring and unappealing. You're my most trusted ally, my oldest and dearest friend. My guardian angel.'

'Am I?'

The trouble with Felicia Kennedy was that she had always been able to corkscrew him around her little finger. In fact, she could twist him into whatever shape she wanted with nothing more than a glance, or the sound of her gentle bubbling laughter. As she bathed him in both, it was on the tip of his tongue to ask her. Straight out beg her for the money he needed. If he meant so much to her, surely she would be only too willing to give it to him? But the moment was fleeting, the weakness gone as soon as it had materialised, from them both. He didn't want her pity – and vice versa.

'Crazy man. Yes. Now – make your phone call and let's get on with it.'

'The will?'

'If it'll make you feel more valued, then yes. Whatever I need to sign, I'll do it today – Patti will witness it and Leo will simply have to give it all to charity if he still doesn't want it once I'm gone. It doesn't seem so important any longer. But I was actually referring to everything. Let's get on with the rest of this trip, the rest of our lives – everything.'

Swallowing his stabbing feelings of guilt, Jeremy nodded, left her standing at the prow of the boat and headed for his cabin, dialling as he walked.

Chapter Thirty

The final full day of the charter was Nikolai Bjerregaard's birthday, and Bella thought it brought with it a definite upturn in the spirits of the guests. The crew, too, she decided as she collected some final breakfast requests and radioed them through to Mel in the galley.

The itinerary for the day had changed, but even Jean-Philippe took the news in good spirits and came to the breakfast table for a chat. Bella couldn't help but smirk as the captain took a seat and Patti made some veiled reference to *Star Trek* to which Jean-Philippe again seemed utterly oblivious. As Bella filled one of the delicate coffee cups with the strong Italian blend Jean-Philippe favoured, leaving it black and sliding it in front of him, she couldn't help but listen in as he enthralled his guests with tales from the high seas. Whether the story about an enormous octopus and four inexperienced sailors was true or simply a fantastical yarn, it didn't matter – the captain may be all sorts of things, many of them went against Bella's sense of the ideal, but he certainly could charm the charter guests.

Instead of hiking to Mount Capanne, Nikolai had decided they would spend the day gently sailing the rest of Elba's beautiful coastline, reaching Portoferraio in time for their dinner reservation. Felicia made him promise he hadn't changed his mind on her behalf. Patti told her not to be so self-absorbed, that Nicki was now officially an old man and probably didn't want to embarrass himself by only managing to get halfway to the summit before he needed a sit-down.

Jeremy rested a hand on a leather document folder while he forked up scrambled eggs with the other. The documents inside had been signed by Felicia before the food had arrived, Jeremy taking care to shield the contents from casual view. Not that Bella cared what Felicia Kennedy was signing, but she did hope the balance had been restored in Leo's favour. Whatever lay in the folder must hold great importance to the lawyer too, Bella supposed, as he shifted and reached for his coffee, all the time with one hand proprietorially on the folder.

As she circled the table again, she made sure to give a wider berth as she passed behind Leo's chair. Another twenty-four hours and he would be gone. Another day of pretending her feelings towards him weren't real, that she'd egged him on for nothing more than a fictional bet between her and Tobias. Another day before she could allow herself to crumble completely.

Was the way Leo's back stiffened every time she walked past in her imagination? When he made a point of leaving the table just as she'd been about to ask him if he needed anything else, there was no way to interpret it except as a direct snub. Could she blame him? Not really.

With her final offers of coffee completed, Bella couldn't hold it together any longer. She slid the coffee pot onto a side table and shot from the room, heading for the quiet of the swimming platform, her mobile out of her pocket and Jay's number dialled before her feet hit the steps.

It was on the tip of Felicia's tongue to call Leo back to the breakfast table, to ask what was wrong – his departure had been that abrupt. He'd caught the edge of her chair on his way past and almost pulled it over backwards in his haste to get away.

He'd left most of his food untouched, his coffee cup half-full. A repeat of the beach lunch, but clearly not for the same reasons. This time Bella remained in the room, her expression tight and wary. Where was the broad smile? The bouncy, bubbly energy that had characterised Bella earlier in the week had gone, replaced by something very sombre. The girl looked immensely sad.

In the melee of Jeremy's revelations, in her discovery that Bella was absolutely no relation, Felicia had found herself absorbed by her own reaction to the information. She'd been processing her own thoughts, dealing with the fact that the disappointment of not finding her daughter was tempered by relief. Tempered by the knowledge that although she would like to know who her daughter was, there was now no need to continue to try and destroy the ties forming between her nephew and Bella.

But something was awry. And when Bella dumped the coffee pot and abruptly left the room, Felicia followed her. Found her on the swimming platform, mobile pressed against an ear as she stared out to sea. Oblivious to Felicia's presence, Bella was talking to her brother – Jay. The breeze whipped away some of Bella's words, but what Felicia heard had her pressing fingers against her lips.

'He told me he'd turned down an entire inheritance . . . for me . . .'

Bella's concentration on the sea, and on her conversation, was total. Felicia remained unnoticed as the girl continued, and the full extent of Felicia's meddling became clear.

'His aunt doesn't think I'm good enough for him. Maybe she's right. He said he didn't care about any of that. But Jay, I couldn't let him throw it all away . . .'

Felicia settled herself on the top step. What had Bella done?

'So, I lied to him. I told him I don't care about him, that it was all a bet. That the chef and I wanted to see which one of us could seduce a charter guest first . . .'

Felicia ran her fingers into her hair, lacing them behind her head. Bella began to cry as she listened to whatever her brother said, her voice cracking as she replied, 'No. I won't. Because this is his whole future, Jay. How can I ask him to give it all up for me?'

The conversation continued, circling around the same carcass like a vulture – and it was all Felicia's fault. When Bella finally ended the call, she stayed put, rubbing at her eyes and sniffing hard in an attempt to regain her composure. Felicia recognised the process, but knew it would take more than that to banish the aftermath of those kinds of tears.

'You'll need to put a cold compress on your eyes,' she said, taking the rest of the steps.

Bella turned, shock and confusion spreading their way in equal measure across her features. Both were replaced within seconds by suspicion, her eyes hooding at Felicia's intrusion.

'Bella, we need to talk.'

Portoferraio was beautiful. Rising from the teal of the water in the horseshoe harbour, the town crowded one colour next to another, buildings washed in bold pinks and yellows, the contrasting greens of their shutters giving a hint at the hidden flora within its streets. Long flights of shallow stone steps were dressed with potted olive and lemon trees at every level, growing in enormous urns which hinted at the town's original heritage – its first settlers predating the Romans, the first people to colonise this amazing place dating all the way back to the ancient Greeks.

Figs and vines grew against crumbling walls, the air heavy with the scent of the sea and the distinctive purple bougainvillea that seemed to cling to every available inch of trellis.

Or perhaps it all looked so beautiful because, for the first time in a very long time, Felicia felt an overwhelming sense of peace.

The charter hadn't gone according to plan, not in the slightest, and even though she wasn't used to things going off plan – especially when the plan was hers – somehow the unexpected spontaneity had brought with it a lifting of expectations, particularly her expectation of herself. The fact that her body hadn't conformed with her wish to keep her illness hidden had forced her to face so many things – properly face them, rather than trying to manipulate her way around them.

And instead of ending this holiday with the black hole of revelation still to come, instead of pretending to enjoy it – because she now recognised that would have been all she would have been able to get out of it – she was free to truly enjoy the rest of it. The rest of everything.

It was possible the rest of everything may even involve meeting her real daughter. The jolt of surprise Felicia felt when Jeremy gave her the name took her unawares. She was grateful for the supportive way he cupped her elbow as he explained that Flora McKinley was a makeup artist, working for the same company as the team contracted to work on MIM. His wry comment about the unexpected coincidence made her smile, then laugh – and finally cry. It would be extremely easy for Felicia to engineer a scenario in which she could meet Flora. If Felicia decided she wanted to. Part of her itched to meet her child; in time, she had no doubt she would do just that. But a large part of her had wanted so badly for it to be Bella, and that part didn't want to relinquish its hold, at least not yet.

She'd done her best to apologise to Bella earlier in the day, to explain that the mix-up with the will had been entirely her doing, and she had been wrong. Totally wrong to try to manipulate her nephew in that way – and that she'd told Leo as much too, begged for his forgiveness. That she thought Bella should tell Leo the truth about her emotions, and they both absolutely had Felicia's blessing – if they cared in the slightest about that, which she understood she didn't deserve, not after what she'd done.

She'd kept quiet about how badly and why she wanted to get to know Bella, how deeply she had felt the tug. Hoped instead she might still have time enough to see her nephew settled and happy, get to know Bella in that way instead.

Understandably, Bella remained cautious, wanted to know what she'd done to set Felicia against her in the first place. And Felicia had fallen back into her old ways. She'd lied; as far as Felicia was concerned this was simply a little white lie, convinced herself this one had less to do with concealment; instead it was one told purely to protect the recipient, or the teller, or in this case, both of them. A lie born out of love. She told Bella it was an effect of the tumour, that she sometimes became confused and imagined things.

Bella seemed placated, skating too close to sympathy until

A Summer on the Riviera

Felicia changed the conversation up and away from her health. It was only later Felicia wondered how long it would be before she really did begin to become confused by things, began to see things that weren't really there.

Not this evening, she prayed.

Because Felicia had decided to manipulate things one more time. She'd spoken with Captain Kirque, asked for Bella to accompany the charter guests into Portoferraio. In case they required anything during dinner. He had agreed without question, no doubt still desperate to curry favour with the person who would be leaving the charter tip, doing his best to make amends for any perceived issues. Ideally, Felicia would have liked Bella to have been able to dress up for the evening, because she had plans for the girl. And the plans had nothing to do with fetching and carrying for Felicia and her guests.

As it was, Bella was wearing her uniform, the turquoise of the shirt over her little beige skirt accentuating the rich mahogany of her hair, and the sheer length of her legs. Watching Bella taking the lead up the steps in front of her, all long legs and easy, athletic youth, Felicia huffed a laugh. She should have known there was no way Bella could have been her daughter, because Felicia would have killed for legs like that.

As she gazed at Bella, a waft of smoke momentarily obscured her view.

'This is possibly the best cigar I have ever smoked.' Nicki took a couple more puffs from it before another cloud of smoke enveloped his face.

'I thought you were planning to keep that until after dinner?'

'I brought more than one. Leo chose well; it is excellent. A very fine birthday gift.'

'I'm glad. What do you plan to eat tonight?'

The conversation that followed, as they discussed the pros and cons of various menu choices, was utterly mundane; but more enjoyable than any she had had in a very long time.

Chapter Thirty-One

Bella felt a rush of confusion when they arrived at the restaurant. Expecting to be sidelined for the duration of the meal, maybe given a seat off to one side of the main dining area, or left to wander the streets, it took her a moment to process what was happening when Felicia led her to a small table, set for two and with an uninterrupted view of the bay. A prime position. She tentatively took a seat, nearly rising to her feet again when Felicia returned, this time with Leo.

'I think the two of you have a lot to discuss,' Felicia said, as she bundled Leo into the chair opposite Bella and fixed them both with an intense stare. 'Make it count.'

Leo looked conflicted, his gaze sliding onto Bella and away again as quickly. For her part, Bella's fingers trembled so badly as she tried to take a sip of water that she nearly spilt the glassful all over the tablecloth.

The scent from the flowers weighing down the trellis behind her was impossible to ignore, filling the night air with a perfume all its own. Darkness was a while off, but the flames from a cluster of candles in a large hurricane lamp danced on the centre of the table, with more of the purple flowers laced around its base.

'I'm sorry, Leo.' One of them had to say something, and Bella decided it might as well be her.

'It's me who should apologise.' Leo sounded as awkward as she felt. He sat ramrod straight in his chair, menu untouched in front of him. 'It was totally inappropriate of me to mention anything about my aunt's will.' His eyebrows arched and he fixed his gaze on her. 'Or perhaps it was just as well I did. At least it got the truth out in the open. My aunt tells me you have something to say about that, but I think you made your position pretty clear.'

'It wasn't the truth, though.'

'What do you mean? Which bit wasn't true? The part about seducing a charter guest? Or placing bets on us? Or the way you pretended to feel about me?'

'No, that part was always real. My feelings for you were real. Are real.'

Leo's brows knotted together. 'I don't understand, then.'

'When you told me you'd chosen me over your inheritance? Leo, I freaked. We'd only known one another a few days, and to think you were willing to risk an entire lifetime's worth of family ties and history for me. I couldn't let you do it. Couldn't allow you to gamble with your future like that.'

'It was my decision to make, though, Bella. And it wasn't a difficult one.' He paused, then a hint of a smile crossed his lips. 'I suppose that either makes me brave, or very stupid. Maybe both. But seriously, I'd never been so sure about anything. I couldn't understand why my aunt had suddenly taken against you like that, but I didn't care.'

'I didn't know what to do. To think that for some reason Felicia hated me enough to do that to you. I panicked, I suppose.' There was more to it, she would need to be brave enough to tell him everything, but for now Bella was enjoying the thawing in his expression. He flicked open the gold-embossed wine list, scanning the range on offer.

'And the bottom fell out of my boat when you said all those things. I don't think you realise how you destroyed me with those few words.' He shook his head, his gaze remaining on the menu.

'I'm so sorry.'

'I think I need a drink,' he said, glancing at her. 'How about some Frascati? Do you like white wine?'

'And that's exactly why I couldn't let you do it.' She watched him pause, then set down the menu.

'What do you mean?'

'We hardly know one another. You don't even know what I like to drink.'

'I know you like hamsters.' His eyes sparkled as he tried for levity. 'And the name Edgar. Also Haribo. And hippos . . .'

'I'm being serious.'

A moment passed, then he said, 'I know how you make me feel every time I look at you. Surely that's more important than knowing your favourite wine? All that other stuff comes over time, doesn't it?' He studied her, his gaze intense.

'But we haven't *got* time, Leo.'

'Fuck it. I wasn't going to do this, but I'll never forgive myself if I don't tell you exactly how I feel.' Even though none of the other tables were within earshot, he lowered his voice and reached across, stretching out a hand towards hers. 'It may have only been a few days, but it's been long enough for me to know this much. I'm like a moth to your flame, Bella – and it's a fucking intense flame. I should have told you earlier, made you understand. You undo me. I'm ripped apart by the way you sound, by your smile and the smell of your hair. How your skin tastes. How you tilt your head when you're not sure about something. Every time you look at me, all I can think is how much I want to—'

'Are you ready to order some wine, *signore*?'

He swore again at the intrusion, this time under his breath. Recovering his composure, he ordered a bottle of Frascati from the sommelier, nodding and smiling as the waiter praised his choice and set about removing the red wine glasses and wine list from the table. With Leo's attention elsewhere, Bella took the opportunity to thread her fingers through his, her grip strengthening as he swung back to focus on her.

'I feel all that too, Leo. I've never wanted anyone like I wanted you.'

His fingers meshed with hers more tightly, his thumb finding the soft skin of her inner wrist and gently circling as he stared at her. His simple action was enough to create an inferno of heat in her belly. Momentarily, she considered how messed up the metaphor would become if they both thought of themselves as the moth and the other as the flame. There would be a lot of fire, a lot of singed wings.

He paused. 'You said "wanted", past tense. Have I blown it?'

They'd been through a rollercoaster of emotions, and maybe at times she'd struggled to hang on to her ability to think straight, but no – he hadn't blown it. Instead, it was possible she had. 'No. But—'

'We're good then? Back on track?' He stared at her with an intensity it was impossible to escape – the edges of Bella's wings began to melt in the heat from his gaze, and she wondered if he felt the same as she held his eye.

It took all her strength to shake her head. To pull her hand away from his.

'No. There's something else you need to know.'

Sucking in a breath, she did her best to ignore the fresh confusion on his face, and the knot tangling itself in her stomach. Time to be honest. Completely honest.

'The captain made me choose.'

'Captain Kirque made you choose what?'

'Between you and my job. After your accident with the jet ski, he told me I was being utterly unprofessional, and I needed to decide which was more important. A holiday romance, or my career. And he was right to ask, because my actions were completely crazy that day.'

'I didn't think you were being crazy; I thought you were awesome.'

He reached for her hand again, but she withdrew it onto her lap. She needed to see this through, needed to be completely transparent. She couldn't bear to deceive him again.

'Leo, I chose my job. I was going to try to explain when you told Captain Kirque you wanted to meet me in the salon. I was going to tell you we couldn't carry on with anything other than a purely professional relationship for the remainder of the charter. I chose my job over you. I think I owe it to you to tell you; I want to be completely honest.'

'He made you choose? What a bastard.' Leo was focusing on the wrong aspect of what she'd just told him.

'No, you're missing the point. I chose my career. Over you. I need you to understand.'

'Oh, I understand all right. Older male employer exerts control over new member of staff by giving her an ultimatum. Threatening her career. I won't even get into the implications of sexual politics.' He shook his head. 'I can't tell you the number of times we've lost young female grooms from the polo yard because my father thinks poorly hidden sex references are still an acceptable form of humour, then gets all uppity when he causes offence.' Leo paused for the arrival of the wine, tasted it and fiddled with his cutlery until the waiter had filled their glasses and moved away again. 'What I'm trying to say is that in my opinion it was completely unacceptable of him to expect you to choose. He shouldn't have asked you to do that.'

'There are standards of professionalism, though.'

'Yes, OK, I suppose there are. But one error of judgement is enough to have you lose your career? That's beyond tough.'

'He told me the chances were you'd walk away at the end of the week and I'd never hear from you again anyway, so why on earth would I want to risk my career?' Spots of heat pricked at her cheeks, but she'd come this far with being honest, needed to get it all out into the open.

'And you considered that as a possibility? That I would walk away – after everything I said?'

He sounded hurt, but she nodded, shrugging at the same time. Mel's advice floated to the forefront of her mind, that very first night in Camogli – one of the second stew's sayings bubbling to the surface. 'I didn't want to consider it, but it's not like this is my first rodeo. I'm not an idiot. I know that what people – what men – say, and what they mean isn't always the same thing.'

'Ouch.'

'Yeah. Well, anyway, I was doing a great job at ignoring all that. I was going to tell you what the captain had said, to try to work out a way to get through the rest of the charter on a professional level, then meet up afterwards. But then you told me about the inheritance, and my plans went out of the window. It was all too intense.'

He drew a long breath, then nodded. 'I'm so sorry. I wish to God I'd kept my mouth shut about that.'

'No. I'm glad you didn't – because it crystallised my feelings for you, even if it meant I did the opposite to what I wanted to do.'

'Which was what? What did you want to do?'

She reached for her glass rather than answering his question. 'I've tried a few white wines before, but I've never had Frascati. Will it be a memorable first?'

Did he understand what she meant? It seemed likely, if the expression spreading across his face was about anything other than the glass of wine he picked up, clinking it against hers. 'I think so,' he said. 'Because, even if I say so myself, it really is very good.'

With an enormous sharing platter of seafood between them, Leo was beginning to relax. A couple of glasses of wine was helping, but his level of contentment had only one important source, and she was sitting opposite.

She'd been impressively candid with him. There had been no need for Bella to even mention the captain's ultimatum. The fact that she had done so was doing strange things to Leo's chest, making it constrict whenever he looked at her. Put that alongside the reason why she'd made up those outrageous lies about her bet with the chef – which, by the way, he was still thanking all available gods had been nothing but lies – and Leo knew he had to make firm plans with Bella. This was not someone he could allow to slip between his fingers.

'Tell me again, when's your birthday?'

'It's the fifth of September.' She sipped her wine, then said, 'Not that it matters all that much.'

'What do you mean? Of course your birthday matters.'

'It's not my actual birthday, though. I don't know my real date of birth. That was just the day they found me.'

'What do you mean "the day they found you"?' He slid his glass onto the table as he studied her.

'Such a cliché, but they found me wrapped in a blanket and left in a satchel bag in a café. Nobody noticed I was there until I started crying, apparently. Then they took me to the hospital.'

'I had no idea.'

'Why would you?'

'And they never found your real mum?'

'Oh yes. The police found her from the CCTV in the street outside, they saw her going in with the bag, then leaving a few minutes later without it.'

'So, how come you were adopted?'

Bella shrugged. 'She was a kid herself; I was an accident and she flatly refused to talk about me, or my dad – wouldn't even tell the hospital when I was born. They never told me much more than that. I could have found out, I suppose, but somehow . . .' She paused, staring off into the middle distance. To take the pressure off her, Leo topped up the water glasses, then set about dissecting a lobster claw. Eventually she carried on. 'I suppose as I got older, I began to understand her choices a bit better. I was angry, of course. And frustrated. I was humiliated at not being wanted. I worked my way through a rainbow of emotions. But in the end, I've always imagined that doing what she did meant she got to have a life of her own. Finish school, get a decent job, all that stuff. I'm one of the lucky ones; I love my family, and I suppose I hoped that she ended up being lucky, too.'

Leo nodded, huffing a breath at how calmly she spoke. He wasn't so sure he would have dealt with that kind of rejection so well. 'In that case, I have an idea. How about I make the entire first week in September your birthday, just to be sure we cover the actual day.'

'Now you're being ridiculous – but . . . OK, I suppose. If

A Summer on the Riviera

you like.' The crinkle in the edges of Bella's eyes gave Leo a fair idea she liked the suggestion, even if she was being circumspect in her words.

'I'm only getting started with being ridiculous. Because I was thinking . . .'

'Dangerous . . .'

He hoped he never got used to her sassy ways. Dropping a piece of lobster shell onto the graveyard plate and wiping his fingers, he took a deep breath. 'Didn't you say you wanted to visit the Amazon rainforest?'

The way her forehead crinkled when she was taken off guard was enough to have Leo desperate to reach out and take her hand, but his were still sticky from the food so he did his best to keep himself under control and instead concentrated on the conversation.

'Yes, I'd love to visit the rainforest one day. Why?'

'How would you feel about taking a trip after your season on *Blue Sky* is finished? I was thinking we could combine the Amazon with my horse shopping in Argentina.'

'But that's in Brazil, not Argentina.'

'So? We could do both. Will you think about it? We could see what this might become, if we give ourselves more time. Just the two of us.'

'You want to go to Brazil with me?'

'I'd go anywhere with you, Bella. That's what I'm trying to say. And I can't think of a better way of being able to spend time with you than on a proper adventure.' The fact that he would need to abandon the end of the competitive polo season, probably cancel his winter tour in the States in order to make the dates work, and the accompanying negative reaction that would bring from his father – all that paled into insignificance when the opportunity to spend unfiltered time with Bella beckoned.

'This evening is too much. I'm not sure . . .' She began to shake her head.

Had he pushed too hard, been too intense? Had he messed

it up again? It suddenly occurred to Leo that he desperately wanted to reach a point at which he'd understand her reactions, a place where they worked on instincts, rather than trial and error.

'We could have a week in Monaco first – you'll probably need time to unwind after a full season on board the yacht. It'll be the perfect opportunity to have someone look after you for a change. Then, if you still want to . . .' Leo was backtracking, revising the idea into something simpler, something less full-on, when Bella's entire face lit up, the glow from the candlelight dancing in her eyes as she leaned forward.

'Could we have a guided tour and actually go into the forest?'

'I don't see why not.'

'Stay in a treehouse?'

'Wait, what?'

'Didn't I mention that? I've always wanted to stay in a treehouse.'

Leo pretended to make a list. 'Guided tour of the rainforest. Tick. Treehouse. Tick.'

She laughed, then the amusement slid away, replaced by a fierce intensity. 'I'm paying my way, though. My flights, the accommodation. All that stuff. OK?'

'If you like. Can I buy you a birthday gift, though?'

'I suppose so.' She thought for a moment, then added, 'What about a boat trip up the Amazon?'

'Another boat?' he groaned. 'Are you completely nuts?'

'Oh my God – I'd almost forgotten.' Pinging her wristband, she added, 'We'll be fine with these, though. Surely?'

'We'll make it work,' he said, grinning.

Bumping fingers against Felicia's hand, Patti gestured to the table where Bella and Leo were deep in conversation.

'What's going on with those two?' Patti said.

'I'm hoping my nephew is about to make an excellent choice.'

'I think they make a great couple.' Patti settled back in her chair, her smile faltering for a moment as she glanced at Hannah, but long enough for Felicia to notice.

'You will allow her to be happy one day, won't you?'

Patti sighed. 'It's never been my intention to stop her from being happy. And it's not like she's worried about what I think – she's always done her own thing.'

'Because of you or despite you?'

Patti's eyes narrowed. 'That's low, Felicia. Even for you. It took everything I had to rebuild my life after Cliff left. You know what all that did to me.'

Felicia hadn't thought about Cliff for years. To be honest, she barely knew Patti's husband, didn't like what she *did* know about his duplicitous nature, and had only met him a handful of strained times before he'd finally been honest with Patti, confessing that he was leaving her for his long-term boyfriend. It went some way towards explaining Patti's complicated relationship with her daughter's sexuality, but while it might be a reason for her to struggle with Hannah's reality, it wasn't an excuse for treating her daughter badly. And Felicia had learned more this week about manipulation and its consequences than she'd been prepared for.

'What he did to you was unforgiveable.' Felicia conceded that point. 'But it's hardly Hannah's fault, is it?'

'And what on earth would you know about dealing with a daughter?'

Not as much as she should – or could have – known. That much was true, Felicia thought. But she was unruffled by Patti's snippy reply. It was appreciated, actually, a step towards the way their relationship had always been. Either scratching one another's backs or doing their best to scratch one another's eyes out.

Across the table, Hannah scrabbled in her bag, pulling out a mobile phone, the ring tone barely audible above the chatter from the insects gathering in the dusk. A glance at her mother, a brief frown, and Felicia pieced together the caller must likely be Hannah's girlfriend. Shoving her napkin on the table, Hannah slipped from the table, answering the call as she went.

'Play nice, Patti,' Felicia said, cradling her glass of wine in one hand. 'You have no idea how lucky you are to have her.'

Patti allowed a long-held sigh to escape her lips, then grinned. 'Much as it irks me to say it, you might be right. Just this once, mind you. Don't go getting any funny ideas.'

As Felicia returned the smile, she felt Patti's hand link its way into hers, and squeeze.

Chapter Thirty-Two

Pushing his plate to one side, Leo emptied his glass of wine in a single mouthful and reached for her hand.

'Would you like dessert, or shall we take a walk around the town?'

'I would say let's check the menu for *panna cotta*, but you'll be seeing the equine one soon, which will probably be better, so that joke might fall a bit flat.'

He appreciated the sentiment, her reference to his horse. 'Plus, it might be difficult to outdo your yacht chef in the actual *panna cotta* dessert department. A walk instead, then?'

'Sure.'

After a brief word with Nicki, assuring him they'd be back in time for coffee, or failing that the tender back to the yacht, Leo retook Bella's hand and they slipped away from the restaurant. Heading up more of the wide steps that seemed so prevalent in Portoferraio, they walked until the pathway was deserted and the town fanned out below them, the twinkling lights from the harbour and the inky blue of the sea beyond making for an incredible view.

And all the time, Leo struggled with what to say. The evening had been going so well, but now time was rapidly running out.

'Thank you for this evening.' Bella broke the awkward silence. 'It's been wonderful.'

'Has it?' He shifted to stare at her. 'Don't bullshit me now.'

'OK. No. You're right, tonight started out awkward as hell.' Bella ran a hand through her hair, looking past him at the view. It felt like hours but was only moments until she fixed her attention back onto him. 'But I'm so very glad we got to sort everything out.'

'I want the rest of this evening to be perfect.' He couldn't stop himself frowning, his free hand balling in a fist of frustration.

'Perfection is overrated,' she said. 'Anyway, it's not over yet.'

Leo glanced at his watch. It was gone half-ten, the evening was all but finished and once they returned to *Blue Sky*, they would have precious little time left together.

'It's almost over, though.'

'Don't be so defeatist,' she said. 'There are plenty of ways to make it last longer.'

'What do you mean?'

'What do you think I mean? We've got all night, if we want it.' The hitch in her eyebrow left him under no illusion as to what she meant; he'd been so determined not to allow himself down that path, to refuse to allow this to become casual, nothing more than the brief intensity of a passing fling, but as she inched closer to him, Leo found it increasingly difficult to hang on to any thoughts, let alone logical ones.

Bella didn't let him speak, didn't give him time to react to what she'd implied. The closer to Leo she got, the more her attempts at logic were evaporating, quicker than water on a hot desert rock. Her step forwards, mirrored by his, bridged the gap between them, hips bumping together leaving no room for pause, no need to check what the other was expecting next. They clashed together, arms wrapping and bodies folding together, lips parting and teeth nipping, tongues searching.

For a moment, Bella thought she could hear the roaring of a motor. In the seconds it took her to realise the noise rumbled through his chest, low in his throat like a growl, full of desire, she almost lost herself to the sudden heat building inside as he pushed her against the rough wall, pressing himself so hard against her it felt as though he was trying to force her into the stones. The palm of his hand etched a path down her ribcage, tugging at the edge of her blouse.

'I've done this with you in every room on the yacht,' she

said, her fingers searching for the skin beneath his shirt. 'In my mind, at least.'

'I've done a lot more than this,' he replied, his voice low and growly, his teeth nipping at the lobe of her ear. 'My imagination seems to have no bounds.'

'Tell me more . . .'

His laugh was like a blast of hot air against her neck, which she had tipped to allow him greater access. 'It always starts the same.'

'With a massive argument and an expensive meal?'

The gruffness of his laugh was swallowed as he reclaimed her mouth, speaking into her. 'If you want . . .'

'Then what?' She rocked her hips against his, wrapping herself even tighter against him.

'Then I do this . . .'

She fought to control her breathing as his fingers encircled her breasts, thumbs rubbing against her nipples, taut and catching in exquisite discomfort against the fabric of her underwear. Their hips crushed together, the stiffness of his erection pressing hard against her belly as their bodies locked against one another.

'Does your imagination have *me* doing anything?' Her words were nothing more than puffs of breathless air, but there was no mistaking his reaction as he cupped her face with teasing fingers.

'Whatever and whenever you like. I'm very open to suggestions.'

'In that case, you could imagine I might do this . . .' Slipping her hands from his back, down past his waistband, she pulled at the backs of his buttocks, where the curve of the muscles became the tops of his thighs. Tugging him towards her, she ran her fingers as far into the curve as she could reach, tilting him and encouraging him to move, to rock slowly up against her again, until there was no mistaking the friction as his erection pushed between them.

'Oh, my imagination likes that.' His words were more of a groan, rushing on an outward breath. 'Very much. And then we could imagine doing this . . .'

His hands dropped abruptly from her face, his movements becoming less measured, more desperate as he felt for the hem of her short khaki skirt and eased it up, taking hold of the backs of her thighs and mirroring her actions with his, the very tips of his fingers reaching and massaging against the soft nakedness of her legs, teasing at the elastic of her underwear, feeling beneath until he was cupping the skin of her buttocks. It was becoming difficult to remain upright, her knees jelly and desperate to open for his touch and he sensed her desperation, heard the whimper that escaped her lips. He wrapped one arm around her back, holding her tight, and she slotted her arms around his neck to stabilise herself.

'This is easily my best imagining to date,' he said, their mouths open against one another, their words and whimpers and growls feeding directly into the other, senses overwhelmed by proximity.

'Mine too.' If it wasn't for the fabric between them – and the fact anyone could walk past – he could be inside her, right now, and she wanted it – wanted him so badly it was scattering any remaining semblance of rational thought.

'God, I want you so badly, Bella.' His fingers were inside her underwear, running backwards and forwards, across and into the very centre of her, and she was liquid under his touch. 'I can't stop.'

'Don't stop.'

Their words were simultaneous, both heavy with desperation. She pressed her mouth against his neck and into the fabric of his shirt, telling him not to stop, never stop, that she wanted to do this for the rest of eternity. That they were only getting started, and she wanted him, needed to feel him, all of him. Needed to do this properly. He was bringing her close to the edge, close enough for the pinpricks of her explosion to build, the bursts of colour beginning to unfurl.

But then his fingers slowed, the wild abandonment in his expression softening, then slipping away. 'No. Not like this.'

'Why?' Confusion surfaced in her mind as his brow furrowed, and his touch slowed further. 'I want you, Leo.'

'And I want you, more than ever. But not like this.' He shook his head. 'I meant what I said about getting to know you. I promised myself.'

'Promised yourself what?' The heavy scent of desire intermingled with the sound of their heavy breathing, her ears ringing from the pounding of her heart.

'That when we do this, we do it properly. Away from here.' Smoothing her skirt down, he stayed pressed against her, the heat from his body and his tantalising proximity frustrating her.

Bella unfurled her arms from his neck, resting them against his chest, instead. 'I don't understand.'

'Much as I want you right now – much as I'd like nothing, and I mean nothing, more than to take you to my cabin and lock us inside for the remainder of this trip – I need you to understand that I don't care what your captain, or anybody else believes about me, or what they think is going on between us. That contrary to popular belief, this is way bigger than a week on *Blue Sky*. It is for me, anyway. And this is my way of proving that to you. To myself, too. Do you see what I mean?'

Bella's brain was scrambled, all over again, and the unexpected turn in conversation was only serving to confuse her further. 'You want to prove how much this means to you by pushing me away?'

'No. The last thing I want is to push you away.' He ran a hand across his forehead, the frustration clear on his face.

Sliding her hands up to cup his face, she paused, waiting for him to settle and look at her. Really look at her. 'What about what I want?' She spoke quietly, with a calmness in direct contrast to the fierce fizzing from every nerve ending she possessed. 'What about what I want. Right now. What about that?'

He shook his head. 'No. You said it yourself. The captain . . .'

'He need never know. I'm not about to tell him. Are you?'

They stumbled their way back to the restaurant, where the remnants of a gateau stood on the table, sparklers and candles abandoned alongside crumbs and splodges of cream. Bella bit her lip when she realised Leo had missed the celebrations, but Nikolai welcomed them back with a broad smile and the offer of cake. Once they'd washed the delicious chocolate orange gateau down with some sharp black coffee and the meal was finished, the group gathered their belongings.

As they headed down to the jetty and Nikolai set light to another of his cigars while they waited for the tender to collect them, Leo was convinced the others could hear the thud of his racing heart, felt sure his – their – intentions must be obvious to anyone giving them more than a passing glance. He didn't release his hold on Bella's hand once during the return trip, as if letting go might cause her to vanish. He was going to have to let her go soon enough; there was no way he was prepared to do so tonight.

At the door to his cabin, she pressed herself against him, their limbs entwined in an even more complicated pattern than their mouths.

Drawing back far enough to be able to whisper in her ear, he said, 'Are you sure?'

'Very.'

As he closed, then locked the cabin door behind them, and their fingers began to search for buttons and their breathing became shallow as words turned into thoughts, when eventually their imaginations became sensations and actions and the heat of explosions, he fleetingly thought it again. Was this going to ruin everything?

Oh so early the following morning, Bella inched her way from Leo's embrace and slipped from his bed. She needed to get back to her cabin before anyone else stirred. Pulling one of his T-shirts over her underwear, she balled the rest of her clothes and did her best to open the cabin door noiselessly.

In the doorway, she took a last look at him. She had to fight the urge to slip back between the sheets, cuddle up with him and pretend nothing else existed. He was impossibly relaxed, and somehow the vulnerability of sleep made him even more attractive. The bruising from his encounter with the jet ski was visible on one shoulder, his arms resting across the space she'd inhabited only moments earlier.

Bella needed to pretend this hadn't happened. This morning she could understand why he'd wanted to wait, why he had been prepared to hold back until they were away from the yacht. She felt guilty here, even though there was nothing to be awkward about. It was as though she had taken something the previous night that wasn't hers to have.

Shaking her head, she pulled his door closed and gently released the handle. She didn't want to feel like she needed to pretend it hadn't happened – the opposite was true. She wanted to shout to the world about him.

Moving soundlessly through the ship, she paused when she thought she heard soft footfalls coming towards her. A quick check of her watch revealed it was before five; changeover on the bridge between the night watch and the member of the deck crew on early duty wasn't for another hour. God forbid the captain was on the prowl at this hour.

Her confusion magnified at the top of the stairs to the crew quarters when Mel padded from the direction of the captain's cabin, similarly dishevelled in her attire and wearing an expression Bella recognised – probably the same as her own: an expression of surprise melting into embarrassed confusion. Pushing hair away from her eyes, Mel halted mid-step and raked her gaze across her, taking in the oversized T-shirt, the bundled clothes and sandals in one hand, the guilt-ridden expression. Her lips twisted in a half-smile.

'Was he good?' Then, shaking her head at Bella's attempts to formulate a sentence without resembling a guppy fish, she added, 'Don't tell me – I genuinely don't want to know.'

'I could ask you the same question.' It was a gamble – there *could* have been another reason why Mel was heading away from Jean-Philippe's cabin at five in the morning with her polo shirt on inside out – but Bella was buggered if she could think of anything.

'But you won't. Not if you want to keep this *entre nous*. As you might now understand, I have the captain's ear. In fact, I have a lot more than that, so bear that in mind.'

'Well, like you said, Leo will probably be gone tomorrow, and there's a good chance I'll never see him again. Whereas it seems Jean-Philippe's going to be making you sneak around all season. Looks like we're both someone's guilty pleasure, doesn't it?'

The arch in Mel's eyebrows was as much of a reply as Bella was going to get; that much was clear as Mel swept past her, and headed for the crew quarters.

Bella sighed, then followed.

A heaviness followed Bella around all morning. It was reminiscent of the final day of a great holiday, that moment when everyone realised all that was left was to pack up and go home. Guests and crew alike were subdued as the yacht headed for its final destination and disembarkation.

Instead of easing her feelings for Leo, all she seemed to have managed was to complicate them. He was awkward around her this morning, the frown darkening his brow and his monosyllabic attempts at conversation compounding her confusion.

Luckily there was plenty to be done, a multitude of ways to avoid him. By the time Jean-Philippe called for the crew to change into their whites, ready for docking and the departure of the guests – and despite everything Leo had said – she'd convinced herself there could only be one conclusion to reach. Leo would wish her a polite farewell and walk away.

As she buttoned her shirt, dressing in the limited space of the cabin while Mel used the bathroom, she almost felt prepared for it.

'There are worse things,' Mel said, pushing the sliding bathroom door to one side. She looked immaculate, without a hair out of place – Bella supposed they both appeared utterly different from when they'd bumped into one another in the early hours of the morning. 'If it isn't him, there's plenty of time to find the right one – and you'll know when it's right.'

'Like you and Jean-Philippe?' Bella caught up her hair into a ponytail, brushing it through and checking it in the mirror before Mel replied.

'Right doesn't always mean easy, or perfect.' Mel straightened her epaulets and nodded at her own reflection. 'Are you fit?'

'Yep.'

'I'm here for you. If he doesn't measure up, I mean.'

'Really?'

The arch in Mel's eyebrows was back. 'Take it or leave it.'

'I'll take it. Thanks, Mel.'

Standing in the line-up of crew as they said their goodbyes to the guests was far harder than Bella had been expecting. If she was going to be like this about every charter, she'd be an emotional husk by the end of the season.

Jeremy and Hannah had already shaken her by the hand – Hannah's grip by far the firmer of the two – and Patti enveloped her in a hug, her freshly sprayed perfume and loosely fitting shirt threatening for a moment to suffocate her. Wishing her all the best, Patti slotted dark glasses over her eyes and moved on. By rights Leo should have been next in line, instead Nikolai took her hand in a double-handed grasp, thanking her for all her kindness before he moved to Tobias and congratulated him effusively on his creation of such excellent food. Next came Felicia – another hug, and this one was accompanied by a whispered message, a hope to see her again. One day very soon. There was no mistaking the message behind the words, and Bella felt tears prick. With thanks uttered and a final hug delivered, she too moved on.

That left Leo. He seemed as baffled about how to act as she felt. Only hours earlier they had been lying entwined in the most intimate way, and now it was as though they should pretend to be strangers. Staring at one another, his expression was impossible to read. Then, as though water finally managed to break through a dam, he stepped forward and slid his arms around her. Her hands felt their way around his ribcage, their bodies settling into an embrace that felt utterly comfortable. His words were quiet, fed directly into her ear as he leaned closer.

'This isn't goodbye. I'll see you soon, OK?'

Blinking rapidly, she refused to allow the tears to form. 'Of course, you will. Say "hi" to Pannacotta from me, will you?'

He laughed. 'I will.' Miming making a phone call, he inched away. 'I'll FaceTime you. We can make plans.'

'Bye, Leo.'

A perfunctory shake of Tobias's hand and Leo moved out of her reach. She did her best to focus on whatever parting comment Patti was making to Jean-Philippe. She was suggesting she hoped he would "Live long and prosper" and the captain smiled politely. Leo turned back to Bella, adopting the weird Vulcan hand sign she hadn't been able to master, his gaze fixed on her. She raised a hand, remaining frozen in place as he took the steps and then the gangway to the quay, and was lost from her sight.

'There is always someone who believes they are the first to make the joke.' Jean-Philippe strode along the line, a thick envelope of cash Felicia had given him as their tip in one hand, muttering as he went. '*Mon Dieu*. It's as if they think nobody in *l'Europe* has heard of *Star Trek*. If I had a euro for every time one of them makes a joke at my expense, I could retire *immédiatement*.'

He halted at the far end of the line, running a hand across his stubbly beard as he studied them. Then he nodded. 'For a first charter, this was not a disaster. Now get back to work. We have new guests arriving tomorrow.'

Epilogue

Bella glanced around the cabin – over the past weeks, she'd grown used to its dimensions; maybe she would even miss its claustrophobic atmosphere, the tiny porthole. She dumped her packed bags onto the lower bunk, now stripped of linen, sliding alongside them as Mel folded the last of her belongings.

A plink from her mobile had Bella checking her messages. She pursed her lips. It was from Jay – a row of emoji sunglasses, shining suns, boats and waves punctuated by sad faces.

It accurately portrayed the end of the charter season, but she would have preferred the message to have been from Leo.

'Is it from him?' Mel glanced her way, eyebrow raised in expectation until Bella shook her head. Turning back to her packing, she said, 'I'm so sorry, babe.'

She hadn't FaceTimed with Leo in a fortnight, hadn't managed to raise any communication with him in the last few days. And if she was being brutally honest – which it might be time to adopt as a safety mechanism – his last few communications had been brusque at best.

'What will you do?'

Bella shrugged. 'Go home, I suppose. It'll be fantastic to see Jay, but . . .'

'But you'd rather be heading off on an adventure with Leo?' Mel didn't wait for an answer, casting around for any unpacked items before she zipped her bag. 'I genuinely thought he might be less of a flaky bastard than most of them. Maybe I was wrong.'

Bella didn't have much to add to the sentiment.

'If you need anything, call me – J-P and I are staying in Monaco for a few days while he hands the yacht over to the owner's crew. They want it in the Bahamas for the winter. So, I'm hanging around until he heads home.'

As Mel spoke, Bella felt it again. Her deeply ingrained desire to tell Mel that what she was saying was so wrong, on every level. To explain her inability to square away Mel's relationship with the captain. As the season progressed, Tobias had revealed that the ongoing situation between Jean-Philippe and his second stewardess was less of a well-kept secret than they'd thought it was, had opened up to Bella how much he'd hoped Mel would realise the folly in her choice one day, and perhaps look his way instead.

'You like Mel?' Bella must have sounded astonished, if Tobias's awkward shrug was anything to go by. 'I thought you two were just good mates.'

'Yeah, we are. And she doesn't know anything about how I feel. Somehow, I always seem to fall for women who aren't interested in a normal bloke. I mean, she's amazing, and yet she allows him to control her career, has her creeping around at all hours. How is that love? I keep telling myself to walk away, leave them to it and find a new boat to work on, but I keep coming back for more. Can't quite bring myself to abandon her, in case.'

'She doesn't like talking about personal stuff much. I've tried to get to know her, but she's intensely private.'

Huffing a laugh, Tobias nodded. 'You're right about that. Pretends the rest of us don't even know about J-P. If she was my girlfriend, I'd shout it from the rooftops, not keep her hidden away like a dirty little secret.'

'She must have her reasons.'

'Yeah, and he's got his. Although his motivations are a hell of a lot easier to work out.' There had been no missing the curl of Tobias's lip, the deep furrows that appeared on his forehead. They hadn't spoken about it again.

Mel was being used. It seemed abundantly clear to Bella that both she and the captain's wife were being taken for fools. But Bella had kept those thoughts to herself all season, and wasn't about to say anything on their last day. Mel had made it abundantly clear it was none of her business, and Bella supposed she was right. It might not be the kind of relationship she wanted for herself, but she understood, however damaging it was, a magnetic attraction of that strength wasn't easy to deny. After all, the one night she'd spent with Leo Kennedy-Edge had meant Bella had barely noticed any of the rest of the season's charter guests, not even the ones who'd done their best to flirt outrageously with her.

When she'd discovered why Mel used the charter season to earn as much money as possible, in order to fund the care plan for her mother, a woman who had – in Mel's own words – had a crap life raising a daughter single-handed while losing the battle against her alcohol demons, Mel's desire to resist a traditional kind of relationship began to make more sense. In fact, everything about Mel made more sense.

'Right. I'm packed.' Mel slotted sunglasses onto her messy blond bun and threaded a handbag across her chest. 'See you next season?'

Bella stood and they hugged. 'Maybe.'

'Hope so. It's been good . . . A lot . . . but good.'

By the time Bella had said her goodbyes to the rest of the departing crew and taken one last walk through *Blue Sky*, Jean-Philippe remained alone on deck, a thermos mug full of strong coffee in one hand.

'This is it, then,' he said. 'Have you enjoyed the season?'

'More than I imagined I would. Thank you for the opportunity, Jean-Philippe.'

'Thank you for rising to the challenge – I would be happy to work with you again.'

'Really?'

'Yes. I do not make jokes about such things. Think about it, will you? Let's call this *adieu*, rather than goodbye. It may have been touch and go at the start of the season, but you pulled it together nicely. Talking of the start, are you expecting to see Mr Kennedy-Edge again?'

'We communicated for a while, but I don't think . . .' Regardless of the way she still felt about him, Bella realised she ought to accept what she'd feared all those weeks ago, when they walked around the beautiful town of Portoferraio, and Leo had been equal parts awkward and irresistible. The evening when she'd decided she wanted all of him, because she secretly believed she would end up with none of him.

Communication had tailed off during recent weeks. Despite his south American plans, despite him telling her he'd found a treehouse in which they could stay if she still wanted to, despite all of that, her inability to get so much as a reply to a text lately seemed to say everything she needed to know. 'I don't think I'll be seeing him again.'

'Maybe you are being hasty, Miss Mason.' Jean-Philippe's face crinkled into the biggest smile she had witnessed all summer as he pointed towards the marina. 'You might wish to look over there.'

A figure stood at the other end of the dock, something in one hand, the other flattened to shade his eyes as he studied *Blue Sky*. Leaning against the guard rail, Bella strained to identify the figure. There was only one person she wanted it to be, and as he started to walk towards *Blue Sky*, Bella caught a breath, her face beaming with astonished joy. It was him. It was Leo.

'Allow me.' Jean-Philippe carried her largest bag down the gangplank, shaking her hand dockside. 'I hope to see you again. *Ciao*, Bella.'

'*Ciao*, Jean-Philippe.'

Leo was halfway along the dock, walking briskly and picking up his pace further as she left her bags in a pile and ran towards him. His expression radiated seriousness, and for a moment Bella thought he was simply here to give her some kind of bad news. Perhaps Felicia Kennedy's health had nosedived . . . Then his features broke into a wide grin, and he held up the bunch of flowers for her to take.

'They're beautiful, thank you.' In truth she didn't even register the flowers; instead she raked her gaze over every inch of his face. Her memory hadn't done him justice. His smile brighter than she remembered, his eyes more sparkly, his voice deeper as he made some comment about the flowers.

'I didn't think you were . . .' She swallowed the rest of the sentence, didn't want to give it credence, not now Leo was here, standing in front of her. With the flowers dangling from one hand, she wrapped the other up and around his shoulder, as he pulled her into a hug.

'I'm so sorry I've been so difficult to get hold of lately . . .' he said. 'I've been looking forward to this – you can't imagine . . .' Leo's words were muffled, his lips nuzzling into her neck.

'I bet I can. Remember, my imagination is just as good as yours.'

His sharp inhalation choreographed perfectly to his arms wrapping her even tighter. 'Yes, I do remember. Vividly.'

After a while she pulled back. 'I thought you'd changed your mind.'

'I'm so sorry, I was always coming – this was always going to happen. It's just that things have been a bit of a nightmare at home.'

Bella flashed hot and cold. 'Oh God, is it your aunt . . . ?'

He shook his head. 'Don't worry, she's doing well. Patti seems to have taken up semi-permanent residence with them and my aunt pretends she hates her being there.'

'Pretends?'

'You know what she's like. Secretly, I think she's enjoying having Patti around.'

'I'm glad your aunt's doing well – that's such good news. How's Hannah?'

'Getting married.'

'Oh, wow – that's great.'

Leo smiled. 'It's been a long time coming. She and Clare are trying to decide between a couple of venues, but wherever the ceremony is, there's going to be one hell of a party afterwards.'

'I'm genuinely happy for her.'

Leo's expression hardened. 'And Jeremy Giles got out of the hospital last week.'

Not long after Felicia's charter group had returned to the UK, Felicia's lawyer had been attacked outside his home, his injuries enough to hospitalise him for months. Leo had told Bella, during one of their FaceTime conversations, how the true extent of Jeremy's gambling and alcohol issues had finally come to light, alongside their link to the attack. How Felicia had insisted on paying off his not insubstantial debts, even though Jeremy had eventually confessed that he'd intended to defraud Felicia. How he'd managed to get the paperwork signed while they were on *Blue Sky*, but in the end, hadn't been able to go through with it. Apparently, Patti had also been visiting the hospital on a regular basis.

'I can't believe any of them still have time for him,' Leo said, then he shrugged. 'I'm not sure I could be so forgiving.'

'But Leo, more importantly, what's been a nightmare?' Bella watched his face soften into concern.

'We've had problems on the yard, lameness and injuries to some of the horses – and . . . it's a pathetic excuse for not even texting you, but Pannacotta's been really ill.'

'What happened to her?'

'I think she caught wind of my plans with you, and like the jealous mare she is, she decided to come down with something to try to scupper my ideas. Colic, to be precise.'

'What's colic? I thought that's what babies get when they eat too fast.'

'Horses get it too, and for them it can be life-threatening. Long story short, she had to have major surgery, and I stayed with her at the vet hospital while she recovered.' The worry lines crowded his forehead, and although his upbeat tone made it sound as if he was making light of the situation, Bella could see how concerned he had been.

'Is she OK now?'

He shook his head. 'No, she's seriously pissed off.' The grin was back.

'What do you mean?'

'I told her she's going to have to share my heart from now on, and she didn't seem at all impressed.'

'Share your heart . . . ?'

Pushing a strand of hair from her face he nodded, suddenly serious. 'Yes. If you don't mind going halfsies, that is?'

'I only get half?' Bella studied him for a while, staring at the man who had taken her through more emotions in a short space of time than anyone she'd ever known. She had no idea what the future would bring, but whatever it was, she knew she wanted to explore it with him.

'Not enough?' Leo pursed his lips. 'Well, how about that's what we tell her. Horses aren't very good at fractions. She'll never know the difference.'

As she laughed, Bella reached up and bunched the front of his shirt in her fingers, pulling until he was close enough to touch, to hold, and to kiss. A kiss they both knew would go on for a very long time.

Acknowledgements

Writing a novel begins as a solitary pursuit, but it ends up being such a team event – and I think mine might just be the dream team.

Firstly, I want to thank my wonderful agent Anne Williams from KHLA. She's utterly calm and always reassuringly positive. Her guidance and support are unparalleled.

The entire team at Embla books are amazing – I'm so lucky to be working with you all – and special thanks go to the editing team, for your invaluable input and attention to detail. Birthday cake . . . need I say more?

A huge thank you to Tanya Gibbins, Hanne Bonczoszek and Clare White for being the best friends anyone could ask for – and for doubling up as cracking beta readers. Fossilers Four Forever!

And even though they are as annoying as they are lovable, I couldn't have done any of this without my family. Support comes in many forms, from unconditional to the 'boot up the backside' kind, and I'm thankful for all of it.

These acknowledgements wouldn't be complete without a heartfelt thank you to the readers – every single one of you is treasured more than you will ever know. Thank you for choosing to pick up my book.

Rachel Barnett

Rachel Barnett lives in the beauty of rural Wiltshire, almost within touching distance of Stonehenge. After a career as a primary school teacher (yes, it is as exhausting as everyone says), and then creating a little monster of her own, a chink of spare time saw her taking as many creative writing courses as she could get her hands on. Suitably equipped, she has finally managed to hide away from everyone for long enough to achieve her life-long ambition of writing a book.

About Embla Books

Embla Books is a digital-first publisher of standout commercial adult fiction. Passionate about storytelling, the team at Embla publish books that will make you 'laugh, love, look over your shoulder and lose sleep'. Launched by Bonnier Books UK in 2021, the imprint is named after the first woman from the creation myth in Norse mythology, who was carved by the gods from a tree trunk found on the seashore – an image of the kind of creative work and crafting that writers do, and a symbol of how stories shape our lives.

Find out about some of our other books and stay in touch:

Twitter, Facebook, Instagram: @emblabooks
Newsletter: https://bit.ly/emblanewsletter

www.ingramcontent.com/pod-product-compliance
Lightning Source LLC
Chambersburg PA
CBHW032100090426
42743CB00007B/186